D1234305

Dear Carole,

Best Wishes,

Integrative Team
Treatment for
**ATTACHMENT
TRAUMA IN
CHILDREN**

A Norton Professional Book

Integrative Team
Treatment for
ATTACHMENT
TRAUMA IN
CHILDREN

Family Therapy and EMDR

Debra Wesselmann

Cathy Schweitzer

Stefanie Armstrong

W. W. Norton & Company
New York • London

For our families.

Thank you for your encouragement
and support throughout this endeavor.

We love you.

CONTENTS

Appendices

Acknowledgments

WE WISH TO THANK all of the parents who have come to our office to work with us week after week, investing their time and energy to help their children heal, and the children who have courageously let down their guards and opened their hearts and minds.

Thank you to Deborah Malmud for her wisdom and expertise. Her suggestions were invaluable and transformed our rough manuscript into a professional book.

We are indebted to Francine Shapiro, Ph.D., for all she has done to help so many individuals around the world find help and healing, and for encouraging us to pursue our work with hurt children.

We are grateful to Meghan Davidson, Ph.D., for her guidance in data collection and research. We have depended upon her expertise over the past several years.

We are indebted to our colleague and good friend, Ann Potter, Ph.D. None of this would have happened without her. Six years ago, she was supervising several child cases involving attachment trauma and recognized the need for a family therapist–EMDR therapist collaboration. Ann's insight and contributions involving the three phases of meltdowns and the "domino effect" have all been integral to the success of the development of the Integrative Team Treatment model.

Thank you to our colleague and good friend, Joan Lovett, M.D. We have co-presented and peer consulted over many years, and her thoughtful conceptualizations and her artistry as a therapist have been an inspiration. Her storytelling method has an important component for helping children make sense of their difficult histories.

Thanks to Daniel Bruckner, LIMHP, for his role as family therapist early on and for his assistance in forming the original Attachment and Trauma Center of Nebraska group.

Thanks, too, to another of our early founders, Mandy Busch, LIMHP. Her "left-brain" thinking was invaluable to the group.

Introduction

IF YOU HAVE FELT overwhelmed in your work with children who have lived through multiple traumas and losses, you are not alone. Wading through the complexity of case management decisions, making appropriate referrals, managing the severe behaviors, addressing the needs of the parents and the schools, and then finding a way to address the traumatic memories in the midst of all of this is a clinical quandary. What if your workload was shared, instead of carried alone? What if you had practical, step-by-step guidelines to address the family system issues as well as the child's traumatic past? This manual provides all of that—a team approach and a protocol for a family therapist and eye movement desensitization and reprocessing (EMDR) therapist team.

There are many and varied circumstances that lead families to seek help for traumatized children in biological, foster, and adoptive families. For the moment, consider one fictional but typical case of a young child and a family preparing to adopt him. . . .

A little boy, age 7 (we'll call him "Josh"), is shopping with his adoptive mom. He's picking out an outfit for adoption day, coming up in a couple of weeks. Mom and Dad have been on a roller coaster ride, navigating this process. Josh came to their home about a year ago as a foster child. Initially, the plan for Josh was reunification with his biological mother. Mom and Dad knew little of Josh's past, except that he had been in and out of his biological mother's care a couple of times. They knew that his mother was a drug user and that Josh had spent a lot of time with his maternal grandmother.

Although Josh is fictional, his situation is very real and surprisingly common. In fact, "during the last 15 years, nearly a million children have been adopted into families in the United States" with "almost three quarters of that total from foster care" (Smith, 2010, p. 9).

Mom and Dad thought that maybe it was a good thing that Josh's maternal grandmother had cared for the little boy at least some of the time, but they didn't know for sure. The caseworker had also mentioned in passing that Josh's mother had never lived in one place for long. This profile represents a common story among foster children, where "chronically neglecting families often are characterized by a chaotic household with changing constellations of adult and child figures" (Polansky, Gaudin, & Kilpatrick, 1992, p. 21). In such situations, households are fluid and chaotic with adults and children living intermittently with various others from grandparents, to aunts, to boyfriends. With regular but unpredictable moves, such children eventually have few possessions but many anxieties. Perhaps, thought Josh's new parents, the frequent moves in his earlier life explained his need to keep the light (not just the night light) on while he slept.

For Josh's new parents the year had been a long one. Their original intent was to provide stability as Josh's foster parents while Josh was having visits with his biological mother. At first, Josh was really excited before each visit, and he returned each time with stories about going to the park or eating at fast-food restaurants. He and his mother spent time at the library, and sometimes they went swimming. However, as time progressed, Josh began to suffer some disappointments. At first, his biological mom missed a visit now and then. Then, she began missing visits more and more often.

Josh became upset each time a visit was canceled. He threw things and slammed doors, whereupon his understanding foster parents worked hard to calm him and distract him with other activities. As the months progressed, the case went to court and his biological mother completely disappeared—no more contact, no more visits. She eventually called the worker and stated that she had to leave town to find work. She would be back sometime, she just didn't know when.

Josh and Mom finished the shopping trip and returned home. Mom could tell that Josh had had enough for the day and was starting to get cranky. She got Josh a snack and sent him outside to ride his bike. Summer was finally here, and he could be outside. Riding his bike was one of the few things that did not make Josh angry. Mom sat down at the window and rifled through some of the final paperwork for the adoption. Her mind wandered back to the beginning when they had first met Josh.

Josh had come to them with sleep and bathroom issues. He often woke really early and silently started searching the kitchen for food. Time and again, Mom reassured him that he could wake her to prepare breakfast. Josh eventually stopped the early morning kitchen trips, but Mom and Dad still regularly found wrappers and food stored under his bed.

Mom remembered the first time that she and Dad had witnessed a meltdown. They had been shocked at how aggressive Josh could become, and they soon discovered that his mood could turn on a dime. They had thought—perhaps naively—that lots of love, comfort, and stability would help Josh settle down. But when Josh really got mad, it was frightening. He destroyed his room, sometimes throwing everything he could get his hands on. He screamed at the top of his lungs that he hated everyone, and there were a few times when he threatened to kill them. His outbursts could last longer than an hour. Not much seemed to work. Thankfully, they were committed to loving and caring for Josh, so they just kept trying different approaches.

Of course, they had grown attached to Josh. They felt like he had really become a member of their family, so they began to pursue adoption. Eventually, the biological mother's rights were terminated, and Mom and Dad told Josh about their plans to adopt him. They knew that the termination process was going to be tough on everyone, and the final "good-bye visit" was heart-wrenching. Even so, mom and dad thought that telling Josh they were going to be his forever family would help ease the pain . . . although it didn't really work out that way.

Josh was in second grade. His first therapist had seemed to work well with him, and she had helped him get a good start to the new school year. But as the weeks had progressed, Josh had become increasingly angry. He not only had meltdowns at home, but he had begun having extensive trouble at school. He could not seem to stay in his seat. At times, he completely shut down and refused to attempt any work. He constantly played with objects that he had squirreled away in his pockets. The therapist was at a loss around Christmas time, especially during the mother's final termination visit. Finally, the therapist stated that she did not have the expertise or skill to help such a challenging child with all of these mounting issues. So, Josh was referred to a new therapist. In January, the school began contacting Mom and Dad one or two times a week, noting Josh's academic and behavioral issues. Mom and Dad gave Josh consequences at home for his misbehaviors at school and continued to work with him academically. Even so, Josh seemed behind his peers and had difficulty understanding and retaining information.

Josh's parents were confronted with a looming truth. Although loving and well intentioned, they simply didn't know what do. In fact, both adoptive and biological parents are not always prepared; they lack important medical information and receive little to no training in how to help their traumatized child with very difficult behaviors. Children are resilient and can make progress when they are placed in a secure environment, but many suffer ongoing, long-term challenges. As in this scenario with Josh, "these challenges often are not fully manifested until the child enters school and has difficulties in adjusting to classroom expectations or mastering academic work" (Smith, 2010, p. 10). Ironically, at a time when most children are gaining confidence and developing improved social skills, Josh and other traumatized children are experiencing increased anxieties and social situations that they are ill-equipped to manage.

Children who experience trauma and disruptions within their earliest attachment relationships may evidence neurological changes in the brain and may exhibit delayed emotional and social growth and development. Such issues can be triggered and magnified by the transition into a school setting. School environments require self-discipline, a positive disposition toward peers and adults, and patience. When things go badly at school, the difficulties often carry over to the home. Children with an abuse history or caregiver changes often exhibit "elevated risks for developmental, physical, psychological, emotional or behavioral challenges" (Smith, 2010, p. 9). Children like Josh are more likely to struggle academically, and they are "more likely than their non-adopted peers to score in the clinical range on standardized behavior problem measures" (Smith, 2010, p. 5). In short, Josh and his parents can expect ongoing difficulties, and they are likely to need capable, ongoing, professional support to overcome these challenges.

After several visits, the new therapist did not feel equipped to work with Josh either. In fact, Mom and Dad began to wonder if anyone was trained to deal with their child. In reality, research "indicates that most health professionals lack relevant training" (Smith, 2010, p. 6). A limited supply of capable professionals means limited access to services and little or no progress for many families struggling to support traumatized or adopted children.

As the year progressed and spring emerged, Josh started to become angry over the smallest things. He couldn't pay attention for longer than a minute or two. The school called every other day with concerns about his academic difficulties and out-of-control behaviors. Mom and Dad had talked with him every night to help him see the errors of his ways and his thinking. It seemed as though Josh's parents were providing more and more consequences, but nothing seemed to have any impact. Mom and Dad had begun to question themselves, and they wondered what could have happened during his early years to cause such problems. Not surprisingly, a study by Briere, Kaltman, and Green (2008) found that cumulative experiences of trauma are directly associated with greater complexity and severity of symptoms. In addition, "many of the behavioral symptoms of adopted children who are seen in mental health settings stem from the effects of trauma" (Smith, 2010, p. 17). Whether they are adopted or remain in the biological home, many traumatized children struggle to succeed at school, with friends, and in the home.

Mom and Dad began to feel desperate. Last spring they decided to undertake a psychological evaluation in the hope that a psychologist could provide some insight into Josh's struggles. The results indicated attention-deficit/hyperactivity disorder (ADHD) and oppositional defiant disorder (ODD), but it also noted something called *reactive attachment disorder*. The parents were not surprised by the first two diagnoses, but they knew nothing about reactive attachment disorder.

Using the Internet, the family searched for alternative ideas to help their child, while learning more about this disorder. They were surprised by the variety of theories and differences in therapeutic interventions. Some professionals recommended holding therapy, whereas others encouraged a gentler approach. Meanwhile, both Mom and Dad had begun to feel increasingly ineffective, as nothing seemed to be working . . . no matter what they did. Even their extended family members, who had originally tried to help, began to encourage them to send Josh away because his behaviors were just too much. Mom had worried, "If I send him away, what message will that send him?" Still, they gathered more information and didn't rule out placing the child they had come to love outside of the home.

The situation was both maddening and humbling. Their love had fueled their desire to find solutions and help Josh. Meanwhile, their lack of success had caused them to question their ability, challenge their resolve, and doubt their child's capacity to adjust to a normal life in their home. One meta-study found that adoptive families are two to five times more likely to seek counseling or other professional help and are four to seven times more likely to seek residential treatment for their children than are families raising the children born to them (Smith, 2010, p. 12). In short, they realize the need for effective professional help.

Mom called out the window that it was getting dark and it was time to come in. After whining a little, Josh put his bike in the garage, came in through the door, walked over, and sat next to Mom. He leaned his head against her shoulder for a minute and said, "Thanks for my new stuff, Mom." Then he raced into the other room to watch television. In moments like these, he was calm and affectionate. These moments rekindled a bit of hope. Like most parents, she desperately wanted to keep Josh at home. With faith and the right help, maybe they could find a way.

This manual is designed to help guide therapeutic work with children like Josh. In the following chapters you will learn how to incorporate the team model into your practice. Chapter 1 explains why the traumatized child's brain, wired for survival, needs a unique approach. Chapter 2 provides an overview of the protocol components, and Chapter 3 specifically addresses case conceptualization and treatment planning, using the adaptive information processing (AIP) model.

Chapter 4 describes detailed therapeutic interventions, provided by the family therapist, which are critical for changing the responses of parents and for building the foundation for the EMDR work. Chapter 5 describes attachment resource development (ARD) exercises used to increase the security of the relationship between the parents and the hurt child. Chapter 6 provides EMDR adaptations for reprocessing with this challenging child population. Chapter 7 outlines complicated cases with specially designed interventions, and Chapter 8 guides clinicians in helping parents who may carry their own attachment issues.

Through ongoing data collection, research, and work with many families over a period of several years, we have developed the Integrative Team Treatment model to improve treatment effectiveness with severely traumatized children. By working as a collaborative team, EMDR and family therapists can simultaneously increase the security of the parent–child attachment and the early experiences that drive the child's behaviors. Affected children and their families are suffering, and they need specialized help. This book is written as a clear and practical treatment guide, outlining the Integrative Team Treatment philosophy and protocols.

You do not have to be a center specializing in treating attachment and trauma to implement this team model. In fact, the members of the team do not have to be practicing at the same location. Two solo clinicians practicing in nearby offices can form a "team" for children with a traumatic history and challenging behaviors. Both clinicians do not have to be EMDR trained, but at least one should be fully trained in EMDR. Naturally, anyone working with this special population should participate in ongoing education through specialty workshops, conferences, and consultations, but don't count yourself out if you are new to the field. The field needs more clinicians who are willing to work with children who exhibit severe behaviors and early neglect, abuse, losses, or other serious traumas. If you are naturally compassionate and patient, enjoy a challenge, and have a love for children, this book may be your first step into the most rewarding (albeit challenging) work in which you will ever engage. If you are an experienced clinician in the field, we believe the Integrative Team Treatment model will provide you with a new and practical approach that will enhance your success. We wish you all the best in your work with the families you serve.

Integrative Team
Treatment for
**ATTACHMENT
TRAUMA IN
CHILDREN**

PART I

CASE CONCEPTUALIZATION AND FOUNDATIONAL WORK

Chapter 1

SCARED CHILDREN, NOT SCARY CHILDREN

The Impact of Neurobiology on the Field of Attachment Therapy

A TRAUMATIC EVENT antedating a diagnosis of posttraumatic stress disorder (PTSD) involves physical or sexual harm or serious physical threat to oneself or another (American Psychiatric Association, 2013). However, problems in functioning are frequently associated with disturbing events that are emotional in nature. Shapiro (2001, 2007) distinguishes between "Big *T*" trauma—events causing actual or threatened injury or sexual violation—and "small *t*" trauma—events that are emotionally distressing, but not physically or sexually harmful. For example, verbal abuse may leave an indelible mark on an individual's sense of security, self-worth, and trust, even when there is no physical danger.

In this manual, the term *attachment trauma* refers to both "Big T" and "small t" traumatic events that take place within significant attachment relationships in childhood. Children are wired by nature to attach to their parents, as closeness with their caregivers allows them to survive. The lives of children revolve around their parents, and most of their early learning takes place through interactions with them. It makes sense that trauma experienced within children's most significant relationships has a profound impact on functioning.

Early attachment trauma may include (1) neglect or physical or sexual abuse by a parent; (2) the witnessing of domestic violence between parents; (3) early pain or medical interventions/ hospitalizations that are perceived by young children as failure on the part of their parents to help them or protect them; or (4) loss or removal from parents followed by foster or orphanage care. Children with a history of attachment trauma frequently suffer from broad problems in functioning that include severe behavioral symptoms (van der Kolk, 2005).

The layperson encountering a child with a history of significant attachment trauma for the first time is typically appalled by the behavioral symptoms. It is common for those who do not understand the traumatic roots of the child's behaviors to perceive the child as "undisciplined" and "spoiled." Aggression, tantrums, lying, stealing, arguing, defiance, enuresis, encopresis, and sexualized behaviors are all commonly observed in children with a traumatic history. Present-day caregivers accompanying the child to treatment may be adoptive or foster parents, guardians, relatives, or biological parents in the case of early medical trauma, circumstances of separation, or reunification after parents' rehabilitation. In all situations, parents feel similarly anxious, overwhelmed, angry, hurt, and powerless. Out of fear and anxiety, caregivers are often entrenched in angry patterns of parenting that include yelling, lecturing, punishing, and spanking. Treating professionals may also experience emotional distress as they encounter the serious challenges presented by struggling families. Due to the broad range of problems and symptoms experienced by affected children, they are frequently diagnosed with multiple psychiatric disorders, including reactive attachment disorder (RAD), oppositional defiant disorder (ODD), conduct disorder (CD), PTSD, attention-deficit/hyperactivity disorder (ADHD), and bipolar disorder.

Many parents of children with a history of attachment trauma look for answers on the Internet and via parent networks, and they frequently run across resources and information that, although not consistent with current knowledge, are still accessible. Some resources present a simplistic and misleading view that the behaviors associated with a diagnosis of RAD are driven by pent-up rage related to infant experiences of abandonment. This conceptualization is associated with the myth that children diagnosed with RAD are sociopaths or "children without a conscience" (Magid, 1988)—a view that was quite popular 15–30 years ago and one that heightens fear and leads to misinformed and ineffective treatment and parenting approaches. Certainly, without adequate treatment and intervention, children who experienced early maltreatment and losses are at heightened risk for mental health problems and unhealthy behaviors that in some cases may include criminal activity. But this is only part of a complex picture involving the impact of adverse childhood events on neurology, emotion regulation, cognitive processes, and social functioning. Children with a history of attachment trauma are handicapped by chronic stress and anxiety and neurological effects of earlier events for which they were not responsible in any way.

A DAWNING AWARENESS: THE NEUROBIOLOGY BEHIND THE BEHAVIORS

The 1990s is referred to as the *decade of the brain* due to the explosion of knowledge regarding the complex processes involved in brain development. Advances were made in brain imaging techniques such as PET (positron emission tomography), SPECT (single photon emission computed tomography), and fMRI (functional magnetic resonance imaging). This new knowledge converged with research in traumatology and attachment to create a more complete picture regarding the development of children with a history of attachment trauma. There was a dawning awareness in the consciousness of mental health providers that some of the common treatment approaches were misguided. Brain scans of children with early relational neglect and trauma provided astonishing pictures of neurological injury. Even though affected children did not have physically visible disabilities (with the exception of their behavioral dysregulation), the lack of appropriate neurological functioning was now visible. Brain scans provided concrete evidence that children impacted by early abuse or neglect may be as neurologically challenged as children suffering from head injury or a brain disease.

THE SECURELY ATTACHED, INTEGRATED BRAIN

Works by Schore (e.g., 1994, 1996, 1997, 2001), Siegel (e.g., 1999, 2001), and Perry (e.g., 1996, 1997) have highlighted the nurturing environment as the key to unlocking the store of genetic potential within the brain of every infant. Siegel (1999, p. 18) states: "A wide range of studies has, in fact, now clarified that development is a product of the effect of experience on the unfolding of genetic potential. . . . Genes do not act in isolation from experience. . . . The social world supplies the most important experiences influencing the expression of genes." Perry (1997, p. 124) concurs: "The major modifier of all human behavior is experience. . . . Experience in early life determines core neurobiology."

Newborn infants operate solely from what could be broadly described as the emotional right hemisphere of the brain; the logical, thinking left brain is undeveloped at the time of birth. Subsequently, infants are bundles of pure, raw sensations and emotions—as mothers everywhere would agree—without the capacity to organize or calm themselves. The disorganized emotional infant brain requires at least one consistent, nurturing adult to create order out of the chaos.

The prefrontal cortex is sometimes referred to as "the seat of the soul" because it seems to be central to the human personality. At birth, the neurons within the infant's prefrontal region are preprogrammed to read emotions on the mother's face (or the father's). Miraculously, once these sensitive neurons "read" the mother's facial expression, circuits are connected within the infant's brain that replicate the mother's circuits and allow the infant to get in synch with the mother's feelings. Like a Vulcan "mind meld," the mother's right brain synchronizes with the infant's right brain, and vice versa. Schore (2001, p. 203) states: "In attachment transactions of affective synchrony, the psychobiologically attuned caregiver interactively regulates the infant's positive and negative states." As the calm, organized brain of the mother attunes to her infant, the infant's brain calms and moves toward becoming more organized. A mother who has a well-organized brain instinctively recognizes when her child is alert and open to play, and when he or she has had too much for now and needs to calm down. She instinctively uses soothing tones when the baby is distressed and a higher pitch when he or she needs stimulation. The mother whose brain is organized is naturally "tuned in" to her infant's moods and rhythms. Without conscious thought, she both follows and leads as she and her infant interact. The infant becomes secure in his or her attachment relationship with the mother as they "dance" in this way, sharing pleasurable experiences, both playful and quiet. Opioids, the "love hormones," rush through their brains, and they yearn to stay near one another. Their attachment to one another keeps them dancing together, and the dance strengthens the bond.

The brain of the securely attached infant develops expertise at self-calming. The infant's prefrontal brain is plugged into the mother's right brain like a battery plugged into a battery recharger, allowing him or her to develop a rich web of circuits within the prefrontal brain. The all-important prefrontal brain becomes Grand Central Station, creating connections between the many neurological structures. The well-integrated brain allows the best parts of the child's innate personality to develop, unimpeded by problems of emotional dysregulation. With a rich web of connections in the prefrontal cortex, the child is equipped to manage and modulate his or her emotions. As the child reaches adolescence, he or she will be less likely to look for methods of changing his or her emotions through drugs, drinking, or other unhealthy means. As an adult, this individual's well-regulated brain will allow him or her to enjoy feelings of love and connection to a significant other, echoing his or her earliest bonds. Later, when he or she becomes a new parent, holding his or her child will tap into stored early memories and associated feelings of love and connection, enhancing his or her feelings of joy in parenthood.

TRAUMA AND NEGLECT: BARRIERS TO NEUROLOGICAL, EMOTIONAL, SOCIAL, AND COGNITIVE DEVELOPMENT

The story of how infants develop a loving and regulated brain is an uplifting one—but the story of the infant who attempts the metaphorical "mind meld" with the parent who is chronically angry, emotionally absent, or abusing substances is extremely concerning. In a famous experiment that has now been replicated many times and is known as the "Still Face Video" (Field & Fogel, 1982; Tronick, Als, Adamson, Wise, & Brazelton, 1978), a loving mother is initially encouraged to speak to her baby and engage in an exchange of happy smiles and sounds. The mother is next asked to keep a "still," unemotional face for 1 minute without speaking. At first, the baby is observed to entice his mother with coos and cuteness. As the agonizing minute wears on, he becomes agitated and angry, until finally, he gives up in despair. His eyes glaze over, his face becomes a reflection of despondency, and he shuts down. At last, the mother is instructed to smile and to repair the misconnection, and thankfully, the baby comes back to life, once again interacting joyfully with his mother.

The despair of the infant whose existence is like an eternal "Still Face" experiment is ongoing and unremitting (Weinberg & Tronick, 1998). But humans are designed to survive, and so the prefrontal brain of the infant who is neglected begins adapting immediately to survive in an environment of deprivation. Cortisol and other stress hormones flood the prefrontal cortex of the infant in distress, destroying brain cells that are unnecessary in a more primitive environment (Perry, 1996, 1997; Schore, 2001). With an underdeveloped prefrontal brain and reduced cortical functioning, the infant is actually more equipped to fend for him- or herself and survive in a harsh world, where quick reactions are more useful than thoughtful plans.

Perry (1996) used imaging techniques to study the brains of 12 severely neglected children who averaged 8 years of age at the time of the study. The cortical structures in the brains of 7 of the 12 severely neglected children were profoundly underdeveloped. Due to lack of attention and nurturing, the frontal brains of these children essentially suffered from a "failure to thrive" (Block & Krebs, 2005).

Chronic stress leaves its own imprint on the developing brain. The release of high levels of cortisol and other stress hormones readies the body for danger, but they are toxic to the brain cells in specific regions of the brain, including the prefrontal cortex (Gunnar & Barr, 1998). If the all-important prefrontal region of a child's brain is already underdeveloped due to early neglect, damage from high levels of stress hormones adds insult to injury. The result is further reduction in the capacity of the child to think things through or self-calm when his or her limbic brain is firing. Survival is everything in the big picture, and the child's reactivity serves this goal.

Another cause for the reactivity observed in a child who has experienced repeated attachment trauma is the effect of trauma on the size of the hippocampus and the amygdala, found within the limbic region. These structures are responsible for either activating or deactivating an emotional reaction to an external event. When the limbic structures are damaged by the "toxic wash" created by stress, the amygdala and the hippocampus function in a more primitive way (LeDoux, 1996; Perry, 1997; Schore, 2001). As a result, the limbic region overinterprets stimuli as dangerous and constantly and unnecessarily activates the nervous system. The child wired for survival has an overly reactive limbic brain as well as the decreased cortical functions that serve to modulate emotions. In real-life terms, the child's brain has been shaped by his or her environment to react on impulse, without the wasted time and frivolity of forethought. Forethought appears to be a luxury that only a lucky child living in a safe environment can afford.

Research has provided direct evidence of the negative impact of early attachment trauma on the development and functioning of young children. For example, an early study by Egeland and Sroufe (1981) followed 200 at-risk families from the third trimester of pregnancy. A number of the families was classified as being physically or emotionally abusive or neglecting. Sadly, although most of the abused and neglected infants were at a normal developmental level at 9 months of age, they appeared to be relatively cognitively delayed at 24 months of age. The infants whose caregivers were emotionally unavailable began showing deterioration by 6 months of age. Although infants suffering any type of mistreatment showed deterioration, emotional unavailability seemed to have the most severe effects. Emotionally neglected infants who were delightful, happy, 3-month-olds were falling apart under stress by 24 months. They exhibited poor emotion regulation, anger, frustration, and noncompliance, and they appeared emotionally nonresponsive to others.

In another classic study, Dodge, Bates, and Pettit (1990) followed 309 children from prekindergarten into elementary school. A full 36% of those with a history of physical abuse were aggressive to others in the deviant range. Researchers reported that these children perceived hostile intentions in others when there was no hostile intent. In other words, their brains had been programmed to read threat even when there was none. The abused kids who were not aggressive toward others were withdrawn and isolated, hiding to survive. Abuse and emotional neglect were clearly detrimental to the children's developing brains and personalities.

Van der Kolk has proposed developmental trauma disorder (DTD) as a formal diagnosis that identifies the pervasive impact of an environment that is chaotic, neglecting, or abusive on children's development and functioning. Whereas a secure attachment with trustworthy parents assists children with processing stressful events in their lives, neglect or maltreatment by parents leads to a breakdown in children's capacity to process their emotions, and their behaviors are maladaptive attempts to self-regulate (van der Kolk, 2005). Children with poor self-regulation have a very narrow window of tolerance (Siegel, 2010) for emotions, leading to frequent hyper- or hypoarousal, or vacillation between the two. Outside of the window of tolerance, they have little ability to think logically, learn, and socialize, leading to delays in their emotional, cognitive, and social development.

Adverse Childhood Experiences (ACE) Study

An enormous 10-year project called the Adverse Childhood Experiences (ACE) study has uncovered the many ways in which trauma impacts the lives of children lifelong (Felitti et al., 1998). Over 9,000 adults completed a questionnaire and responded to questions about early experiences, mental and physical health, and habits of behavior. Participants received up to 7 points, scoring 1 point for each category of abuse experienced. As the score went up, so did the likelihood for obesity, mental illness, promiscuity, alcoholism, drug use, and death. The study concluded that adverse childhood experiences affect neurodevelopment, and that unhealthy, high-risk behaviors are attempts to alleviate emotional pain.

The Vagal Nerve Response to Trauma

Children with a history of attachment trauma may exhibit a variety of responses to environmental stress. Porges (1995) explains that the body's responses to threat are regulated by the vagal nerve. Branches of the vagal nervous system reach from the medulla to the lungs, heart, and abdomen. The most primitive part of the vagal system, termed the *vegetative vagal response*, can be traced all the way back to our reptilian ancestors. When words won't work and fighting or running is impossible, humans are programmed to "freeze" like a reptile trying to blend into its surroundings.

The mammalian response to stress involves suppressing the vegetative vagus and instead readying the body for flight or fight through activation of the sympathetic nervous system. Adrenaline flow, heart rate, and respiration increase as the brain is flooded with stress hormones.

The most evolved vagal response modulates the fight–flight system and activates the social and communication skills (e.g., eye contact, facial expressions, vocal intonation, listening) needed to communicate quickly and effectively in a perilous situation. This response requires, of course, some well-developed higher cortical functions.

In abuse situations, the communication response is typically useless. As a result, the skill of communication remains underdeveloped. The fight–flight response is useful for older children who are living with abuse, but running or fighting is impossible for infants and toddlers. When the social and mammalian responses to stress are useless, the more primitive vagus response is activated. Termed the vegetative *freeze* response, this system slows all the body's metabolic processes to preserve energy. The child in the vegetative vagal nerve response visibly appears very still and shut down. This shut down state is useful for the very young, as the child avoids attracting attention by essentially "feigning death." This survival mechanism can be observed in the animal world and is the only recourse for someone who is vulnerable and powerless.

When an infant or toddler experiences the vegetative vagal response repeatedly, it may become an entrenched pattern, leading to chronic hypoarousal. The slowing of heart and respiration in the face of threat manifests as dissociation in situations of duress. Dissociation and hypoarousal can take many forms, but they always disconnect the child from a conscious experience of his or her emotional or physical pain. Many children vacillate between hyper- and hypoarousal. The ability to access logical thought or to learn, problem-solve, or relate to others is equally impaired in hypo- and hyperarousal.

Impact of Trauma on the Corpus Callosum and Temporal Regions

Researchers have observed numerous ways in which complex childhood trauma impacts the functioning and structures of the developing brain. Teicher (2002) observed that the corpus callosum, the band between the right and left hemispheres of the brain, facilitates communication between the hemispheres and is significantly smaller in people who were seriously abused in childhood— more evidence of the impact of trauma on neurological structure and integration. Trauma also appears to impact electrical functioning in the brain. Data collected from electroencephalograms (EEGs) showed that 72% of the children and teens admitted to a psychiatric hospital with a history of serious physical and sexual abuse exhibited abnormal activity in the frontal and temporal regions of the brain, especially in the left temporal area. In contrast, only 27% of the nonabused inpatient youngsters showed EEG irregularities. Furthermore, symptoms resembling temporal lobe epilepsy were 113% more common in psychiatric patients with a history of physical and sexual abuse than in psychiatric patients with no abuse history. Symptoms of temporal lobe epilepsy include feelings of unreality or dissociation, numbness, vertigo, staring, nausea, or upset in the pit of the stomach.

Clearly, individuals with a history of complex trauma in childhood are lacking what Siegel (2001, 2007,) and Siegel and Bryson (2011) describe as *brain integration*, in which the left, logical hemisphere is able to communicate and work together with the emotional and creative right hemisphere for greater synthesis of thoughts and emotions. Neurological integration also allows the higher cortical regions to modulate the limbic brain and thereby facilitate emotional stability. The dearth of neural connections in the prefrontal cortex and the corpus callosum, the more primitive functioning in the limbic region, and the mammalian and vegetative vagal responses are all pieces in the puzzle to understanding the functional problems experienced by severely traumatized children.

Attachment Deprivation, Disorganization, and Loss

Ainsworth (1967) and Bowlby (1989), both pioneers in the field of human attachment, recognized that the infant's innate fear of abandonment and the drive to engage the mother are critical to human survival. When a mother responds with sensitivity to her infant's fears and needs, the infant's anxiety is lessened and he or she is able to relax. The baby's sense of trust in the responsive caregiver grows over time, and his or her positive expectations generalize to the world at large. Infants whose needs are met only intermittently, however, remain anxious about the possibility of getting their needs met and about their safety in the world, generally. These infants adapt to their situation by learning to be demanding; the term *ambivalent/resistant* describes the quality of their attachment. In other infant–mother dyads, the infants learn that the mother moves away when they cry. These infants adapt to their situation by repressing their feelings and needs, which allows their mothers to stay close. These infants are categorized as *avoidant* in their attachment, They are insecure and anxious, despite an appearance of indifference (Ainsworth, 1982).

Attachment researchers have discovered that when children become fearful in the presence of their caregiver, the conflict and confusion create mental disorganization. This is the case when the parent is abusive or has symptoms related to a traumatic history that are frightening to the child (Main & Hesse, 1990; Main & Solomon, 1990; Lyons-Ruth & Jacobvitz, 1999). Children with a disorganized/disoriented attachment appear to be predisposed to dissociation (Liotti, 1999). By school age, children with disorganized/disoriented attachment may be characterized by punishing and controlling behaviors toward their parents or controlled and caretaking behaviors (Lyons-Ruth, Alpern, & Repacholi, 1993).

Whether temporary or permanent, the placement of children in orphanage, foster, adoptive, or guardianship care is associated with loss and separation from the biological parents. During the late 1940s and early 1950s Bowlby studied children who had been separated from attachment figures due to World War II or lengthy hospitalizations. He observed that children separated from their attachment figures are devastated by the loss and move through stages of protest, despair, and resignation. He noted that the children who experienced attachment separations continued to have superficial attachments even after reunification, and that they were at risk for behavioral problems later on (Bowlby, 1973).

Some children who have suffered severe neglect or perhaps frequent changes in caregivers appear to have missed a window of opportunity for developing the capacity to experience deep connectedness to others. They appear shut down to relationships, a condition described by Zeanah and Boris (2000) as a disorder of "nonattachment."

Children with a history of attachment trauma presenting for treatment may suffer from some combination of nonattachment, attachment separations or losses, attachment disorganization, and attachment insecurity. Unfortunately, the symptoms of children with a history of attachment trauma can worsen when they are placed into state care due to ongoing "Big T" and "small t" experiences and lack of opportunity for healthy attachments. By the time the child is placed with a family, the behaviors may be so challenging that the placement disrupts, sending the child further into a downward spiral.

UNDERSTANDING CHILDREN WITH A HISTORY OF ATTACHMENT TRAUMA THROUGH THE EMDR ADAPTIVE INFORMATION PROCESSING MODEL

The adaptive information processing (AIP) model proposed by Shapiro (2007) provides the theoretical underpinnings for the EMDR approach and a helpful way to understand the symptoms and behaviors of children with a history of attachment trauma. The model posits that all human beings have a natural information processing system, which involves activation of important centers in the right and left hemispheres that help metabolize emotions and life experiences. When events are extremely disturbing, this natural information processing system may become overwhelmed and shut down. Highly distressing events are stored physiologically in an unprocessed form. Images, emotions, body sensations, and beliefs are encapsulated within separate neural networks in the limbic region of the brain. Later, when the un-metabolized traumatic memories are triggered by some type of emotional, sensory, or visual reminder, the child or adult suddenly experiences thoughts, emotions, sensations, or visual images associated with the memory (van der Kolk & Fisler, 1992).

According to the most recent U.S. Department of Health and Human Services (2012) data, which were calculated for the year

2011, the highest rate of victimization of children takes place in the first year of life. There was a time when that was considered fortunate because it meant that the early abuse was not consciously remembered. However, it is now clear that, although preverbal trauma is not recorded in the "explicit" memory system, the trauma memory is stored in an unprocessed form within the "implicit" memory system (Siegel, 2001; van der Kolk & Fisler, 1992).

Children with a history of attachment trauma have a store of disturbing, unmetabolized attachment memories. The negative emotions, sensations, and images associated with the memories are encapsulated within neural networks in the limbic brain and are easily accessed by interactions with present-day caregivers. Children do not need to have conscious memories of their traumatic past to experience the associated anxiety, hurt, sadness, and fear. These children are trapped in a double bind: They feel a survival-driven need for love and closeness with their present-day attachment figures, but they simultaneously must avoid the closeness to feel safe.

EMDR addresses the memories that are entrenched in the neurology of traumatized children by facilitating integration of the unprocessed, stored trauma with the logical, adaptive information of the left brain. EMDR moves beyond just talking about memories and reaches the subcortical, right-brain structures (van der Kolk, 2002). Numerous studies have demonstrated that EMDR effectively reduces traumatic stress in children (e.g., Ahmad, Larsson, & Sundelin-Wahlsten, 2007; Chemtob, Nakashima, & Carlson, 2002; de Roos et al., 2011; Jaberghaderi, Greenwald, Rubin, Dolatabadim, & Zand, 2004; Kemp, Drummond, & McDermott, 2010). Preliminary studies have shown EMDR to have a positive effect on attachments (Madrid, Skolek, & Shapiro, 2006; Potter, Davidson, & Wesselmann, 2013; Robredo, 2011; Taylor, 2002; Wesselmann & Potter, 2009). In our ongoing research, we have found that children with a history of attachment trauma show significant improvement in scores on behavioral and attachment measures following 24 weeks or more of Integrative Team Treatment involving EMDR and family therapy (Attachment and Trauma Center of Nebraska, 2011; Wesselmann, 2013; Wesselmann & Shapiro, 2013; Wesselmann et al., 2012).

CONCLUSION

Think about the children whose development and brain functioning have been compromised by early family neglect and abuse. They are unable to self-regulate due to poor neurological integration and an overactive limbic brain. They live largely in a state of hyper- or hypoarousal, and they perceive a threatening world where they are unable to trust the people who are caring for them. If they are removed from their family-of-origin by the authorities, they are then physically safe but grief-stricken over the loss of their parents, to whom they had an attachment—albeit, a disorganized one. If they enter foster care or care by relatives, they remain in survival mode, reacting with aggression to their present caregivers' attempts to parent them. At other times, they become emotionally shut down and unreachable. Their caregivers become increasingly punitive as they attempt to control alarming behaviors. These behaviors escalate in response, until the caregivers make a call to their caseworker and ask to have the children moved. The move reinforces these children's belief that they have no place in the world.

Children with stored, unprocessed trauma and a brain structured to be reactive are commonly delayed in their emotional, social, and cognitive development. Due to their neurological and psychological injuries and their poor ability to manage stress, they may receive multiple diagnoses over the years. They may also have a genetic predisposition to mental health disorders.

Many children with a history of attachment trauma have been removed from abusive or neglectful biological families and placed with new caregivers. Others are reunified with their rehabilitated biological parents. Despite an end to the mistreatment, the children are left with stored, unprocessed memories and their associated emotions, sensations, thoughts, and images. They continue to function with a brain structured to be emotionally reactive and self-protective, and they continue to self-regulate through maladaptive behaviors. When their current caregivers become frustrated and punitive, their negative beliefs about themselves and others are reinforced.

Due to an increased understanding of the causes of the severe symptoms and behaviors in affected children, there is new hope. The Integrative Team Treatment, involving collaboration between family and EMDR therapists, is designed to overcome the special challenges to treating this special population. The foundational work provided through the parent education and family therapy component helps ensure successful implementation of the EMDR.

There is an enormous population of children who are suffering from attachment trauma. Traumatized children require compassionate and effective help from the society that has failed to provide them with an appropriate, nurturing environment during the first months or years of life. They deserve treatment that will reduce reactivity and fear, facilitate neurological integration, and allow them to discover the joy of human connection, trust, and love.

Chapter 2
OVERVIEW OF THE EMDR INTEGRATIVE TEAM TREATMENT MODEL

TEAMWORK IS A COMMON term, but it can be difficult to execute in a therapeutic situation. The EMDR and family therapy Integrative Team Treatment model is founded upon the necessity of teamwork. Children who experience attachment trauma truly require a team to help them learn to manage day-to-day life, successfully regulate their feelings, remove obstacles related to past trauma, and establish lasting and loving relationships with others. The complexity of these children and their lives requires trained clinicians and parents working together to heal the whole child and repair the family. Without a team, the process of healing can be overwhelming for all involved: the client, the family, and the provider.

The team includes an EMDR therapist and a family therapist. Each therapist has a distinct role and follows specific protocol criteria necessary for building healthy attachments in the family and for removing obstacles to closeness created by trauma in the child's past. The collaboration between the therapists enhances effectiveness and efficiency of the treatment. The family therapist provides the foundational preparation work for the EMDR, and the EMDR therapist begins implementing protocols for strengthening attachment and self-regulation. The therapists continue to collaborate and integrate their work as treatment progresses toward desensitization and reprocessing of triggers and past memories and the development of future templates.

The four primary components of the EMDR and family therapy Integrative Team Treatment model include:

1. Parent education
2. Family therapy
3. EMDR therapy
4. Peer consultation

Following is an overview of the four components and the progression of the treatment model.

BEGINNING TREATMENT

Once the family has committed to participation in the team approach, an appointment is made for the first session. The initial sessions are critical in setting the tone for the therapeutic environment. Ideally, if the child has two parents, both participate in the therapy, but realistically, one parent may participate with more frequency than the other. Both the family therapist and EMDR therapist focus on developing a collaborative therapeutic relationship with the parents and the child that focuses on healing for the whole family.

Assessments

Formal assessments can provide useful information regarding specific behaviors, traumatic stress, dissociation, attentional problems, impulsivity, and attachment that cannot be determined through a history-taking interview. Assessments can be repeated in the latter part of treatment to accurately assess change. As clinical scores reach nonclinical level, frequency of sessions can be reduced, typically beginning at 6–12 months of treatment. The frequency continues to be reduced until the par-

21

ents and therapeutic team agree that the family is ready for discharge. See Appendix B for information regarding assessment tools that we have found helpful. Parents can be asked to complete assessments prior to the history-taking session to determine the severity of the problems and the appropriateness of the full Integrative Team Treatment protocol.

History-Taking

It is recommended that both the family therapist and the EMDR therapist meet with the parents without the child present for most of the initial history-taking. The therapists talk with the parents and gather the child's history, including information about the prenatal period, birth, infancy, and early childhood, as well as losses and caregiver changes and separations, medical trauma, and any other traumatic experiences. At times there is little information about the child's history, and the therapists must do the best they can with the information given, relying on the child's memories. Sometimes it is possible to contact current or previous caseworkers or social workers, who may be able to provide additional information. The therapists assess current behaviors at home and school, past and current medications, and gather the history of previous mental health treatments. Releases of information are signed and other mental health records are requested. School, cultural, or religious issues are identified.

During the initial session, the parents should be given information about the structure of the integrative protocol, the importance of having at least one parent in attendance at all sessions during the therapeutic process, and the importance of regular attendance. The therapist explains that the child and one or both parents will probably be attending therapy 2 hours per week for approximately 6–12 months, with gradual decrease in frequency as the child's behaviors improve. We have discovered that regular attendance with each therapist on a weekly basis is critical to the success of the treatment, and this point should be emphasized when meeting with the parents. Reducing frequency before new patterns of behavior and interactions have become fully established will result in backsliding.

During the initial history-taking session, the therapists can go over the checklist in Appendix A with the parents. Besides providing information the therapists can use to conceptualize the case, this discussion regarding the checklist can assist the therapists in helping the parents to begin hypothesizing about the source of the child's negative beliefs and understanding the traumatic roots of the child's behaviors. The checklist can also be given to the parents along with formal assessments prior to the history-taking session.

As the information-gathering session progresses, therapists are directly and indirectly assessing the parents' level of understanding regarding attachment issues, their parenting skills, their support system, their marital or other relationship, and their emotional well-being. Questions regarding the parents' extended family support and the style of parenting in which they were raised can help determine whether or not the parents may suffer from a traumatic past.

The therapists should describe the ups and downs of the therapeutic process, including the gains and setbacks that are likely to occur. This discussion provides a good opportunity for the family therapist to plant a seed with the parents regarding the idea of participation in their own individual therapy by acknowledging the stress related to raising traumatized children and by mentioning that many parents do seek therapeutic support for themselves during the child's treatment process.

Following the history-taking session, the weekly sessions with the family therapist and EMDR therapist are scheduled. If possible, the therapists should schedule the appointments back-to-back, with the EMDR session following the family session. Although this is an ideal way to schedule the appointments, the protocol is also effective if the family must come in for two separate appointments, as long as there is good weekly communication between the therapists.

INTEGRATIVE PARENTING: THE EDUCATIONAL COMPONENT

Parent education is an important component of this treatment model. The accompanying guide, *Integrative Parenting: Strategies for Raising Children Affected by Attachment Trauma* (Wesselmann, Schweitzer, & Armstrong, 2013) was developed to facilitate parents' understanding of attachment, trauma, and brain development and to provide parents with a unique set of parenting tools that will enhance the therapeutic work. This book acts as a springboard for ongoing discussion, guidance, and support for the parents in the weekly therapy sessions and helps them shift from emotion-driven responses to calmer, more attuned *integrative parenting* strategies.

The therapeutic team also has the option of providing the information in the parent guide to a group of parents in a class format. This format can be an efficient method of presenting and discussing the material, and also allows parents to receive support from one another. Each of the five chapters can be presented and discussed in approximately 2 hours.

Following is a brief explanation of the content contained in each of the guide's five chapters:

1. "Scared Children, Not Scary Children" helps parents understand how attachment trauma has impacted their child's neurology and belief system. This chapter facilitates a paradigm shift in parents from viewing their child's behaviors as intentional to viewing the behaviors as driven by past trauma and a brain stuck in "survival mode."

2. "Creating Connections" teaches parents how to develop mindfulness in themselves and how to encourage mindful-

ness in their child. It focuses on the importance of creating experiences of closeness and connection with their child and encourages playfulness as an important method of strengthening the relationship.

3. "Solutions to Challenging Behaviors" reviews the most common troubling behaviors of traumatized children and describes the underlying beliefs and emotions driving the behaviors, as well as effective, integrative parenting strategies. Learning to understand and effectively respond to the three phases of a meltdown is emphasized.

4. "Becoming a Happier Parent" helps parents to reflect on the thoughts and feelings that are driving their reactions to their child. The class helps parents find methods that help them cope in the face of these struggles.

5. "Boundaries and Consequences with Love and Attunement" provides parents with new tools to help them create safe and appropriate boundaries and manage the day-to-day behaviors presented by the child. The chapter clearly delineates the differences between *emotion-driven* and *integrative parenting* methods.

By reading the parent guide or attending a class based on the material, parents begin to understand that their hurt children appear manipulative and rage-filled only because their brains are in survival mode. Children in "survival brain" view the world as an unsafe and dangerous place that requires them to take charge and control even the most minor situations. When traumatized children are given instructions or redirected, they become triggered, and out of the drive to survive, they attempt to gain control of the situation through manipulation or anger. Prior to participation in the Integrative Team Treatment model, parents often use severe words, a harsh tone of voice, and punishments in an attempt to match the severity of the child's behaviors. The parent guide points out that emotion-driven parenting approaches are triggers for traumatized children and only serve to further reinforce their negative beliefs. The guide is designed to give parents an opportunity to gain insight into the root cause of their children's behaviors and to develop effective tools for calming the children (which can happen only by calming brain processes), thereby fostering more rapid change.

OVERVIEW OF THE FAMILY THERAPIST ROLE

During the beginning of family sessions, the therapist meets with parents one-on-one and creates a nonjudgmental, warm environment that allows parents to open up and share their feelings honestly, while discussing both successes and challenges.

The family therapist provides the foundational work for the EMDR therapist. The family therapist intervenes to shift the parents from emotion-driven parenting to the integrative parenting method for calming and integrating the child's reactive brain. The family therapist must be able to balance emotional attunement and empathy toward parents while giving them direct feedback regarding parenting techniques. The family therapist encourages self-care for parents and refers parents to individual and/or couple therapy as needed.

The family therapist supports the introduction of EMDR by increasing parents' recognition of the impact of the child's traumatic history on his or her behaviors. The family therapist helps the child and parent understand how trauma is stored and how the associated cognitions and affects are repeatedly triggered, driving the child's behaviors. Through the use of a variety of therapeutic techniques, the child becomes more aware of thoughts, past events, and emotions influencing his or her choices and behaviors in current-day situations. The family therapist lays the groundwork for the EMDR therapist by helping the child identify negative cognitions, current triggers, and traumatic memories. The cognitive work completed in the family therapy session is then carried over to the EMDR session and reprocessed for deeper understanding and the creation of new, healthy, adaptive neurological connections in the child's brain.

OVERVIEW OF THE EMDR THERAPIST ROLE

The EMDR therapist plays a unique role in the integrative model. EMDR appears to facilitate a natural associative process that leads to the creation of new neurological connections between neural networks holding unprocessed disturbing events and helpful, adaptive information stored within other parts of the brain.

"To ensure the successful use of EMDR with children, the clinician must pay special attention to creating a safe psychological environment, and as with any other procedure, EMDR should not be used unless the clinician is already comfortable working with them" (Shapiro, 2001, p. 281). The EMDR therapist provides both the child and parent with a warm, accepting atmosphere and explains EMDR to the family and child in simple terms.

Preparation Phase of EMDR

EMDR memory work can bring up strong emotions for the parents who are present in the room as well as for the child. The family work and the EMDR preparation work help to ensure that the child and parents have the support and resources they need to experience the feelings related to difficult, hurtful, and confusing memories.

One of the major roles of the EMDR therapist utilizing the Integrative Team Treatment model is attachment resource development (ARD), which involves a series of exercises (described in detail in Chapter 5) that create closeness and positive feelings between the parent and child to establish and strengthen the current attachment relationship. The EMDR therapist uses other traditional resource development methods to help the child create a safe or calm place, a container, and to reinforce the "most

27

grown-up child" state. Self-regulation development and installation (S-RDI) is a protocol designed to reinforce the child's ability to self-regulate.

Assessment Phase of EMDR

The third phase of EMDR (assessment) presents challenges for children with a history of attachment trauma due to the lack of self-awareness and their poor vocabulary for describing feelings. Although the children are full of complex emotions, *happy* and *mad* are often the only emotions they recognize. They also struggle to find the words to formulate a negative or positive cognition. Chapter 6 describes adaptations to help children learn how to identify emotions, sensations, and cognitions.

The EMDR therapist who is fortunate enough to have a treatment team can rely on the family therapist to assist with the assessment phase of EMDR. The "detective work" initiated in family therapy often identifies useful triggers, cognitions, and touchstone events, and this information is passed along to the EMDR therapist, who is able to begin processing the material almost immediately.

Desensitization and Reprocessing

During desensitization and reprocessing of recent and past events, the EMDR therapist implements necessary creative adaptations to handle the reality that children who have been exposed to abuse and neglect frequently have difficulty sitting still and concentrating, are easily dysregulated, and lack appropriate, adaptive information. Chapter 6 describes how the EMDR therapist utilizes the emotional support of the parents as well as a variety of tools, including drawings, sand trays, stuffed animals, and empowering interweaves, to assist children in optimally reprocessing upsetting memories. The family therapist lays much groundwork for successful EMDR reprocessing by providing children with helpful knowledge and coaching them to express their thoughts and feelings.

Future Templates

When implementing the steps involved in creating future templates (see Chapter 6), the EMDR therapist utilizes role play or a mental movie, in conjunction with bilateral stimulation, to reinforce a positive response to a challenging situation. The family therapist supports the work by teaching skills that can be reinforced during the work involved in creating future templates.

COLLABORATION

Figure 2.1 is a flow chart that provides a visual aid to help both the family therapist and EMDR therapist stay mindful of the progressive steps involved in the collaborative treatment. It may be helpful to refer to this chart while reading Chapters 4–6.

The foundational work conducted in family therapy saves the EMDR therapist time and allows him or her to implement EMDR weekly, moving the therapy along as efficiently as possible. It is not necessary for the EMDR therapist to negotiate whether or not EMDR will be utilized, as parents and child expect the EMDR to take place each week. Because much of the material for EMDR reprocessing is identified during family therapy and communicated directly to the EMDR therapist, the EMDR therapist is able to implement the treatment quite early in the session, allowing adequate time for processing. When the family therapy session directly precedes the EMDR session, the child and parents enter EMDR therapy with the family session fresh in their minds.

PEER CONSULTATION COMPONENT

Peer consultation is the final component in the treatment model. It is recommended that clinicians gather on a weekly or twice-weekly basis with treatment plans, updates, and challenges in hand to discuss client progress and consider where clients and

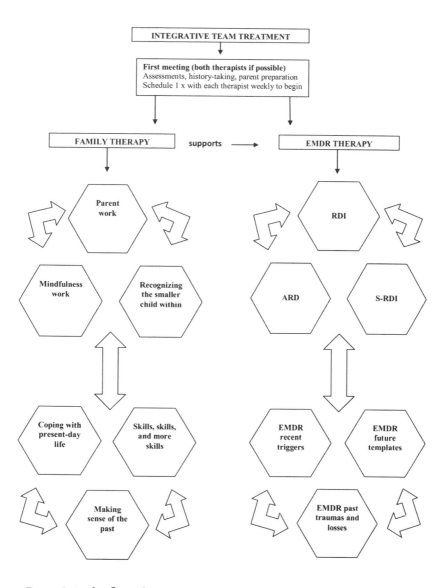

FIGURE 2.1. The flow chart provides a general sequence for the family therapist and EMDR therapist interventions, although both therapists strategically weave back and forth within the protocol. The work of the family therapist (left column) informs and supports the work of the EMDR therapist (on the right). Clinical judgment determines readiness for each new step of the protocol.

families are stuck. Each team will need to make its own decision regarding the length of the consultation. We prefer meeting twice weekly for 2 hours each time. We begin consultation with a mindfulness activity to assist therapists in maintaining self-regulation while discussing challenging cases. Next, we write the meeting agenda on a dry-erase board, prioritizing the cases appropriately. The peer consultation form in Appendix D helps structure and increase the effectiveness of the consultation.

Peer consultation is designed to address high-priority cases first—cases in which there are serious safety issues occurring in the home or in which the child's placement is at risk of disruption. In this consultation meeting a brief history of the child's life and traumatic events is outlined. The therapeutic team summarizes therapeutic gains or challenges by reviewing what has been covered during sessions. Following the summary, a brainstorming session begins with thoughts, suggestions, or insights offered regarding ways to solve a current issue or ideas for quickly stabilizing a jeopardized placement. Members of the peer consultation team should also consider involving other professionals, such as caseworkers, psychologists, and psychiatrists, as necessary. Although it may not be possible to have all these members present during each peer consultation meeting, having them participate via phone/Skype can be very beneficial and is strongly advised when dealing with difficult cases.

After covering the high-priority cases, therapists are asked to discuss cases where parents, children, or both seem to be stuck. The team collaborates to conceptualize what is blocking progress in the families and brainstorms ideas regarding what part of the protocol should be implemented, the need for an additional service, or how to best address a parent-related issue. We often role-play to prepare for initiating a difficult discussion with parents who are overly punitive. We frequently brainstorm to successfully identify negative cognitions and emotions driving a child's very stuck behaviors. Peer consultation can ignite the creative energy of a treatment team to meet the challenges presented by the families in treatment. Many exciting and sometimes unique approaches to a problem are discovered during the therapeutic brainstorm.

The peer consultation time should be safe and supportive for each therapist. The shared time can provide an opportunity to ask for and provide helpful feedback for one another and sometimes discuss personal feelings related to the difficult cases. It is normal for therapists to experience a variety of emotions when working with complex and challenging cases, such as disappointment in a parent's decision to place a child outside the home, self-doubt about providing a certain intervention, or countertransference issues with a parent. An important part of the peer consultation is the opportunity to experience mutual support and to talk through the personal challenges, problem-solve, role-play, or find a helpful perspective. Part of the recipe for treatment success is the therapists' positive morale and enthusiasm for the work.

SENSITIVE THERAPEUTIC ATTUNEMENT

Traumatized children and traumatized parents provide a unique challenge in the therapeutic setting. Parents come into session battered, sometimes both physically and emotionally, and at a loss as to how to handle their child. They may be angry and resentful toward this child due to many overwhelming problems and behaviors, and they may be hoping to temporarily place the child outside their home or disrupt the adoption or placement. Parents are often isolated from friends and extended family members and feel as if their entire world revolves around the child. Children also come to therapy angry, hurt and, defensive. They may have been involved in previous therapies, and they are resistant to starting over once again. The therapist must attune to the emotions of everyone in the family and create a therapeutic environment that entices both the parents and the child to participate.

Some parents feel uncomfortable and unsure about their role in the weekly sessions. The philosophy of the treatment may be completely new and feel quite foreign to the parents. Part of the job of the therapists is to help parents feel like they are part of the child's therapeutic team.

The first 15–20 minutes of each family therapy and EMDR therapy session are spent meeting with the parent alone. This allows parents to report on the child's behaviors and share their feelings privately, and it gives them an opportunity to review what may be asked of them during the session. The time alone also helps build positive rapport between therapist and parents.

Working with severely traumatized children in therapy is work. Therapists implementing this model must be ready to attune to the emotional state of the child and adjust voice tone, volume, and physical proximity to create a "secure, holding environment" (Winnicott, 1965) for the child. For the anxious child who is either fidgety or dissociative, the therapist may need to move his or her chair very close in proximity to the child's chair and speak in a gentle voice to calm the child. In contrast, some children may be triggered by closeness and require more physical distance. It is important for the therapist to consistently assess the child's emotional state to ensure that the child feels safe, heard, and accepted before beginning any therapeutic work.

Children who have been traumatized are often emotionally delayed. A child's chronological age may be 9, but emotionally he or she may behave, think, and react as a 4-year-old. The team of therapists must adjust their language, activities, and expectations to match the child's abilities. As the child moves through therapy and begins to change and grasp new insights, both therapists should adjust their expectations and language along the way.

Most therapists who work with children know that although

plans are helpful, they sometimes have to be set aside to address something that comes up in the moment. Something that happens in the car ride to therapy or even in the waiting room can change the course of a session. Therapists using this model attune to any pressing current emotional needs first and then move on to a strategy chosen from the protocol.

It is important to note that the protocol is not designed to be implemented in a linear fashion. Although there is an overall beginning, middle, and end to the therapy, both the family and EMDR therapist repeatedly weave back and forth through the protocol as needed.

Children with a history of attachment trauma are wonderfully unique and challenging. They require special flexibility, attunement, humor, creative ideas, and patience.

CONCLUSION

This model combines the work of an EMDR therapist and a family therapist, working in synch with one another to interrupt negative patterns of relating within the family. As therapy progresses, the child and the parents experience more positive interactions, and their connection grows stronger. As the parents move to a more mindful, attuned, and nurturing approach, the child becomes more regulated and more trusting. As the child opens up emotionally, he or she is able to utilize the EMDR to reprocess past hurts, and the family begins to heal. Children who have participated in this treatment model feel better and do better; likewise, families feel better and do better. When relationships are positive and close, the ups and downs of everyday life can be tolerated. It takes teamwork—two therapists, parents, the child, and other supportive services—to initiate and sustain change. Moving hurt children toward healthier functioning is exciting and meaningful work. One mom said, "You gave our family our life back."

Chapter 3

CASE CONCEPTUALIZATION AND TREATMENT PLANNING USING THE AIP MODEL

ACCORDING TO SHAPIRO's AIP model (2007), the human brain regularly processes emotions and information related to daily life events through a natural process in which the experience is synthesized with other previously stored, adaptive information in the brain. When children experience neglect, abuse, or loss related to attachment figures, disturbing images, emotions, and sensations are stored in an unprocessed form in their limbic brain. When children are removed from their maltreating families, they continue to exhibit severe symptoms and behaviors, as the stored maladaptive beliefs and distressing emotions negatively skew their interpretation of interpersonal and other situations, interfering with relationships and adaptive functioning overall. When the problems and symptoms of children with a history of attachment trauma are examined with an eye to the "Big T" and "small t" life events, the family–EMDR therapist team is able to develop a roadmap for therapy.

A large part of the case conceptualization takes place in conjunction with the child's parents, which also helps the parents develop greater insight into, and compassion for, the traumatic roots of the child's behaviors. The History-Taking Checklist in Appendix A can be used by the therapist and the parents to help identify current symptoms and behaviors, triggers for the child's behaviors, possible early traumas, hypothesized negative cognitions (NCs), desired positive cognitions (PCs), and behaviors.

The history-taking session is a first opportunity to begin the educational component of the treatment model by taking time to explain how early traumas are stored in the child's brain. The concept of trauma-driven behaviors is new to most parents, and the information is likely in direct conflict with the parents' previously held beliefs. As therapy proceeds, it is common for parents to vacillate between the newfound understanding of their child's behaviors as rooted in traumatic past events and their previously held beliefs that the child's behaviors are simply the result of "bad choices." Parents typically need ongoing assistance to internalize and hold onto the trauma model.

BEHAVIORS AS SYMPTOMS

Both therapists or one member of the child's treatment team may conduct the initial history-taking. Parents may feel overwhelmed as they make checkmarks by behavior after behavior on the History-Taking Checklist, but at the same time, they may be comforted by the fact that their child's behaviors are on the list, proving that other children and families also deal with such challenges. As the therapist and the parents look over the list, the therapist explains that these behaviors are rooted in fear and negative beliefs associated with the early distressing events also noted on the checklist, and that chronic early stress also interferes with children's development in many areas. The therapist should reassure the parents that the team will be working closely with them to help their child heal.

In the following vignette, the therapist helps Mark's parents identify his most concerning symptoms and behaviors. (Note: Names and other identifying details in this case and all other cases in this manual have been changed to preserve anonymity.)

MARK'S ASSESSMENT

Mark is an 8-year-old boy who was removed from his biological mother at age 4 due to her neglect, abuse, and drug and alcohol use. He spent a year in foster care and then came to live with his adoptive family at age 6. During the history-taking session, the family therapist and the parents look together at the History-Taking Checklist and identify Mark's most concerning behaviors:

- Arguing
- Meltdowns
- Aggression
- Clingy with parents
- Lying
- Stealing

IDENTIFYING TRAUMATIC EVENTS

The therapist and parents can use the list of traumas in the History-Taking Checklist as a starting point. Often, after therapy has begun and the child is feeling comfortable, the child reveals more detail regarding his or her own memories.

Sometimes case files or previous caseworkers can fill in missing information from the child's earliest months or years. Therapists should ask the parents what the children know about their preverbal experiences, how they were told, and how they tell their story to others. Children have mental "pictures" that they have developed related to what they know or believe to be true, and these mental pictures can later be used in EMDR therapy as a way of accessing and processing the emotions and sensations associated with the preverbal trauma that is stored in the implicit memory system. The therapist explains to the parents that preverbal material may be driving the child's current behaviors, despite the child's inability to consciously remember the event.

Attachment trauma can happen at any point in a child's life. The therapist should ask the child's parents about any known experiences of abuse, neglect, frightening parental behaviors, separations, and losses, criticism, or ridicule. Ask about any painful illnesses or medical interventions that may have been perceived by the child as a failure on the part of the parents to make him or her feel better. Look for trauma outside of the family environment as well, including car accidents, abuse by neighbors or teachers, and experiences of bullying or rejection by peers, and any recent traumas, as any of the child's traumatic experiences may be contributing to current symptoms and behaviors.

> The therapist assists Mark's parents in identifying important traumas from his past by jointly examining the list of traumas on the History-Taking Checklist and discussing what the parents know from recollections Mark has recounted as well as information they had received from his caseworker. "Big T" and "small t" traumatic incidents included:
>
> • Being ignored when his mother was drinking
> • Being locked in his bedroom by his birth mother's boyfriend
> • Witnessing a violent episode involving birth mother's boyfriend
> • Being distraught at the good-bye visit with his birth mother

CURRENT TRIGGERS

As part of the history-taking and the development of the treatment plan, the therapist and parents work together to identify the present-day situations or triggers that seem to be associated with the child's concerning behaviors. Again, the History-Taking Checklist can be used as a resource. The therapist explains that in family therapy, the child will be assisted in recognizing his or her triggers and learning coping skills, and EMDR will be implemented to reduce the emotional charge associated with the triggers.

The therapist and Mark identify the following situations as triggers for Mark's challenging behaviors:

- Parents' attention focused on others
- Parents busy
- Being asked to do a chore
- Being sent to his room
- Being told "no"

IDENTIFYING THE NEGATIVE COGNITIONS

Although the child is not present for the initial history-taking, the therapist should invite the parents to look at the History-Taking Checklist while considering the child's trauma history and current behaviors in order to make some educated guesses about the negative cognitions (NCs) that might be fueling the child's actions. Explain to the parents that their child may know one thing intellectually, but believe something entirely different on a "gut" level. Explain that the child's trauma has led to very stuck, very irrational thinking that may not be at all consistent with reality. Identifying hypothesized NCs helps the therapists develop a beginning treatment plan and helps the parents immediately begin to develop greater insight and a more compassionate perspective regarding their child's actions.

Mark's parents collaborate with the therapist in identifying his NCs. As the therapist discusses Mark's traumatic memories with his parents, she encourages them to consider the overwhelming feelings of abandonment, rejection, and isolation he must have felt, as well as the disappointment in the grown-ups who were supposed to take care of him. Next, the therapist and parents examine the relationship between Mark's early traumas and his present-day behaviors and conclude that Mark must be interpreting his parents' behaviors as evidence that they don't care about him. Mark seems especially triggered whenever he thinks he is being ignored or sent away, or when he thinks his parents don't care about what he wants. Mark's parents gain insight into Mark's struggles with trauma-related feelings of abandonment and hurt. They hypothesized the following NCs:

- "I'm alone."
- "My parents don't care about me."
- "Parents are mean."
- "I'll be rejected."
- "I don't belong."
- "I'm not good enough."

POSITIVE COGNITIONS

During the history-taking, the therapist asks the parents about the positive cognitions (PCs) they would like the child to adopt to replace the current NCs. There is a sample list of desired positive cognitions in the History-taking Checklist that might be helpful. This is probably the first time that most parents have given thought to their child's belief system and its impact on his or her behaviors.

The therapist assists Mark's parents in identifying PCs by pointing out that his behaviors would not be the same if he had a different belief system. The parents grow thoughtful when the therapist suggests that they consider how Mark might respond to redirection or inattention if he truly believed that he belonged, that he was loved, and that he was good. They identified the following PCs they hoped Mark could adopt over time:

- "I belong."
- "My parents love me and will always take care of me.
- "My parents care about my feelings and want me to be happy."
- "I'm lovable and good."

Even though this session is focused on getting a good history for planning treatment, the family therapist implements an early intervention by encouraging Mark's parents to begin countering Mark's NCs by increasing verbal affirmations of their love for him and avoiding use of time-outs in his room, as the isolation appears to reinforce his negative beliefs.

DESIRED FUTURE BEHAVIORS

By now, the parents are beginning to understand that changing the child's belief system is a crucial component to changing the way the child responds to his or her environment. However, the therapist should point out that the child has been trapped in feelings, thoughts, and behaviors related to his or her traumatic past for a very long time, and therefore the child will also need assistance in learning alternative behavioral skills. Together, the therapist and parents can identify desired behaviors and skills the child needs.

Mark's parents easily identify four behaviors they would like Mark to be able to adopt in the future:

- Positive coping when parents' attention is focused elsewhere
- Following directions and redirections
- Accepting a "no" answer
- Staying honest

THE TREATMENT PLAN

Following the history-taking session, the treatment team creates a beginning treatment plan for the child and parents. The overall goals of the treatment team typically include (1) increasing attachment security and emotional support from the parents, (2) eliminating or reducing the child's problem behaviors, (3) restructuring the child's belief system, (4) removing the emotional charge related to the child's memories and triggers, and (5) developing new behavioral skills.

In order to accomplish the overall goals, the family and EMDR therapists each carry out specific objectives. The family therapist assists the parents in the implementation of integrative parenting strategies, as outlined in the parent guide, *Integrative Parenting: Strategies for Raising Children Affected by Attachment Trauma* (Wesselmann et al., 2013) to improve the home environment. The family therapist coaches the child in mindfulness and self-regulation skills and lays the foundation for EMDR by developing a timeline and a narrative of the child's life story that identifies traumas, NCs, and desired PCs. (See Chapter 4.)

The specific objectives of the EMDR therapist include implementation of positive resource development and installation (RDI), attachment resource development (ARD) for enhancing feelings of closeness, and self-regulation development and installation (S-RDI). The EMDR therapist also reprocesses triggers and memories and develops positive templates for the future. (See Chapters 5 and 6.)

MARK'S TREATMENT PLAN

The family therapist will . . .

1. Help the parents implement integrative parenting strategies to increase Mark's sense of security and calm his reactive brain.
2. Assist Mark in developing mindfulness and self-regulation

skills to help him cope with triggers and prepare him for managing emotions during EMDR.

3. Help Mark develop a time line and narrative of his life story, identifying major events, NCs, and desired PCs. (See Chapter 4.)

4. Assist Mark and his parents in an examination of all problematic interactions to look for the NCs and triggers.

5. Provide the EMDR therapist with all identified triggers, memories, NCs, and PCs for reprocessing.

6. Assist Mark in developing new skills and behaviors, such as finding something to do when his parents are busy, following directions, and giving honest answers to questions.

The EMDR therapist will . . .

1. Implement RDI, ARD, and S-RDI with Mark to strengthen a positive view of self, feelings of closeness with his parents, and capacity to self-regulate.

2. Implement EMDR to desensitize current triggers and restructure beliefs related to situations in which Mark's parents are focused on someone else or telling him no.

3. Implement EMDR with Mark to reprocess memories and reinforce new positive cognitions related to being ignored when his birth mother was drinking, being locked in his bedroom, witnessing domestic violence, and saying goodbye to his birth mother.

4. Use EMDR with Mark to reinforce positive future templates involving new behavioral skills developed during family therapy.

Certainly not everything that therapists need to know is uncovered during the history-taking session. The work of the family therapist to identify triggers and NCs is ongoing throughout treatment. As various situations arise, they become opportunities to learn more about the child and his or her beliefs and triggers. As the family and EMDR work continues, it is not uncommon for the child to share additional memories not previously known to the parents; these added memories allow therapists to help the child address all of his or her significant "Big T" and "small t" traumas.

DEANNA: ADOPTED CHILD WITH DEVELOPMENTAL DELAY AND A HISTORY OF ORPHANAGE CARE

Deanna is a 13-year-old Russian female who resided in an orphanage in Russia for the first 7 months of her life. Deanna is mildly mentally handicapped and has a speech impairment. She is the only child of a single, adoptive mother.

Deanna's Presenting Symptoms/Behaviors

The first day Deanna walked into the waiting room, she clung to her mother and complained loudly that she did not feel safe with the other children and infants in the waiting room. In the therapy office, she curled up into a fetal position on the couch and said in a loud voice, "Everyone always says I am the problem. But I think everyone else is the problem." Her mother explained that she suffered from extreme anxiety and phobias about children and babies; she constantly argued with her mother and with peers and teachers at school; she suffered from panic attacks when she was in public places; and she had frequent angry meltdowns in public and at home. She also avoided physical closeness or affection with her mother.

Deanna's Trauma History

During the history-taking session, Deanna's mother reported that Deanna had experienced a great deal of "small t" rejection in preschool, and the therapist agreed that rejection by peers has great impact on children. The mother also explained that Deanna had been abandoned as an infant and that she had adopted Deanna from a Russian orphanage when Deanna was 7 months old. Deanna's mother asked the therapist how events so early in Deanna's life could still be impacting her behaviors. The therapist explained that preverbal trauma is stored as emotional memory in the implicit memory system, and that the stored emotions can be triggered without any conscious recall of the memory itself. The therapist also suggested that Deanna had likely created pictures in her mind of what she imagined had happened, and that these mental pictures were traumatic to her. Later, in therapy, it became clear that Deanna had created pictures in her mind related to what she knew of her early life, and in fact, Deanna was adamant that she could remember life in the orphanage at 7 months of age.

Deanna's Triggers

During the history-taking session, the therapist learned that Deanna was triggered to become argumentative or explosive when she was corrected or told no by her mother or teachers. She often exhibited angry reactions to any type of interaction with peers. She became especially anxious and agitated around young children or babies, and she frequently complained that babies and children in her vicinity were attempting to "argue" with her.

Deanna's NCs

Together, the therapist and Deanna's mother thought about her history, her behaviors, and her triggers, and they hypothesized several important NCs:

- "I'm not safe around babies and children."
- "Babies and children want to argue with me."

- "I have to be in control to be safe."
- "I have to be in charge of getting what I need."
- "I can't control my feelings and urges."
- "I can't trust or depend on grown-ups to take care of me."

Desired PCs

The therapist and mother identified beliefs that they hoped Deanna would adopt through the therapy:

- "I'm safe around children and babies."
- "I'm safe without arguing."
- "It's safe to remain calm."
- "I can trust my mom to take care of me and keep me safe."
- "I can trust my teachers to be in charge and keep me safe."
- "I don't have to act on my feelings and urges."

Deanna's Future Templates

The therapist encouraged Deanna's mother to describe how she would ideally wish to see her daughter functioning at home and school, and in this way, they identified behaviors that would later be taught, rehearsed, and then reinforced with EMDR. Deanna's mother wanted Deanna to be able to remain calm and cooperative in the classroom, interact appropriately with peers and teachers, remain calm in public places around children and babies, accept directions and corrections from her mother at home, and give and receive affection with her mother.

Deanna's Treatment Plan

After Deanna's behaviors, traumas, triggers, NCs, and PCs had been identified, the therapists were able to develop a beginning treatment plan—subject to change as they began working with Deanna and learning more about her:

The family therapist will . . .

1. Help Deanna's mother implement integrative parenting strategies to help calm Deanna's reactive brain.
2. Assist Deanna in developing mindfulness and self-regulation skills to help her cope with her emotions in the presence of children and babies, whenever her mother and teachers correct her, and during EMDR.
3. Begin helping Deanna develop a timeline and a narrative of her life story, identifying major events, NCs, and desired PCs. (See Chapter 4.) Assist Deanna and her mother in examining all problematic interactions and identifying the NCs and triggers.
4. Provide the EMDR therapist with all identified triggers, memories, NCs, and PCs for reprocessing.
5. Assist Deanna in developing new interpersonal behaviors such as following directions, saying "OK," and other appropriate social skills.

The EMDR therapist will . . .

1. Implement EMDR resource work with Deanna (RDI, ARD, and S-RDI) to strengthen a calm, positive affect state, feelings of closeness with her mother, and capacity to self-regulate.
2. Implement EMDR with Deanna to desensitize current triggers and restructure beliefs related to being around other children and babies and receiving directions or corrections from adults.
3. Implement EMDR with Deanna to process memories and develop new positive cognitions related to past experiences of rejection in preschool as well as mental pictures and emotions related to her preverbal trauma.
4. Use EMDR with Deanna to reinforce positive future templates related to new positive behaviors taught by the family therapist.

Deanna's therapy is described further in Chapter 7.

EVAN, LIVING WITH BIOLOGICAL FATHER AND STEPMOTHER

Evan was an 11-year-old boy who had lived with his father and stepmother for 1 year. He had been removed from the care of his biological mother due to physical abuse.

Evan's Presenting Symptoms/Behaviors

Evan had been hospitalized twice after becoming out of control. He exhibited violent meltdowns in the home, avoided closeness with his parents, and refused to accept their directions. He was uncooperative with teachers and had poor social skills and no friends. His father and stepmother were exhausted and angry. In the therapy office, he presented as angry and withdrawn.

Evan's Trauma History

Evan had shared with investigators and previous therapists memories of being physically beaten by his biological mother.

Evan's Current Triggers

Evan's defiant and aggressive behaviors were triggered when he was asked to do a chore or homework or told no by his father or stepmother. He was triggered at school by redirection from teachers or teasing or confrontation by classmates.

Evan's NCs

Together, the therapist and Evan's parents thought about his behaviors, his history, and his triggers, and they hypothesized his NCs:

- "Parents and other adults are mean."
- "I can't trust parents or other adults to be in charge."
- "No one loves me."
- "I'll always be rejected."
- "I'm bad and shameful."

Desired PCs

Together, the therapist and Evan's parents identified PCs they hoped Evan would be able to adopt through the therapy:

- "Parents and other important adults do care about me."
- "I can trust parents and other important adults to be in charge."
- "I'm loved."
- "I have a lot to offer, and I can learn to make friends."
- "I'm lovable and good."

Evan's Future Templates

The therapist and parents agreed that to have a happy life, Evan needed to learn to accept affection, follow directions, accept corrections, and apply friendship skills.

Evan's Treatment Plan

The therapists developed a beginning treatment plan. The family therapist's initial goal was to help Evan's parents learn and apply integrative parenting strategies in the home. She also planned to begin helping Evan develop skills for self-regulation, a timeline, and a narrative of his life story as foundational work for EMDR. (See Chapter 4.) Throughout the therapy, the family therapist planned to help Evan and his parents examine any current crises in terms of identifying problem triggers and NCs and teaching Evan appropriate new behavioral responses.

The EMDR therapist's initial goal was to implement

EMDR to reinforce positive experiences of closeness, help Evan develop affect tolerance, and desensitize his most common triggers at home and at school. The EMDR therapist planned to use EMDR to help Evan process the previously reported memories of abuse and to reinforce positive future templates related to cooperative responses at home and friendship skills at school.

JUSTIN: ADOPTED AFTER 2 YEARS IN THE HOSPITAL

Justin was a 6-year-old boy who had been born in the United States with severe intestinal issues. His birth parents relinquished him at birth due to the complicated medical issues and their limited capacity to meet his needs. Justin resided in the hospital for an entire 6 months with no caregiver other than doctors and nurses. Around the age of 6 months, he was transferred to another medical facility where he underwent an organ transplant. When Justin was 18 months old, a couple read an article about his situation and decided to pursue adoption. After beginning the paperwork, the couple was allowed to meet the little boy. They were shocked to discover that Justin had become emotionally attached to his IV pole. Justin had spent his entire life thus far with the pole, which he held onto while sucking his fingers. He did not sit up on his own and was highly sensitive to touch. Justin had to remain in the hospital for another 6 months before coming to his "forever home."

Justin's Presenting Symptoms/Behaviors.

During history-taking, Justin's parents described him as argumentative and angry. He only allowed touch from his adoptive mother. He had to follow a very strict diet and power-struggled over the food. He had poor friendship skills and few friends and did not seem to know how to play.

Justin's Trauma History

Justin had suffered numerous painful medical interventions and had experienced no attachment figures before 2 years of age.

Justin's Triggers

Justin was triggered by mealtimes, unwanted or surprise touch, being told "no," and interactions with peers.

Justin's NCs

The therapist and Justin's parents hypothesized his NCs:

- "I'm in charge of myself and don't need anyone."
- "Parents are mean."
- "I should get to eat what I want, like other kids."
- "I'm not likeable."
- "Touch hurts and is unsafe."

Desired PCs

Justin's parents hoped that Justin could adopt the following PCs through the therapy:

- "It's good to allow my mom and dad to be in charge; they will keep me safe and love me."
- "I have a forever mom who will keep me and love me no matter what."
- "I can work with my mom and dad to figure out good things to eat that I like."
- "Touch can be enjoyed."
- "I can have friends who like me and want to play with me."
- "I can play by myself and be OK."

Justin's Future Templates

The therapist and Justin's parents agreed that, in the future, they would like to see Justin staying calm while eating a meal, accepting the word "no," playing, and exhibiting friendship skills.

Justin's Treatment Plan

Justin's treatment plan for family therapy focused on helping his parents with integrative parenting strategies, building Justin's capacity to self-regulate and manage triggers, and developing a timeline, narrative of his life story, and positive interpersonal skills. The plan for EMDR therapy focused on processing Justin's mental pictures related to the preverbal traumas, desensitizing current triggers related to food and touch, and developing future templates for handling the word *no* and managing mealtime. Because of the extent of the preverbal attachment trauma, the EMDR therapist elaborated the resource development for attachment security, as described in detail in Chapter 7.

SUSAN: BIOLOGICAL CHILD WITH A HISTORY OF MEDICAL TRAUMA

Susan, a 17-year-old girl with developmental delay, had undergone several painful surgeries for medical problems between ages 2 and 7, and her devoted mother was always present following each surgery.

Susan's Presenting Symptoms/Behaviors

Susan's mother described problems with aggressive outbursts that were most frequent when her mother was present.

Susan's Trauma History

As Susan's mother listed the many painful medical interventions that Susan had endured in her life, it occurred to the therapist to ask where the mother was during the events. Susan's mother replied, "Well, of course I was right there with her as soon as they allowed me into the recovery room after every surgery. I always wanted to make sure my face was the first thing she saw." It dawned on the therapist that the mother's face had probably become associated with the painful experiences, and she explained this to Susan's mother, who nodded and said, "I had never thought of it that way. Worse yet, I had to be trained to insert a feeding tube when she was little. I know she didn't understand why I was doing this horrible thing to her."

Susan's Current Triggers

Susan was especially triggered whenever her mother gave her a direction, corrected a behavior, asked her to do a chore, or said no to a request.

Susan's NCs

The therapist and Susan's mother examined Susan's behaviors, triggers, and traumas and identified the following NCs:

- "My mom is mean."
- "My mom doesn't really care about me."
- "I have to be in charge to be safe."

Desired PCs

Susan's mother hoped that Susan could come to believe the following PCs:

- "My mom loves me and wants me to be happy."
- "I can let my mom be in charge."
- "My mom keeps me safe."

Susan's Future Templates

Susan's mother wished that Susan would accept affection, redirection, and help from her without anger.

Susan's Treatment Plan

The family therapist made a plan to help Susan's mother implement integrative parenting strategies and to help Susan develop the capacity for self-regulation. The family therapist also made a plan to help Susan develop a time-line, a narrative of her life story, and new interpersonal skills. The EMDR therapist's goals included reinforcing experiences of closeness between Susan and her mother and reprocessing the triggers in their relationship. This work would be interspersed with EMDR reprocessing of memories related to painful medical experiences and her mother's involvement. Future template work was planned to reinforce new interpersonal skills. As treatment progressed, Susan and her mother made great gains in their relationship. Susan discovered the trust and security she had felt prior to age 2 and was discharged after 9 months of treatment.

CONCLUSION

Identification of the negative cognitions, memories, and triggers driving troubled children's behaviors through the AIP model allows both the family therapist and EMDR therapist to focus their interventions meaningfully and in tandem. Understanding severe child behaviors through the AIP lens immediately increases parents' empathy and attunement and provides a clear rationale for the integrative parenting strategies they are learning. As the traumatized and attachment-disordered child senses his or her parents' attunement and compassion, he or she can open up emotionally and begin reprocessing traumas and triggers in order to heal.

Chapter 4

PROVIDING THE FOUNDATIONAL WORK IN THE FAMILY THERAPY COMPONENT

Often, parents arrive at yet another therapy session disillusioned, angry, and proclaiming, "This is the last stop. If this doesn't work, our child has to leave our home!" In short, the families are desperate. Through data collection and collaborative work with many families over several years time, we developed this model to provide therapists with a practical protocol for healing traumatized children in the most efficient manner possible.

The family therapist has a direct and active role in changing interpersonal patterns in the parent-child dyad. He or she helps parents recognize the impact of children's traumatic experiences and losses on their perceptions of themselves and the world. The family therapist helps parents (and sometimes siblings) to look beyond children's troubled behaviors, attune to their emotions and thoughts, and respond with sensitivity. The increased emotional support enables these children to open up emotionally during EMDR reprocessing. The family therapist's role requires sensitivity and understanding to nurture the family and facilitate success.

The family therapist propels affected children toward healing by helping them develop the ability to self-reflect and self-regulate. The family therapist guides children in becoming aware of their own thoughts and feelings, thereby bringing unconscious material to conscious awareness. When coupled with skills for self-calming, children's new perceptions improve their capacity to freely associate and reprocess trauma and triggers during EMDR.

Finally, the family therapist proactively integrates the family therapy session with the EMDR therapy by providing the EMDR therapist with information following each family session. The family therapist communicates discoveries and insights such as traumatic memories, current triggers, and negative beliefs that can be used for EMDR reprocessing. Additionally, the family therapist identifies self-regulation skills or communication skills that were learned or rehearsed during the family session that might be reinforced with EMDR. The family therapist also develops a therapeutic story that ultimately becomes a roadmap for the EMDR therapy. The EMDR therapist often conducts the EMDR session directly from the material provided by the family therapist. As noted previously, if scheduling and child tolerance allow, the EMDR therapy session directly follows the family therapy session.

THE BEGINNING

At the onset of therapy, the family therapist creates a nonjudgmental and warm atmosphere that enables both the child and the parents to feel safe, cared for, and accepted, so the healing work can begin. In some child therapeutic approaches, parents feel left out of the process. This model emphasizes the importance of parent involvement in all family and EMDR sessions. Parents are often traumatized by the extreme behavioral challenges presented by the child in the home, and so the parents themselves may present as angry, reactive, tearful, or argumentative. It is important that the therapist maintain calm, attune emotionally, and validate the extreme stress that the parents have endured.

The Integrative Team Treatment model considers the family system as a whole. It is important to remember that the family is the client—not just the troubled child. Healing the family system is crucial to healing the child.

Throughout the course of therapy, the family therapist usually begins each session by meeting with the parents alone for 15–20 minutes, as we've noted previously, so they can share their perspectives on the week without upsetting the child, and so the therapist can begin implementing interventions with the parents. Children may be defensive in the beginning, because they imagine their parents telling "all the bad stuff" about the preceding week. The family therapist should take time to explain that "Mom and Dad come first because they have work to do in therapy, too." It is important for the family therapist to be aware of the child's level of sensitivity, as some weeks are much harder than the others. There are cases in which the child and parents come in together at the beginning, or the child is unable to sit out for longer than 5 or 10 minutes, due to the child's age or capacity to tolerate waiting. Sometimes families are able to bring along a friend or extended family member to stay with the child in the waiting room. Otherwise, the family therapist may want to communicate initially with the parents through email or phone prior to each session.

Toward the end of the parents' check-in time, the family therapist should emphasize the highlights and successes of the week (while being sensitive to the parents' need for validation regarding the severity of the challenges) and then explain the plan for the rest of the session.

THE PARENT WORK

The family therapist's work with the parents is equal in importance to the work with the child. Preparing children for addressing traumas in EMDR includes the development of a positive, attuned atmosphere both in the office and with parents at home, so that children can safely let down their defenses, verbalize their innermost thoughts and feelings, and experience vulnerability. Parent work includes (1) helping parents view the child through the trauma lens, (2) parent coaching, (3) facilitating emotional attunement, and (4) guiding parents in managing meltdowns.

Helping Parents View the Child Through the Trauma Lens

The first challenge in the healing process is helping parents learn to understand that their child's behaviors are rooted in trauma. Many parents enter treatment believing that their misbehaving child is angry, controlling, manipulative, and intentionally out to destroy the entire family. The family therapist assists parents in gradually shifting their point of view to understand their child's behaviors as driven by fear and anxiety. Together, the family therapist and parents examine the child's behaviors and early history to identify the negative beliefs driving the child's behaviors; for example, "I'm not lovable," "I'm not safe," "I can't trust anybody," and "I'll be rejected and abandoned." Ultimately, the goal is to help parents shift their negative beliefs about their child and adopt an approach in which they attune to the child's thoughts and emotions, calm the child, and improve his or her capacity to reason.

The family therapist's work with the parents is vital to the success of the therapeutic process. These interactions allow parents to confer with the therapist and feel heard and understood regarding their parenting struggles with a very difficult child. It also allows the family therapist to guide the parents in responding effectively to specific behaviors.

Parent Coaching

The parent guide, *Integrative Parenting: Strategies for Raising Children Affected by Attachment Trauma* (Wesselmann et al., 2013), is used as an ongoing resource during family therapy, as mentioned previously. Integrative parenting strategies involve staying calm and mindful; intentionally calming the child (which means, in turn, calming the child's "survival brain"); emotionally attuning and responding to the feelings and thoughts underlying the child's behaviors; and increasing experiences of closeness through physical touch, playfulness, and empathy. The strategies are consistent with recommendations by Siegel and Bryson (2011) to connect emotionally with children before activating the higher cortical regions through teaching or redirecting. The goal is to integrate the upper and lower regions of the brain, as well as the right and left hemispheres. Brain integration leads to healthier emotional and cognitive functioning. Although integrative parenting methods help parents decrease the child's reactivity at home, Integrative Team Treatment works to integrate the child's neurology through a synthesis of family therapy and EMDR reprocessing.

Facilitating Emotional Attunement

An important component of family therapy is the facilitation of emotional attunement during the session. The family therapist emphasizes to the parents the importance of children feeling supported and understood at a deep emotional level in order to reprocess trauma. Children who have been traumatized are triggered on a daily basis to experience thoughts and feelings that cause meltdowns, promote power struggles, and fuel endless arguments. It can feel counterintuitive to attune to a child's emotions when the emotions are an overreaction based on what appears to be illogical thinking. The automatic response for most parents is to argue with the logic behind the emotions. The family therapist emphasizes the importance of helping the child feel understood and connected *before* employing logic.

Emotional attunement involves (1) listening intently, even when the child's behaviors or words seem illogical; (2) avoiding judgments or corrections; (3) paraphrasing; and (4) providing a sensitive response. It is important to emphasize that attunement takes patience and the ability to listen more while speaking less. The family therapist models emotional attunement for the parents during each therapy session. The parents are present as the therapist listens nonjudgmentally to the child's feelings, paraphrases them, and responds with sensitivity.

Parents often need as much encouragement and as many chances to practice new skills during sessions as the child. The family therapist carefully constructs a relationship with the parent that demonstrates empathy and support, so that when it appears that the parent has mishandled a situation, the family therapist is able to encourage, support, and correct the parent's behavior in a way that facilitates positive changes in the child.

As the therapist works with the child on uncovering the beliefs, feelings, and early memories driving many of the troublesome behaviors, the parent's level of anger naturally decreases, while emotional attunement and feelings of empathy for the child increase. The foundation for trauma-informed integrative parenting is emotional attunement, which is the ability to respond sensitively to the feelings and beliefs driving the behaviors instead of reacting to the behaviors themselves. Parents are frequently reminded that the goal is to calm and integrate the child's brain, versus "teaching the child a lesson" through punishments. However, parents still need and want practical strategies for motivating and managing their child on a daily basis, in addition to tools for calming the child's brain, reducing his or her fears, and providing reassurance.

The family therapist must be prepared to handle difficult and stressful conversations with parents. Parents can become extremely defensive in attempting to justify their actions. If a strong therapeutic relationship has been established with the parents, the family therapist is able to be more frank and honest regarding the parents' actions. When the therapeutic relationship is still in the formative stage, the therapist must be careful to balance corrections of the parents' behaviors with validation of their emotions. At times, most of a family therapy session may be spent helping parents become regulated and calm so that the EMDR session can be more productive and helpful for the child.

When the family therapist is able to provide a nonjudgmental, warm, and attuned atmosphere for the parents, the positive rapport allows the parents to take in the family therapist's directive regarding their need for improved self-care. Caring for children with a history of attachment trauma often triggers reactions in parents that are rooted in their own childhood experiences of rejection, abandonment, or abuse. Parents may also be suffering from unresolved grief related to infertility or other losses. (See Chapter 8 for more information regarding parent issues.) The level of traumatic stress or dysfunction in either parent may warrant a referral, perhaps for individual EMDR therapy, or infertility or adoptive parent support groups. Furthermore, the challenges of raising affected children can put undue stress on the couple relationship that might be remediated by a couple therapist. Other discussions in family therapy may include the need for parents to have more respite or to engage in more stress-reducing activities such as exercise, meditation, or fun forms of entertainment.

Guiding Parents in Managing Major Meltdowns

Meltdowns are common among children with attachment and trauma issues. Our colleague, Ann Potter (2011a), has conceptualized the child meltdown in a way that we have found very useful in our work with families. This concept is described further in the accompanying parent guide (Wesselmann et al., 2014). She has identified three readily recognizable phases of a meltdown:

- Phase 1: acting out (panic)
- Phase 2: acting in (shame)
- Phase 3: repair and reconnection (emotional pain)

The family therapist can work with the parents to identify when their child is in which phase and which strategies are most helpful with their child. We find that when parents conceptualize their child's meltdown in this way, they immediately feel less anger and more empathy, resulting in calmer, more attuned responses that lead to shorter, less intense, and less frequent meltdowns.

Phase 1 of a meltdown is essentially an enormous child version of a panic attack. The child's brain is stuck. The child has catapulted into a state of extreme hyperarousal, and his or her ability to make good judgments and engage in cause-and-effect thinking has shut down. Some children in Phase 1 cannot tell the difference between the past and the present. The survival brain has been activated, and the child is verbally and physically out of control. Usually, during this stage, the child will tolerate no touch or closeness whatsoever.

During Phase 2, the child's brain is still stuck. The survival brain remains in hyperarousal, and the behavior is fueled by shame and fear of rejection or abandonment. Although the child is more grounded in the present, he or she may continue to push the parent away due to the flood of shame and fear, and may or may not tolerate touch.

During Phase 3, the child's brain is unstuck, and he or she has returned to present time. Flooded by feelings of shame and anxiety regarding the meltdown, now the child yearns for reconnection and physical closeness or touch.

Each phase of the meltdown requires different parenting skills (Potter, 2011). The family therapist can help parents understand that in Phase 1, the child's brain has become flooded with cortisol and adrenaline, deactivating the logic-bearing regions of the brain. Lecturing or scolding literally "goes in one ear and out the other" when a child is operating in this type of survival mode. The family therapist emphasizes that emotional attunement may help shorten the meltdown and ready the child for reconnection more quickly. The therapist also explains that, due to the panicky state, the child cannot tolerate any physical closeness. Forcibly moving closer to the child will cause further escalation. Explain to parents that they can help the child move into a space where there is less concern about harm to him- or herself or to property. Next it is important for parents to give the child space, while avoiding triggering the child's abandonment fears. The parent should stay nearby and give messages such as, "I'm here," "I'm not going anywhere," "We can talk when you're calm," "You're safe," "It's going to be OK." Coach parents on how to use a calm tone of voice while reassuring the child as a way to shorten the meltdown. Caution parents that sarcasm, threats, or a raised voice during Phase 1 will only escalate the panic and lengthen the meltdown.

During Phase 2, the primary emotion is shame. Encourage parents to attune emotionally and reassure the child at this point and to move closer if the child seems ready. The child may or may not be ready for physical touch; parents should closely observe for cues in one direction or the other. Explain that reassuring messages of love and safety are extremely helpful for moving the child through Phase 2. Parents can help their children become more fully "grounded" in the present by gently asking questions such as, "Can you feel your feet on the floor?" or "What color is the room we are sitting in?"

The family therapist explains that the child in Phase 3 needs reconnection and repair. At this point, it is vitally important for the child and parent to connect either physically or emotionally in order to repair the relationship. This phase gives parents a chance to strengthen the attachment relationship with even the most guarded child, because the extreme vulnerability encourages him or her to accept comforting. When parents show physical affection and provide nurturing messages during this phase, it can be a powerful experience of healing for the child. However, parents may be resistant to this suggestion due to their own hurt, anger, and exhaustion, and they may fear that if they are physically and verbally comforting, they are "rewarding" the meltdown. The family therapist should attune to the parents' emotions but explain that meltdowns cannot be prevented by "teaching the child a lesson," because meltdowns are reflexive and automatic responses that a cognitive-style lesson cannot affect. Repairing and restoring the relationship will, in the end, help change the child's negative perceptions of his or her world and calm the reflexive brain.

Meltdowns are tough to handle, and some children experience many meltdowns in one day. The family therapist plays an instrumental role in helping parents shift their thoughts and responses during the three phases of the meltdown.

MINDFULNESS WORK

The family therapist helps children become mindful by learning to think about their thoughts, feelings, and body sensations. Tolerance for everyday issues, managing emotional triggers, thinking things through, and solving problems are essential skills for traumatized children. In order to be able to carry out any of these skills, children who have been traumatized must first learn to simply notice and tolerate their internal state. Conducting the mindfulness work in the context of the family session allows parents and children to speak the same mindfulness language and encourages parents to use mindfulness and self-regulation skills for themselves.

The mindfulness work includes the following strategies: (1) feelings come and feelings go, (2) teaching the window of tolerance, and (3) teaching "belly breath" and "cooked noodle."

Feelings Come and Feelings Go . . .

When asked about emotions, the traumatized child often identifies just two—happy and mad. Helping the child identify all of his or her feelings and be able to tolerate them is crucial.

With the parents listening, the family therapist teaches the child a mindful, more accepting attitude toward emotions by explaining that "all feelings come and go." We say to the child, "Feelings are similar to ocean waves in that they can wash up very suddenly and be very big, but then they always go away, little by little. We don't have to do anything or act out of the feelings, and if we give it a little time, the feelings go away." In the Feelings Come and Feelings Go activity (Schweitzer, 2011), the family therapist tells a story that highlights the transitory nature of emotions. While telling the story, the family therapist holds up large, age-appropriate cutouts of faces to illustrate the various emotions in the story. Following is a short vignette demonstrating the Feelings Come and Feelings Go activity. The family therapist is speaking to Hannah, age 11.

Teaching the Feelings Come and Feelings Go Activity

Family Therapist: Tell me, where do your feelings come from? *(Hannah shrugs her shoulders.)* Do you get them from a store?

Hannah: (Laughs and shakes her head.) No.

Family Therapist: Think for a minute . . . where do your feelings come from?

Hannah: Your head?

Family Therapist: Yes, that's right. They come from your head. Do you feel your feelings only in your head or in other places too?

Hannah: I only feel them in my head.

Family Therapist: OK. I know that if I feel scared sometimes, I get a funny feeling in my stomach. Does that ever happen to you?

Hannah: (Thinks for a minute and then agrees.) Yes, that happens to me, too.

Family Therapist: When I feel worried, I sometimes feel it in my stomach or my chest.

Hannah: Yes, that happens to me sometimes.

Family Therapist: So, we know that feelings start in your brain, and that sometimes you feel them in your body. Good. Now, when you feel a feeling, does it stay around for a while, a long time, or do all our feelings come and go?

Hannah: (Thinks for a few seconds, then shrugs her shoulders.)

Family Therapist: Well, this is what happens to me. *(Picks up the various cutouts of feelings as she tells a story about her day.)* I heard my alarm go off this morning, and I thought, "Oh, no. It's dark and cold out. I don't want to get up." *(Holds up the face that looks tired, and then the face that looks frustrated.)* Then I got up and got all dressed for work. As I was driving to my office, I thought, "Oh no, I'm going to be late." *(Puts down the tired and frustrated faces, and then holds up a face that looks worried.)* I got to work on time, and then my phone rang. It was my friend calling me from Colorado. *(Puts down the cutout of the worried face and holds up the cutout of the happy face.)* I had not talked to my friend in a long time, so I had the feeling of happy when I was talking with her. After I hung up the phone, it was almost lunchtime, and I noticed that I had the feeling of hunger in my stomach. *(Puts down the happy feeling and holds up another face to represent hunger.)*

This story continued until the therapist was sure that the child had a full understanding of the concept.

Teaching the Window of Tolerance

Siegel (2010, pp. 137–139) describes the window of tolerance as the range of emotional intensity that an individual is able to experience while still remaining connected in his or her relationships, able to process information, and able to learn. Children who have experienced chronic trauma typically have a narrow window of tolerance for emotional intensity. When the child leaves this calm window and goes into sympathetic nervous system arousal, he is emotionally reactive, aggressive, and impulsive or frozen, but internally aroused. Alternatively, the triggered child may move to hypoarousal when the parasympathetic system is activated. During hypoarousal, the child has "flat affect" and a numb response; he or she is collapsed and internally may have a "dead" feeling. Demonstrating this concept reduces judgments and helps both the parents and the child become more sensitive and mindful of the child's emotional state and heightens parents' awareness of their own emotional tolerance, as well.

Following is a transcript of a family therapy session in which the therapist demonstrated the window of tolerance with a 12-year-old boy who was chronically angry. Jacob was adopted at age 4, and he claimed that he had been "mad ever since." When triggered by a directive from either parent, Jacob usually yelled and argued, resulting in lengthy timeouts in his room.

NOTE: In the following vignette and in other vignettes throughout the manual, the therapist addresses the parents directly using the terms "Dad" or "Mom" as opposed to an adult-to-adult style of conversation in which the parents are addressed by name. This style of speaking more effectively attunes to the child's perspective and helps to keep the child present in the conversation.

Family Therapist: Jacob, do you know what a window looks like?

Jacob: (Rolling his eyes) Yes, of course.

Family Therapist: Draw me a window on this dry erase board. *(Jacob draws a picture of a window on the board.)* You know how a window can be opened and shut, right? We open a window . . .

Jacob: To let the air in?

Family Therapist: And we close the window . . .

Jacob: Because it's raining, or it's cold, and Mom yells at me to close it.

Family Therapist: Exactly. Now, let's think of this same window and connect it to feelings. *(Draws another window.)* When your "feelings window" is open fairly wide, your body and brain are working together, because you can feel your feelings, but still think and solve problems or make choices—like when your mom asks you to get off the Wii to do your homework, right?

Jacob: Yeah, I hate that. It really makes me mad. She never lets me play the Wii.

Family Therapist: So you are telling me that your brain and your body feel angry, right?

Jacob: Yep.

Family Therapist: When your window is open a bit, you know how to handle it. You complain a little bit and maybe say, "Aw, Mom, do I have to?" Mom says, "Yes." Then, you get off and go get your homework. Your body and brain are feeling a mad feeling, yet you can still use your brain to decide to go ahead and do your homework, because you know and remember that you can come back to the Wii later. Is this right, Jacob? Does your mom let you play the Wii if your homework is done and all put away? Is that true?

Jacob: Yes, that's true.

Family Therapist: See, Jacob, this is when your window is open. You let yourself feel the upsetting or angry feeling, knowing that the feeling will pass.

Jacob: OK, OK.

Family Therapist: Sometimes, Jacob, when you get triggered or have a big feeling, your window slams shut. Remember this past week, when your dad asked you to empty all the bathroom trash cans and take the garbage out to the curb for pickup?

Jacob: Yeah, I remember. I got really mad and told him that I hated him, and that it wasn't fair. I said, "No one else in the family has to take out the trash except me."

Family Therapist: Yes, that did happen, and that wasn't very much fun for you or Dad, was it?

Jacob: No. I got grounded from the Wii for a day because of that.

Family Therapist: I know. See, you didn't have your window open very much at all that day, and so you didn't think and remember that your brother Billy had just done this chore last week, and that the job is supposed to rotate between the two of you.

Jacob: Yes, I know.

Family Therapist: We remember that feelings come and go, right? When you feel a feeling, what are you supposed to do?

Jacob: Just notice the feeling, and use my words to tell my dad that I'm mad.

Family Therapist: Yeah, that would help your window stay open wide so that you could think. Then, if you told your dad you were mad, and you forgot it was your turn to do the chore, your dad could still talk to you and remind you, because your brain would still be working. Then there would have been no arguing or yelling, and of course no consequence.

Jacob: Yeah, you're right.

Family Therapist: (Turning to Dad) Is this true, Dad? Would you have helped Jacob with his angry feeling and reminded him about chores and your system?

Dad: Yes, I would have. We did talk about it the next day, and then Jacob did remember that Billy did trash duty last week. Jacob even apologized to me.

Family Therapist: That's great, Jacob. See what happens when your window is open?

During this session, the family therapist included the father in this conversation, which taught Dad more about Jacob's window of tolerance. The family therapist continued to work with the father on implementing the steps of attunement to help Jacob's brain come back "online" and keep him within his calm window.

Teaching Belly Breath and Cooked Noodle

Traumatized children often have great difficulty feeling calm and happy in their own skin. Mindfulness skills for calming the body increase children's capacity for self-regulation overall and help them become prepared for EMDR reprocessing. The family therapist should explain to the child and parents that there are healthy and mindful ways to breathe that can make our bodies and our brains calm and help us keep our window of tolerance open wide. Of course, it is easiest to practice these skills before the window slams all the way shut. Teach the child and the parents that regular practice of mindful breathing keeps us feeling happier and more relaxed. Instruct the entire family how to breathe in slowly through the nose and then exhale slowly through the mouth, and just to "pay attention to the breath in, and the breath out." Ask the family members to notice how the body feels after a minute of mindful breathing. The entire family can practice diaphragmatic breathing, or "belly breathing," by placing a hand or a small toy on the belly and "filling the stomach with air on the inhale" and "letting the air go from the stomach on the exhale." Again, ask the family members just to pay attention to the breath and then to notice how it feels after a minute of belly breathing. Return to mindful breathing, or belly breathing, on a regular basis for review and practice throughout treatment.

Another fun skill is called *cooked noodle*. Children are fascinated by the family therapist's comparison of the body with spaghetti noodles. The cooked noodle activity and the breathing skills increase the child's self-awareness and capacity for self-regulation and can be used at bedtime to help with sleep. Following is a transcript of the cooked noodle exercise.

Family Therapist: Have you ever eaten spaghetti?

Maya: Yeah, I've eaten spaghetti.

Family Therapist: What does an uncooked noodle look like or feel like?

[It can be helpful to keep a package of uncooked spaghetti noodles in the office as a visual aid. Some cooked noodles can also be prepared ahead of time.]

Maya: It's hard.

Family Therapist: What happens if you bend a piece of uncooked spaghetti?

71

Maya: It breaks.

Family Therapist: You're right . . . and it usually flies all over the place. Now, let's compare an uncooked piece of spaghetti to a cooked piece. What's the difference?

Maya: The cooked piece is warm and soft.

Family Therapist: Can it bend?

Maya: Yeah.

Family Therapist: Let's imagine your body is a spaghetti noodle. *(Instructs Maya to lie on the floor and invites her dad to come down on the floor next to her. She asks Maya to stiffen her body and "pretend" to be an uncooked noodle. She asks her dad to lift Maya's arm and leg and to attempt to bend her arms at the elbow.)* What does your body feel like as an uncooked noodle?

Maya: I feel stiff.

Family Therapist: Is it a comfortable feeling or an uncomfortable feeling?

Maya: It's not comfortable.

Family Therapist: Now, see if you can change your body to feel like a cooked noodle. *(Asks Maya's dad to lift her arms and legs and describe what he notices.)* Maya, what does your body feel like as a cooked noodle?

Maya: It feels looser.

Family Therapist: Is it a comfortable or an uncomfortable feeling in your body as a cooked noodle?

Maya: It's more comfortable. *(Instructs both Maya and her dad to sit back up and explains how relaxing the body also relaxes the brain. Maya has trouble with sleep, and the therapist suggests she practice "belly breath" and "cooked noodle" at bedtime.)*

Coach both the parent and the child to practice this activity at home and have both the mom or dad help the child develop more awareness of his or her body and how it is responding. After this activity has been taught and practiced in the family therapy session, the child's internal experience of self-regulation can be reinforced with bilateral simulation during the EMDR session. (See explanation in Chapter 5.)

Recognizing the Smaller Child Within

Whether children suffer from acute or mild dissociation related to unprocessed trauma, the "inner child" model is a way to both normalize and work with the dissociated affect in a compassionate and gentle way. Both parents and their traumatized children tend to instinctively understand this concept, and they are encouraged to work together to heal the "smaller child within."

This section includes the following strategies to help children recognize the smaller child within themselves: (1) use of nesting dolls as a visual aid, (2) expressing of appreciation for the actions of the younger parts of self, and (3) teaching what babies need and the cycle of trust.

Russian Nesting Dolls as Visual Aid

To begin, the family therapist can say something like the following:

> "Each one of us has an inner child who lives inside our hearts. The little scared or hurt child inside your heart gets triggered and has big feelings when certain things happen. We want this little one inside to heal, feel safe, and let go of worry."

A hands-on method of helping the child understand this important concept is by using Russian nesting dolls as a visual aid. These dolls can be found at some toy stores or through an online toy company. Ultimately, the family therapist, parents, and the child dialogue with the younger child within, gathering information about feelings of safety and trust and working through daily issues.

Following is a vignette that illustrates the use of the dolls and inner child work with Emily, age 9, who was severely neglected and malnourished before moving to her adoptive home. This particular family session centered around the issue of food hoarding. The family therapist began by separating a set of Russian dolls so that each was standing individually. (Note that the number of dolls in different sets of stacking dolls varies.)

Family Therapist: Emily, let's figure out the age of each of these Emily dolls. The biggest doll is your most grown-up 9-year-old self. The littlest one is Baby Emily. What about the ones in-between?

Emily: (Pointing to the various dolls) This one is the 2-year-old Emily, and this one is the 4- or 5-year-old Emily, and this last one is the 8-year-old Emily.

Family Therapist: OK, Emily, now remind me, how big is the little Emily who came to live with your forever mom and dad?

Emily: (Pointing to the age 2 Emily) This one. I was 2 when I came to your house, right, Mom?

Mom: That's about right, Emily. You were just turning 2 years old when you came to live with us. You were so tiny and cute.

Family Therapist: Mom, you mentioned that Emily was really tiny? How come?

Mom: Emily's birth mom did not always remember to feed little Emily, so she was really tiny and didn't weigh very much.

Family Therapist: [Emily is ready for this information, because the family therapist has addressed this part of her story previously. Emily understands that her birth mother had loved her, but had been too young to know how to take good care of her.] Is this true, Emily? [The therapist is checking to make sure that Emily is tolerating the conversation.]

Emily: Yes, that's true.

Family Therapist: Well, we know that your birth mom loved you, but she was so young, and she didn't know the best way to keep you safe and give you what you needed to grow. That is sad, isn't it?

Emily: Yes, it's sad, but I'm glad I live with you and Dad now, Mom.

Mom: Yes, it is sad, and we are so glad that you are here with us.

Family Therapist: Let's talk a little bit about how eating and asking for food is going at your house.

Emily: I've been working really hard on remembering to ask for snacks, and I'm eating all of my meals.

Mom: This is true. Emily is doing really well at mealtime, slowing down and eating her dinner and asking for seconds if she still feels hungry. We are still working on asking for snacks, aren't we, Emily? This week, I went in your closet to put away some of your shoes, and I found an empty box of graham crackers. We had just bought the box of crackers a couple of days before.

Emily: (Hanging her head) I got hungry the other night, and you were too busy on the computer, Mom, so I just took the box of crackers into my room, and now they're all gone.

Family Therapist: Mom, were you too busy to answer Emily's question about the crackers?

Mom: No, of course not. Emily knows that she can always ask me for things. She may have to wait a minute, but I always have time to help her.

Family Therapist: Let's use these dolls to see if we can figure out what is going on, Emily *(picks up the 2-year-old Emily doll).* Emily, I think the 2-year-old Emily gets hungry a lot, because when she was 2 and even younger, she was always worried about whether or not there was going to be enough food. I think the little Emily felt hungry a lot. *(Speaking to the 2-year-old Emily doll)* Is this true, little Emily?

Emily: (Nodding) Yes, that's true. My mom sometimes forgot to feed me, right Mom? That's why I was so tiny?

Mom: Yes, that's right.

Family Therapist: (Still addressing the little Emily doll) Little Emily, now that you are living with this mom and dad, do you still think that sometimes you have to sneak food and eat it in your closet because you are worried that this mom is going to forget to feed you?

Emily: (Speaking for the 2-year-old doll) Yes, that's true. She is too busy to feed me.

Family Therapist: (Picking up the 9-year-old Emily doll) Is this true, 9-year-old Emily*?*

Emily: (Shrugs her shoulders, and the therapist waits quietly.) No, that's not true. I know I can ask my mom if I can have a snack.

Family Therapist: I think the little Emily still gets scared and worried that there won't be enough food, and this is when she goes and gets things for herself without asking.

Emily: I think so, too.

Family Therapist: (Handing the 2-year-old Emily doll to Mom for her to hold) Mom, what would you say to little 2-year-old Emily?

Mom: (Speaking to the little doll in her hand) I would say, "Emily, you don't have to worry anymore. I will always remember to feed you, and if you are still hungry, no matter what I'm doing, you can always ask me for food."

Emily: (Listens to Mom intently.)

Family Therapist: Emily, did you hear what your mom said to little Emily? Do you think little Emily thinks this is true?

Emily: Yes . . . I don't know.

Family Therapist: Let's let the 9-year-old Emily talk to the little Emily and remind her that it *is* true that her forever mom will always feed her, and that she can ask for food when she is hungry. *(Picks up the 9-year-old Emily doll and pretends that the bigger doll is speaking to the 2-year-old Emily doll that the mom is holding.)* "Little Emily, it is OK, now you are safe with your forever mom and dad who love you and will always feed you. Little Emily, it is OK to ask for food if you are hungry. You are safe now." *(Emily watches and listens intently. The therapist looks at her.)* OK, big 9-year-old Emily, can you talk to little Emily?

Emily: (Speaking to the 2-year-old Emily doll) "OK, little Emily, you are safe now. You can ask for snacks and you don't have to sneak stuff."

Family Therapist: (Setting the dolls aside) Now, let's practice for real. Nine-year-old Emily, please ask your mom for a snack.

Emily: Mom, can I have a snack?

Mom: Of course, you can. What do you think would be a good choice?

As homework, Emily is encouraged to practice asking for snacks at home from her most grown-up, 9-year-old self.

In this session, the family therapist laid the groundwork for the EMDR therapist to implement bilateral stimulation to reinforce feelings of safety and the mature, competent state. By working in tandem this way, the family therapist and EMDR therapist expedited the child's healing.

Expressing Appreciation for the Actions of Younger Parts of Self

The therapist should never refer to "good parts" or "bad parts" of a child. Often, parents will refer to their child's "evil twin" or "bad part." The family therapist should explain that the "angry younger part within" was a necessary adaptation for surviving in a harsh early environment. When speaking of the child's anger or acting out as an expression of the "inner child" or "inner toddler," the therapist should speak with great compassion and admiration for how the strong anger and acting out behaviors helped the child to survive either mentally or physically or both. This younger part of the self deserves gratitude and needs help to understand that he or she is safe now. Following is a sample transcript of how such an exchange might proceed.

Family Therapist: Davey, what do you suppose was the trigger when you blew up at your mom this morning?

Davey: Mom told me to hurry up and get in the car. I think it was her tone of voice that triggered me. I thought she was being mean.

Family Therapist: What do you think about that right now?

Davey: Well, I guess that Mom just wanted me to be on time for school. I guess she was trying to help me.

Family Therapist: Do you think those mistrusting feelings might have been coming from toddler Davey?

Davey: Yeah, toddler Davey is a real pain.

Family Therapist: No, toddler Davey really is not a pain at all. Let's remember that the toddler part of you had to be wary of grown-ups, because some of the grown-ups in your life back when you were little weren't always safe to be with. The toddler part of you also did a good job developing those giant mad feelings for self-protection. I think we should thank the littler Davey for working so hard to stay safe. We need to help him understand that today he is safe, and let him know that he can stay in the safe place, and that big Davey can handle life now.

More Inner Child Work: "What Babies Need and the Cycle of Trust"

Helping children to assimilate and make sense of their story is an important component of the healing process. Hurt children need to understand the root of their behaviors in order to shift away from shame and self-blame. This process begins by teaching both the parents and the child about where and how babies learn to trust the world. With the help of a baby doll or a drawing, the family therapist explains how babies need many things when they are born. The therapist and parents can help the child think about what a baby needs. The therapist invites the parents to explain how a baby communicates by crying, and how the parents' job is to provide the baby with comfort and anything else he or she needs. The child learns that through this "cycle of trust," babies discover that the world is a safe place and that they can trust their parents to take good care of them. The therapist then guides the child to think about how babies might feel when no one responds to their cries or needs over and over again. Through the discussion, the child discovers that the cycle of trust is broken or interrupted when this happens and that babies who are neglected cannot trust others to meet their needs. The family therapist explains that this broken cycle eventually causes babies to feel unsafe and to wonder if there is something wrong with them. As children begin to understand the impact of a broken cycle of trust, they come to recognize why they have trouble, and it is easier for them to address their problems because the blame has shifted away from them.

Following is a conversation about the cycle of trust with 9-year-old Lisa, who was neglected as an infant in her biological home. The therapist has brought out a baby doll wrapped in a blanket to use as a prop during the discussion.

Lisa: What are we going to do with the baby?

Family Therapist: Well, I thought we could spend some time thinking about what babies need. What do you think babies need, Lisa?

Lisa: They need a bottle.

Family Therapist: Yes, that's right, they do need a bottle. Do they just need one in a day or how many do you think?

Lisa: They need three.

Family Therapist: Only three . . . did you know that a tiny baby eats every 3 or 4 hours? Plus, they need blankets to stay warm and feel safe.

Lisa: Wow, I didn't know that babies need blankets.

Family Therapist: Yes, they do. What else do babies need?

Lisa: Clean pants.

Family Therapist: Yes, that's right. How does a baby ask for what it needs? Does it say, "Hey Mom, I'm hungry"?

Lisa: No, a baby can't talk. It cries.

Family Therapist: Yes, you are so smart. Did you know that a mom and a dad learn to understand the baby's cry? They can tell if the baby is crying because he or she is hungry, or tired, or needs some attention.

Lisa: That's cool. *(Turning toward her adoptive mom)* Did I do that?

Mom: Well, Lisa, you didn't live with me when you were a tiny baby, but I know that is what you did. If I'd had you as a tiny baby, I know that I would have known why you were crying.

Family Therapist: That's right, Mom, I bet you would have. Now, Lisa, we know that some confusing things and some wonderful things happened to you when you were little. I think we know that your birth mom and birth dad had mixed-up brains, and when you cried, they just didn't do what they needed to do to take good care of you.

Lisa: I don't remember that.

Family Therapist: I'm sure you don't. Do you think that sometimes now . . . in the present . . . when you get really hungry, and your forever mom says, "No, you can't have a snack because it's right before dinner," you get really mad because that tiny baby who lives inside your heart is scared that she won't get enough food? I wonder if the tiny baby Lisa could have talked, what she would have said to birth mom.

Lisa: She would have said, "Hey, Mom, Where are you? I'm hungry!"

Family Therapist: I bet that is what baby Lisa would have said. I wonder today, when you don't get that snack, if you have big feelings that come from baby Susan in your heart, who believes that if you don't get that snack, you will die. *(Lisa is thinking quietly.)*

Mom: I bet that's right, Lisa. Sometimes, I'll say, "Lisa, we will eat very soon, and at dinner you can have as much food as you would like." It's like you don't believe me! But don't I always give you enough food?

Lisa: Yes, you give me enough food, but I'm hungry all the time, and you won't let me have snacks whenever I want.

Mom: Yes, that's true, because I want you to be able to eat your dinner.

Lisa: I hate that.

Mom: I know you don't like it, but do you understand why I don't want you to fill up on snacks before dinner?

Family Therapist: Do you think you understand, Lisa, even though it is really hard?

Lisa: Yes. . . .

Family Therapist: Well, let's let your brain do a little more work when you go to Stefanie's office.

Lisa: OK.

Teaching the cycle of trust helps children gain insight into where their big feelings originated, and it helps parents view their child's behaviors as rooted in the earliest experiences of life. Following the family session with Lisa, the family therapist communicated their discoveries to the EMDR therapist, who targeted the trigger of hunger and "baby Lisa's" belief, "If I don't get food right now, I just might die." In addition, the EMDR therapist developed and reinforced a future template in which Lisa managed the feelings of hunger and accepted "You have to wait" as an answer from her mom.

COPING WITH PRESENT-DAY LIFE

Due to their unprocessed memories and the social, emotional, and cognitive effects of early relational trauma, traumatized children have difficulty coping with everyday routines and situations involving their parents, teachers, peers, homework, chores, bedtime, morning, and so on. Parents and children need a common language and shared strategies to use at home to sort out difficulties and solve problems.

This section helps children and their parents cope with present-day life through the following strategies: (1) teaching the jobs of moms and dads, (2) brain work (feeling/thinking brain and talking to the brain), (3) teaching past, present, and future, (4) detective work: understanding and implementing the domino effect, and (5) zeroing in on triggers and applying skills.

Teaching the Jobs of Moms and Dads

Children who hold the underlying negative belief "My mom is mean" or "My dad is mean" may interpret almost every direction, correction, or request as motivated by "meanness." The EMDR therapist will be processing these parenting behaviors as current triggers, but in order to reprocess successfully, the child will need to be able to associate to the corrective, adaptive information. The family therapist can help by making a list, together with the parents and child, identifying "the jobs of moms and dads." Get as much input from the child as possible before providing the information directly. Our lists usually include such jobs as "keeping kids safe," "keeping kids healthy," "making sure kids get their education so they can have a smart brain," "teaching kids how to take care of their things," and "teaching kids appropriate behaviors so they will have friends and be successful in life." This list will help the EMDR therapist with cognitive interweaves, such as, "Was Mom really being mean, or was there another reason she said 'no' to that candy bar?"

Brain Work

Understanding how brains work is a relatively new component of the family therapist role. Teaching children and parents about brain development and how the brain works reduces shame and leads to important insights.

Illustrating the "Feeling Brain" and the "Thinking Brain"

With the help of a dry erase board or a piece of paper, the family therapist teaches the child what a brain looks like and how it works. The family therapist explains how the thinking part of the brain and the feeling part of the brain work together when we play, solve problems, and do schoolwork.

The therapist can create a picture of the brain to help explain to the child and parents that the right hemisphere is the center of emotions and the left is the center of logical thoughts. The therapist can say something like this: "Everyone has feelings, and feelings are not right, wrong, good, or bad. Feelings are very necessary and an important part of being human. But our left brain can work with our right brain to help us notice our feelings, think about our feelings, and think about what to do if we are having an upset feeling."

The family therapist can go on to explain, "Sometimes, when something really upsetting and confusing happens, the upsetting memory and the feelings connected to the memory can get 'stuck' in the right side of the brain." The therapist can illustrate the concept for the child and parents by making a clay model of the brain and then inserting a piece of paper into the clay to represent the child's memory, lodged in the limbic brain. The therapist can say something like, "This piece of paper contains not only the memory of what happened, but all the feelings you had when it happened. When something occurs now that reminds you of the past, these old feelings light up, even though everything is really OK now" (Schweitzer, 2011, p.1).

Talking to the Brain

The family therapist teaches the child to notice the feelings and "talk to the brain" or "self-talk" rather than letting the feelings be the "boss." The therapist can use him- or herself as an example and describe times when he or she used "self-talk" to cope with a difficult situation. Encourage the child to identify self-talk statements to use to "talk to his brain" in various triggering situations, such as "I'm safe" or "My mom and dad love me." It is important that the parents are fully engaged in this activity, as they are often unfamiliar with the concept of self-talk, and they can learn to attune to the child's emotions and then provide encouragement through helpful reminders. The parent and child can role-play recent situations that caused upset, and the parent can rehearse providing encouragement by saying, for example, "I'm noticing that you are having a big feeling. Use your self-talk and remind your brain that you can depend on me, and I love you."

Teaching Past, Present, and Future

Past, present, and *future* are powerful concepts that can be confusing to traumatized children. Teaching children about the meanings of these three words can be vitally important in grounding them in the present (Schweitzer, 2011, p. 2). One such session occurred with 10-year-old Cade, who had been removed from his biological mother by social services at age 8 due to neglect, and adopted by his paternal grandparents at age 9. Cade had revealed that he had been sexually abused from age 5 to age 8 by an older cousin, and he had entered therapy with symptoms of traumatic stress, including nightmares, severe anxiety, and frequent meltdowns.

Therapist: Today, I'm going to pretend that I am your teacher, and we are going to learn about three new words. *(Writes the three words on the dry erase board and asks the child about the meaning of each.)* What does the word *past* mean?

Cade: (Shrugging his shoulders) Something that happened a long time ago.

Family Therapist: Yes, that's right. Can you tell me one or two things that you remember from your past that are good memories?

Cade: Yes, my birthday last year—I had that really cool cake with cars on it. And I went swimming last weekend.

Family Therapist: Yes, those are great examples. Those things did happen in the past, and when you thought about those things, what were your feelings?

Cade: Happy.

Family Therapist: Good. I'm glad . . . there are things that happened to you in your past that do bring back happy feelings. Now, let's talk about the next word *present.*

Cade: Yeah. It's something you get at Christmas.

Family Therapist: You're right again, you do get presents at Christmas time. Does this word have another meaning?

Cade: (Shrugs his shoulders.)

Family Therapist: Well, where are you right now?

Cade: In therapy with you.

Family Therapist: Yep, you are. So this is happening in the *present.*

Cade: Yeah, I guess.

Family Therapist: So, the present is stuff that is going on right now. Tell me, where do you live right now?

Cade: At my mom's house . . .

Family Therapist: Right. You live in your forever mom's house right now. It's a nice, safe house, right?

Cade: Yes.

Family Therapist: What about the last word, *future*? What does that mean?

Cade: Something that will happen in the future.

Family Therapist: OK, can you name something that will happen to you in the future?

Cade: I'm going to be 11 on my next birthday.

Family Therapist: Yes, that's a good example. Sometimes our brains get mixed up about what is happening to us right now in the present and what happened to us in the past. It's like the clock in our brain does not know what time of day it is. Sometimes, when we get triggered or we have a lot of upsetting memories, our brain thinks that we are still in the past. Then we react or behave like we are living in the past. The truth is, sometimes, we have to remind our brain that we are in the present . . . living in a safe home with a safe mom and dad who are taking good care of us. Do you think you get confused sometimes?

Cade: Yeah, I do.

Family Therapist: Mom, do you think he gets confused sometimes?

Mom: Yes, I think he does. Sometimes, I think he believes that I am his birth mom.

Family Therapist: That does happen, doesn't it? OK, Mom and

Cade, what can you do if you think Cade's brain is getting confused?

Mom: I could remind him . . . gently. Hey, it's me—your forever mom—do you remember where you are? [This is a grounding method the mother learned previously.]

Cade: I could talk to my brain and tell it that I'm in the present.

Family Therapist: Exactly. Good idea. We're going to keep working on upsetting stuff from your past, but we will always remember that it is over now. We can talk about it, and even though your brain will always remember some of that yucky stuff, it will also be able to remember that you are safe now . . . in the present, and you have lots to look forward to in your future.

The family therapist will need to continue to reinforce this concept as she weaves back and forth between present-day triggers, unresolved issues, and past memories. The work completed in this family session was also used as the foundation for an EMDR session that addressed an old upsetting memory, and then closed by strengthening the current attachment relationship and sense of safety in the present. The family and EMDR therapists worked in tandem to efficiently and effectively help Cade heal.

Detective Work: Understanding and Interrupting the Domino Effect

Like the detective who gathers clues and solves crimes, the family therapist works closely with the child and parents to bring the clues of unconscious feelings and thoughts to conscious awareness. The family therapist invites the child and parent to work with him or her as a team to search for clues into the child's NCs, feelings, body sensations, and triggers by carefully examining the daily problems that the child and family bring to the session.

A concept used in dialectical behavioral therapy (Linehan, 1993), called the *behavior chain analysis*, examines the thoughts, feelings, and actions leading to a problem behavior in an effort to discover where the path could be interrupted by implementing a skill. Potter (2011b) has used the term *domino effect* to describe this process with families, because it makes more sense to children.

The behavior chain analysis, or the domino effect, is used to help both parents and children reflect upon the thoughts, emotions, sensations, and actions each has contributed to any crises experienced during the past week. The family therapist may wish to guide the parents in examining their part without the child present. When parents can learn to identify their own triggers and manage them, the child ultimately benefits.

The game of dominoes has been popular since it first originated in China during the 12th century. Over the years, millions of children have carefully stood dominoes on end in long rows, just for the fun of watching what happens after the first domino in the row is pushed over. Children are fascinated with the chain reaction that tips numerous dominoes over within seconds. The therapist can demonstrate the effect in the office with real dominoes, and then explain that meltdowns and other big behaviors are usually the end result of toppling thoughts, feelings, and actions. This demonstration can help the child and parent to understand the chain reaction and look for ways to "pull dominoes" and interrupt the cascade of falling dominoes.

To utilize the domino effect intervention, work with the child and parent to identify the following key elements in relation to a specific event:

- Factors that increased the child's vulnerability
- Situational or environmental triggers
- The child's emotions
- The child's NCs
- The child's body sensations
- The last domino that signaled the beginning of the meltdown

Following is a conversation with 12-year-old Steve and his biological mother in family therapy. Steve had experienced many surgeries and lengthy hospitalizations in his early life that had interrupted his emotional development and interfered with the development of a secure attachment to his mom. Steve's mom entered the session expressing frustration that Steve continued to have huge meltdowns over seemingly small, everyday occurrences such as the completion of homework. She complained that Steve should be used to the routine of doing daily homework and that he should no longer be having fits about it.

Family Therapist: Today, we are going to use the white board to see if we can figure out the dominoes that lead to these big upsets about homework, Steve. Does this sound like a good idea?

Steve: Yeah, I guess.

Family Therapist: (Pulling out the dry erase board and markers) OK, we know that the other day you had some homework, right?

Steve: Yep, that's right. I hate homework. It's a waste of time.

Family Therapist: Well, I know that you really don't like it. Let's take a closer look at what happened. It sounds like at some point you went stomping out of the room and didn't get it finished. Does that sound right?

Steve: Yes, that's right. I already said I was sorry.

Family Therapist: Yes, I know. I'm glad it's over, aren't you? OK, we are going to write that toward the bottom of the dry erase board. Let's work backwards, because sometimes that is easier. What happened right before you left the kitchen table?

Steve: I was sitting there. . . .

Mom: Yes, he was. He had his head down on the table, and he was screaming at me.

Family Therapist: What were you screaming? *(Therapist writes exactly what had happened on the dry erase board.)*

Steve: I don't remember.

Mom: You were telling me how stupid I was . . . and that the whole world was stupid. So was homework, and you weren't going to do it.

Steve: Oh . . . yeah. . . .

Family Therapist: Well, let's write that down. What happened before that?

Steve: I was trying to do my math assignment. It was such a waste of time.

Family Therapist: What did you have to do?

Steve: We're adding and subtracting fractions. I hate fractions.

Family Therapist: OK, let's write that down—and yes, fractions are hard. What happened before that?

As the therapist, the mother, and Steve moved through the discussion, the therapist wrote each single action, thought, and feeling on the dry erase board. When the incident was completely logged, they all took a look back, and the therapist asked questions that helped ascertain other feelings and body sensations at different points in the chain of dominoes, and any other triggers and NCs that were driving the incident. Once those factors were identified and noted, they all reviewed the series of dominoes to identify where any one of them could have changed something to stop the dominoes from continuing to fall. Perhaps, pulling one domino from the series of dominoes could have prevented the whole reaction and prevented the meltdown.

In this case, his mother had yelled at Steve because he'd had his head down on the table. This was Steve's triggering event. He was also very behind in math class, and his teacher was really putting pressure on him to get caught up. His mom knew that Steve was under pressure, and as she looked at the dominoes on the dry erase board, she realized that she could have adjusted and attuned to Steve's feelings instead of raising her voice. As Mom recognized her part in the domino effect, Steve felt understood, and Mom and Steve were able to talk and come up with a plan during the session to address math homework in the future.

With the dry erase board in hand, Mom and Steve went next door to see their EMDR therapist, who quickly reviewed the dominoes on the board. It contained the feelings, body sensations, and NCs that enabled Steve to target and reprocess the event, and finally, install a PC. Afterwards, Steve had more positive thoughts about himself and his homework, so he was better able to tolerate his feelings and actually finish the work without meltdowns.

Integrative Team Treatment enabled Steve's therapists to collaborate effectively to eliminate the meltdowns that limited Steve's academic progress and strained his relationship with his mother. Integrating the family work into the EMDR session proved both effective and time-saving.

In the next example, the therapist helps 9-year-old John and his adoptive mother interrupt the domino effect. John was adopted from Ethiopia at 2 years of age, and he had entered therapy with symptoms of defiance and aggression. John was continuing to engage in provoking bedtime behaviors that had culminated in a physical confrontation the previous evening. Before John was invited to participate, his mother was helped to look at her part in the domino cascade and discover her own trigger as the parent. After this exercise, she was able to change her thinking, become more mindful, and successfully guide John through the bedtime routine.

Family Therapist: So, let's take a closer look at what is going on at bedtime.

Mom: Every night is a battle. Last night was awful. John came flying out of the bathroom and hit me several times.

Family Therapist: Before we bring John in here, let's do a domino exercise to see if we can discover the factors that led up to the outburst.

Mom: OK.

Family Therapist: (*Begins writing down each "domino"—each thought, feeling, sensation, or action—on the dry erase board, as John's mother recalls what happened in detail. In the middle of the exercise, Mom remembers that her son had been in the bathroom, and he had been singing.)*

Mom: (Staring at the board) That's it. I'm triggered by his singing.

Family Therapist: Singing? Tell me more about that.

Mom: When he sings, I think he isn't listening to me and doesn't care about what I have asked him to do *(discovering her own NC)*. He doesn't care what I say. He's just in there singing. He's just standing there doing nothing.

Family Therapist: (Gently) Do you know for sure that he is not brushing his teeth and washing his face . . . ?

Mom: No. . . .

Family Therapist: (Addressing the NC very gently) Is it true that he never listens to you?

Mom: No, that's not true. *(Now smiling)* But sometimes it *is* true.

Family Therapist: (Laughing) Of course, our children don't always listen to us, do they?

Mom: No, I guess that singing is just a trigger for me. I think that if you're in the bathroom doing what you need to be doing, there should be no singing.

Family Therapist: (With a smile) That's understandable, but it could be true that in between song verses, he is getting it done.

Mom: True . . . I guess I will let the singing thing go, and try not to worry about it.

Family Therapist: Yes, let's see how that goes. If he starts singing tonight, just notice how you are feeling, consider your thoughts, and don't say anything. Just let the feeling pass. Now, let's bring him in, so we can go through this same event with him. If you are comfortable with it, I'd like you to share your trigger, how it makes you feel, and we'll see what he comes up.

Mom: OK. You know, I just want the very best for him.

Therapist: I know.

As the session continued, the domino exercise was repeated with John. As the therapist and John walked through the evening's events, Mom revealed her trigger. In addition, John figured out that he was triggered whenever his mom told him what to do. John realized his NC: "I should get to do what I want. I'm in charge of myself." The therapist discussed this belief with Mom and John, noting that "while it is true that you can do some things by yourself, like brushing your own teeth and washing your own face, is it also true, John, that you need a mom to help your remember that there is a bedtime, because getting enough sleep is important."

Though he recognized that this statement was logically true, John had a hard time really believing it deep down. The family therapist described what John had discovered regarding his trigger and NC to the EMDR therapist, who took all of this great detective work and came up with a plan for the EMDR.

John began the EMDR session by bringing up the triggering situation (his mom telling him what to do) and pairing it with his NC, "I should get to do what I want because I'm in charge of myself." John's desired PC was, "It's OK for my mom to help take care of me." When John got stuck, the EMDR therapist asked, "When did you first learn that you have to be in charge of yourself?" John recalled an early memory in an orphanage in Ethiopia when he felt scared and lonely, with no one to take care of him. After reprocessing the earlier trauma, John was able to adopt the positive cognition and believe it as "completely true" in his life today. This case example helps illustrate the efficiency of the collaborating family therapist and EMDR therapist team in accessing vital information and reprocessing it effectively.

Zeroing in on Triggers

The detective work in sessions often focuses on the initial falling domino that escalates behavior. The family therapist teaches children and parents about triggers and helps children identify their own triggers. Explain to the child that triggers can be almost anything—a situation, a look on someone's face, a thought, a smell, or a sound that creates sudden big feelings inside. Very common triggers for a child with a history of attachment trauma include a parent or teacher saying "no" or directing him or her to begin homework, get up in the morning, or go to bed. Many children are triggered by complicated feelings related to special occasions such as holidays or birthdays.

Applying Skills to Triggers

Once the child has identified many of his or her triggers, skills to cope with the triggers can be developed and practiced with the family therapist and then reinforced by the EMDR therapist. Alice, age 15, and her family therapist figured out that she was triggered to explode in anger whenever she was corrected, redirected, or questioned about a behavior. Her NC was, "I'm always in trouble for nothing." This information was provided to the EMDR therapist, who taught Alice how to give herself nurturing messages while using the butterfly tap (see Chapter 5). Alice learned to notice her triggers by reading her own body cues. When she started to feel the upset feeling, she learned to initiate her own tapping while running the self-nurturing affirmations through her mind. Remarkably, Alice also allowed her mother to give her nurturing messages while tapping slowly on her shoulders. Alice's mother learned to identify her daughter's triggers and thereby helped her become more self-aware. The child, the parent, the family therapist, and the EMDR therapist working as a collaborative team were able to effectively interrupt Alice's self-defeating behaviors and eliminate the escalating anger between Alice and her parents.

Once therapy is well under way, the family therapist regularly helps the child and family find strategies to interrupt their falling dominoes. The family therapist continues to look for triggers and negative beliefs and help the child and family understand the connection between current triggers and the child's early experiences. This work helps the parents make sense of the child's behaviors in relationship to negative beliefs and his or her traumatic past. The family therapist also reminds parents, again and again, that children impacted by trauma cannot understand reason or logic when the emotional brain is triggered. Healing can happen only in an environment of attunement, validation, and support.

SKILLS, SKILLS, AND MORE SKILLS

The last major area of importance in the family therapy component of the integrative team approach is the development of interpersonal and behavioral skills. Traumatized children are often behind developmentally, emotionally, and socially. Parents understand this lag at an intellectual level, but they have a hard time recognizing and effectively managing the reality of it in daily situations. It is common for a parent to say something like, "My child is 12 years old—she should know how to behave in this situation!" Technically, this parent is correct, as a child on a typical developmental pathway has developed many basic skills by the age of 12—but this is not the case for many traumatized children. The child's lack of skills becomes a source of conflict when parents become frustrated and fearful that their child will never learn to behave appropriately. Missing skills frequently include:

- Asking for help
- Seeking comfort appropriately
- Accepting help or comfort when offered
- Accepting the answer "no" appropriately
- Accepting redirection or feedback
- Social skills, such as sharing, taking turns, waiting, communicating, and losing a game

This section outlines the following strategies: (1) creative practice, (2) the communication game, and (3) teaching high-alert/low-alert language.

Creative Practice

Working in conjunction with the parents, the family therapist explores and prioritizes the missing skills, then helps the child gain insight and feelings of success through practice with the new skills in session. The family therapist can call upon his or her creative side to teach and reinforce skills. Drawings, sand trays, stuffed animals, action figures, and live role plays can be used to demonstrate and practice skills. Some social skills can be practiced during board games and card games. The family therapist should find what works most effectively with each individual child, taking into account his or her cognitive abilities, emotional maturity, and learning style.

In the following example, the family therapist teaches the skill of waiting to speak. Nine-year-old Bette was adopted from abroad. She had very poor frustration tolerance and real issues around waiting for anything. Her mother was very triggered by the child's habit of interrupting her, and it was causing regular arguments in the home on a daily basis.

Family Therapist: So let's talk about this interruption thing, shall we? *(Bette nods.)* Tell me, what does *interrupting* mean, anyway?

Bette: It means someone else is talking or doing something, and another person butts in.

Family Therapist: That's right. Good thinking. Do you think that all people do this sometimes?

Bette: Yes, kids in my class interrupt the teacher all the time.

Family Therapist: Yes, I bet that does happen. Do you interrupt your teacher?

Bette: Yes, I do. But everyone else does it.

Family Therapist: True. How do you think the teacher feels when she is interrupted?

Bette: Well, she yells at the person, and then makes them have a consequence.

Family Therapist: Yes, but how do you think the teacher feels?

Bette: Probably frustrated.

Family Therapist: Can you tell when she is frustrated?

Bette: Yes, she sighs a lot and gets this look on her face.

Family Therapist: So . . . tell me about yourself and your interruptions.

Bette: What do you mean?

Family Therapist: Well, when do you find yourself interrupting during the school day . . . and do you do it a lot?

Bette: (Thinking) I do it a lot . . . I guess . . . I have no idea. I just want to say something or tell someone else something.

Family Therapist: Do you think it is hard to wait?

Bette: No.

Family Therapist: Hmmm . . . I wonder about that.

Bette: Well, maybe *(smiling)*.

Family Therapist: It's hard to wait sometimes. I know I have a hard time waiting. I think all people do. Do you think you interrupt your mom a lot?

Bette: (Looking at her mom's face) Yes, I know I do.

Family Therapist: (Addressing the mother) Is this true? Does she interrupt a lot?

Mom: Yes, it is true.

Family Therapist: How do you feel, Mom, when she interrupts you?

Mom: I think I feel like her teacher—frustrated. Sometimes, I think if she would only just let me finish my sentence, then she would get her answer or understand what I am trying to tell her. It's like she always thinks I'm going to say "no" or tell her something that she doesn't want to hear. Sometimes that's true, but it is not always true. Sometimes I just want to tell her something simple.

Family Therapist: Oh, that is interesting, Mom, can you give us an example?

Mom: Well, the other day, she asked me if she could go to a friend's house after school. I was trying to tell her that on that particular afternoon, I had to go to a meeting at the church, but before I could finish, she interrupted me and started arguing. She didn't even know what I was going to say.

Family Therapist: What happened?

Bette: Well, we got into a great big argument, and I couldn't go.

Family Therapist: You didn't get to go because . . .

Bette: I argued.

Family Therapist: What would have happened if you would have let your mom finish talking about this meeting?

Bette: I would have known that her meeting wasn't going to get over until 5:30. So, if I was going to my friend's house, I should ask her mom if it would be OK if I stayed that late. If it was OK with my friend's mom, I guess I would have gotten to go.

Family Therapist: What do you think your brain is thinking or doing when it is interrupting?

Bette: I think my brain thinks . . . I have to talk.

Family Therapist: I think you're right. What do you think might be the upsetting thought? [The therapist is looking for the NC.]

Bette: I hate waiting.

Family Therapist: Well, that's a true thought, for sure. I wonder about the thought, "I can't wait."

Bette: Yep, that's it.

Family Therapist: Now, what do you think is going to happen to you if you have to wait?

Bette: I'm not sure, I just don't like it.

Family Therapist: Let's think about it for a minute.

Bette: I know—I think I won't get what I want.

Family Therapist: OK, so your thought is that if you interrupt, you will get what you want . . . like, in this case, wanting to go to your friend's house, right?

Bette: Right, but I would have gotten to go . . . *(sighing)*

Family Therapist: Yes, that is true, isn't it? Maybe this upsetting thought is really getting in your way. Do you think we could practice waiting to talk when your mom is talking? Mom, would you be willing to practice?

Mom: Sure.

As the session progressed, Bette, her mother, and the therapist role-played a variety of different scenarios in which Bette had to wait until her mom finished speaking. Her mother was willing to practice her attunement skills when she noticed that Bette was becoming anxious during the role-play. Mom and Bette came up with a plan. Mom would point out what she had observed by saying, "Bette, I am noticing that you are getting anxious about this conversation. Remember to tell your brain, 'It is OK to wait and let Mom finish.'" After the family session, the EMDR therapist followed up by targeting and reprocessing the recent situations that had triggered Bette's NC, "If I interrupt, I will get what I want." Bette was able to adopt the PC, "It's OK to wait." Teamwork between the two therapists and the family allowed Bette to move through the whole process in 1 hour of work with each therapist.

The Communication Game

The skill of communicating involves both listening and expressing feelings and thoughts. Both traumatized children and their parents lack good communication habits and skills. The "communication game" is an exercise that is traditionally used in couple therapy. The parent and child take turns as *speaker* and *listener*. If the mother volunteers to speak first, ask her to talk about her feelings for a minute or so regarding any issue. The child is told to remain quiet until the mother is finished, at which time the child will be asked to tell the mother what he or she heard her say. The mother is instructed to give the child a rating, such as "You understood about 75% of what I said. The part you missed is. . . . " Younger children can be told, "You understood most of what I said. Here's one part you missed. . . ." Then the roles are switched, and the child gets to be the speaker while the mother practices listening.

Encourage the parent and child to look at, and speak directly to, one another, not to the therapist. Sometimes the therapist must be very directive in jumping in and stopping one or the other from interrupting. If it is really difficult, hand the speaker a toy microphone or some other object and playfully command, "Only the person who holds this microphone can be heard right now. But don't worry, each of you will have your turn with the microphone, so you have a chance to be heard."

Teaching High-Alert/Low-Alert Language

High-alert/low-alert language is nonjudgmental language that helps traumatized children recognize when they are moving into hyperarousal. The language allows parents to help the child notice what is happening in a supportive manner. The therapist, child, and parents discuss each term, identifying situations that might cause a high-alert state and a low-alert state, as well as the body sensations associated with each. Next, the therapist, child, and parents identify the upsetting thoughts that might lead them to a state of high alert, and thoughts that might lead to low alert. The therapist and child then brainstorm strategies the child might use to bring him- or herself to low alert. Parents can use this neutral language as another way to attune to the child's feelings by simply saying, for example, "It looks like you are moving into high alert. What would help to bring you back down to low alert? Remember what Deb said? In low alert, we can think and solve problems more clearly." Children sometimes begin to notice that a parent is going into high alert and gently redirect his or her escalation. The EMDR therapist can follow up the high-alert/low-alert discussion by helping the child experience low alert in session and then reinforcing the experience with bilateral stimulation (see the discussion of S-RDI in Chapter 5). Following is an example of the use of high-alert/low-alert language with 11-year-old Jolie. Adopted at age 5, Jolie had a tendency to whine and flail when something didn't go her way or when she made a mistake.

Family Therapist: Jolie, today we are going to learn about low alert and high alert. Can you tell me what you think these might be?

Jolie: (Silence for a few seconds.) Maybe when something is really big and then littler?

Family Therapist: That's right. It is like that and there's more. Let's get out the dry erase board and talk about this. Do you want to help your mom write on the board, or do you just want her to do it?

Jolie: I want to help.

Family Therapist: OK, Jolie, can you write "Jolie's high alerts" on the board?" *(The therapist, the mother, and Jolie begin to brainstorm times when Jolie has been on high alert.)*

Mom: Jolie, I notice that when I say "no," you begin to go into high alert—also, when you know you have made a mistake—that sometimes sends you into high alert.

Jolie: I hate it when you say "no." Sometimes you say "no" when you could say "yes."

Mom: I know it's hard when I say "no."

Jolie: I know another time—when I'm at school and my friends don't play what I want to play.

Family Therapist: What happens?

Jolie: Well, they want to play tag, and I don't want to.

Family Therapist: Do you start to feel the high alert?

Jolie: Maybe . . .

Family Therapist: Well, what does your body look like and do when you don't want to play tag?

Jolie: (Starting to feel some shame, Jolie moves closer to her mother.) I don't know.

Family Therapist: Jolie, you are not in trouble. We are just trying to solve a problem. It looks like you want your friends to play with you, but sometimes your high alert gets in the way. We want to help make that better for you.

Jolie: It looks like I'm mad, and I yell at them.

Family Therapist: OK, that's just your high alert turning on. Let's find ways to notice your high alert and practice calming down.

As the session progressed, the therapist drew a gauge on the dry erase board with HIGH ALERT written at the top and LOW ALERT written at the bottom. The therapist and Jolie identified a time when Jolie was on high alert with her mom and wrote the uncomfortable thoughts and sensations at the top. Then, at the bottom, the therapist, Jolie, and Mom brainstormed calming thoughts and behaviors Jolie could practice to keep herself in low alert. Next, they all discussed what moving into high alert felt like in the brain and the body.

At the end of the session, the family therapist asked Jolie and her mother to practice paying attention to the high-alert and low-alert signals in-between sessions. A possible scenario of noticing high-alert signals was practiced with a role play. Next, the family therapist passed along the insights to the EMDR therapist, who incorporated the high-alert/low-alert language in her session, targeting negative thoughts associated with high alert and reinforcing future templates in which the child used her skills to bring herself to low alert.

The intervention provides a nonshaming way for parents to help their child implement skills for self-calming that can prevent meltdowns and other big behaviors.

MAKING SENSE OF THE PAST

Helping children make sense of the events of the past is important for increasing their ability to talk about their earlier life and resolve their trauma. Making sense of the child's past involves (1) creating a timeline and (2) creating a therapeutic story.

Beginning with a Timeline

After the child has gained some trust and self-regulation skills and is a little more comfortable with discussing his or her past, the family therapist begins developing the child's story through creation of a timeline. The therapist may use a large sheet of paper on which to draw a horizontal line, using spaced vertical lines to represent each year of the child's life. The therapist chats with the parents and child and gradually gathers information about the child's life, using clinical judgment regarding the child's tolerance. The child and parents are invited to help place the events, people, and locations into chronological order on the timeline. Because traumatic memories are stored differently in the brain than typical memories and can feel very "current" when triggered, traumatized children often operate out of "trauma time" and have memories of events all mixed up. The creation of a timeline helps organize the child's disorganized brain. In addition, the family therapist emphasizes the terms *past*, *present*, and *future* during this work, so that the child remains grounded in the present. The family therapist can do a little "detective work" in creating the timeline by asking the child, "How do you think this event caused you to feel?" and "What do you think this event caused you to believe?" as the various events on the timeline are discussed. This information should be noted on the timeline. The family therapist and parent can use the discussion to begin providing clarification to the child's story and correcting misinformation and incorrect beliefs.

Preverbal Trauma

Although the child does not remember being placed in an orphanage as a newborn or being removed from his or her biological home at 18 months, he or she has been impacted nonetheless by the early trauma. Although the child does not have conscious memories, he or she has probably heard this early story in bits and pieces and holds pictures, feelings, and beliefs related to it. The timeline work can help straighten out misinformation and clarify the child's story.

Creating a Therapeutic Story

In her book *Small Wonders: Healing Childhood Trauma with EMDR*, Joan Lovett, MD (1999), describes a method of writing a therapeutic story and then integrating the narrative method with EMDR. We use Lovett's therapeutic story method within the overall Integrative Team Treatment approach. The family therapist is responsible for writing the story, and the EMDR therapist uses the story, first in its entirety, and then by pulling out single events to reprocess, as described in Chapter 6.

Appendix E provides an outline that assists the therapist and parents in writing a therapeutic story for a child with a history of attachment trauma. The story has three parts: a beginning with current, positive information about the child; a middle section, with a brief description of the challenging situation; and a concluding section with positive cognitions that distinguish present from past.

A sample therapeutic story is provided in Appendix F. Lovett (1999, 2009) suggests writing the story in the third person to make it easier for the child to hear and discuss. She recommends beginning the story with something positive about the child and his current life. As an example, the first sentence might read: "There was a boy who lived with his parents, his two dogs, and his two cats." The first paragraph of the story demonstrates that the child's parents know him very well—what he likes, his strengths, what they enjoy doing together. It also describes some of the ways the parents reliably take care of their child, for example, "Every day his parents made sure he had a good breakfast, lunch, dinner, and snacks. They took him to school and picked him up every day. They made sure he had clean clothes and some toys he liked." For younger children, you may wish to begin with "Once upon a time. . . ." The positive, current-day beginning grounds the child in the present before focusing on the past.

The next sentence, as recommended by Lovett (1999, 2009), normalizes the mix of positive and negative events in the child's life. For example, this sentence might read: "Like everybody else in the world, the child had some things that were wonderful in his [her] life and some things that were confusing [hard, sad, or scary, or hard to understand]." Next, the story describes a positive event in the past. For children who are adopted, this part might read: "One wonderful thing was that this baby was born good and lovable." A confusing point might be introduced with a sentence like the following: "One confusing thing was that the baby's birth mother couldn't take care of a baby."

The timeline forms the foundation of the therapeutic story. We often have the timeline in front of us while we write the story along with the parents and the child in session. Lovett (1999, 2009) recommends first discussing with the parents what should or should not be included in the story, and writing the story with the parents alone. Writing in session can be anxiety-provoking for the therapist who is new to this therapeutic activity. Alternatively, the clinician may choose to write a rough draft or outline of the story outside of the family session.

The first draft should be informational, true, and developmentally appropriate, but without a description of thoughts or feelings. Lovett recommends inviting the child to help "fill in the blanks" by inserting the thoughts and feelings for the child in the prepared story. The child and family therapist are ready for this task, because they have already identified many negative beliefs during work on the timeline and during "detective work."

The child is usually prepared to discuss his or her story, because it describes events that have already been included on the timeline. That said, neither the timeline nor the story should go into elaborate detail or cover too many events. Keep the story as simple as possible. A child may have a very complicated history wrought with terrible events, which could easily overwhelm him or her. Use clinical judgment regarding what should be included and what should be left out of the child's story. The therapeutic story for children with a history of attachment trauma typically begins with preverbal events, including the child's birth, and includes, for example, an explanation for why the child is not living with his or her biological family. Lovett (1999, 2009) provides adaptive information in the story by stating something like,

"Now that he is older, he can understand that . . ." or, "His forever mom wants him to know that. . . ." We often simply state, "The truth is. . . ." The positive, accurate information differentiates the present from the past situation and includes the desired PCs that the therapist and the child's parents want the child to understand.

Because the story is written while the child is still struggling, we usually end the story by saying something like this: "Sometimes the child still struggles with believing she is safe and loved and worthwhile. Luckily, her parents and therapists are helping her feel better about herself, and she is gradually learning to trust her parents to keep her safe and love her each and every day."

After completing the story, the family therapist passes it along to the EMDR therapist, who reads through the entire story while the child sits with the parent and holds bilateral tactile pulsars (Lovett, 1999). Later, the EMDR therapist returns to the story again and again to process specific events. The story allows the EMDR therapist to tap into stored preverbal material by targeting emotions, sensations, images, and cognitions associated with that part of the story. (The use of the therapeutic story by the EMDR therapist is described further in Chapter 6.)

By delegating the writing of the story to the family therapist, the team makes the most efficient use of therapeutic time. While the family therapist is devoting time to developing and writing the child's story, the EMDR clinician is preparing the child for EMDR memory work.

PREPARATION FOR DISCHARGE

At the beginning of the treatment, the child and parents attend one family session and one EMDR session weekly. It is imperative to maintain the frequency until the child's behaviors have stabilized. To ensure that the child is ready for a decrease in frequency, parents may be asked to complete assessments to determine if scores have reached nonclinical level. (Suggested assessments are provided in Appendix B.) At that point, frequency can gradually be decreased until the child is discharged.

The family therapist should reassure parents and children that therapeutic "tune-ups" are available following a discharge from treatment. New environmental triggers, hormonal changes, or new developmental tasks as the children grow and mature may lead to a need for therapeutic support, and the sooner the situation is addressed, the easier it is for the child—and parents—to get back on track. Children and parents who have a positive experience during Integrative Team Treatment are more likely to continue seeking help when needed, preventing smaller crises from turning into bigger crises.

CONCLUSION

The family therapist's role in the Integrative Team Treatment model is to provide the foundational work for the EMDR therapy by helping both parents and children develop insight, self-regulation, and more positive interactions. Parents often begin treatment with their child in a state of frustration, anger, and hurt. The family therapist is able to embrace the parents by surrounding them with a safe and secure environment through listening and attunement. Parents make a vital paradigm shift as they begin to view their child through the lens of attachment and trauma realities. When parents have a clearer view, they are able to respond more effectively to the hurt child.

As children develop mindfulness, self-regulation, and interpersonal skills they become less reactive. As children begin to talk about their life story and identify memories, triggers, and negative beliefs, they develop readiness for trauma work in EMDR. The Integrative Team Treatment model is a direct and active model that also allows for flexibility in response to the specific needs of children and families. Look again at the flow chart in Chapter 2 (Figure 2.1, p. 30). Although there is a general flow to the family therapy, the therapist is free to use clinical judgment and intuition regarding choice of strategies for the session, depending upon the needs of the child and parents. The family therapist also moves back and forth among the various strategies, repeating components as needed. For example, the family therapist naturally returns to parent work again and again, as parents often lose sight of what is fueling disruptive behaviors in the home and revert back to old thinking and emotion-driven parenting behaviors. Likewise, the family therapist regularly returns to mindfulness work with the child because the child inevitably experiences various emotions, memories, and thoughts throughout the treatment process.

In the Integrative Team Treatment model, children are embraced within a collaborative, nonjudgmental environment that helps them gain the ability to trust the world again. The family therapist, EMDR therapist, and parents become part of the same team, working together to build a healthy, regulated family and a healthy, regulated child.

Following is a reference list for the family therapy strategies described in Chapter 4:

Parent work
1) Helping parents view the child through the trauma lens
2) Parent coaching
3) Facilitating emotional attunement
4) Guiding parents in managing meltdowns

Mindfulness Work
1) Feelings come and feelings go
2) Teaching the window of tolerance
3) Teaching "belly breath" and "cooked noodle"

Recognizing the Smaller Child Within
1) Use of nesting dolls as a visual aid

2) Expressing appreciation for the actions of the younger parts of self

3) Teaching what babies need and the cycle of trust.

Coping with Present-day Life

1) Teaching the jobs of moms and dads

2) Brain work (feeling/thinking brain and talking to the brain)

3) Teaching past, present, and future

4) Detective work: zeroing in on triggers and applying skills

Skills, Skills, and More Skills

1) Creative practice

2) The communication game

3) Teach high-alert/low alert language

Making Sense of the Past

1) Beginning with a timeline

2) Creating a therapeutic story

PART II
EMDR Strategies

Chapter 5

ATTACHMENT RESOURCE DEVELOPMENT AND OTHER EMDR PREPARATION ACTIVITIES

EMDR FACILITATES A natural associative process to achieve the integration of unprocessed, disturbing memories with stored, adaptive information through eight phases: (1) history-taking, (2) preparation, (3) assessment, (4) desensitization, (5) installation, (6) body scan, (7) closure, and (8) reevaluation. EMDR is a three-pronged approach, addressing past events, identifying current triggers, and developing future templates for desired behaviors.

Children with single-event traumas and secure attachments need minimal preparation for reprocessing, as they have an emotionally supportive environment and a store of adaptive information available for synthesis with the unprocessed trauma. Children who have suffered emotional deprivation and complex trauma, however, have an altogether different situation. First, they lack an adequate store of positive experiences and adaptive information upon which to draw, and may have processing problems due to inadequate neurological integration. Second, children with disordered attachments have difficulty trusting adults or turning to them for support, and therefore they reasonably cannot allow themselves to open up emotionally and work through painful emotions and memories.

The EMDR preparation work described in this chapter, along with the work of the collaborating family therapist, can create parent–child closeness and increase the store of adaptive information for more effective EMDR reprocessing. The work with both the EMDR therapist and the family therapist wraps children in a nurturing cocoon, enabling them to open up emotionally and face their most vulnerable feelings and memories during EMDR Phases 3–8.

This chapter describes how the EMDR member of the team can use EMDR during the preparation phase. The chapter describes (1) traditional resource development and installation (RDI) helpful with traumatized children; (2) the use of attachment resource development (ARD) to increase the sense of connection for children with attachment disorder; (3) self-regulation development and installation (S-RDI), and (4) optional helpful EMDR activities.

INTRODUCING EMDR

By introducing EMDR to parents and children in a simple way without scientific jargon, therapists can help them feel comfortable with the idea. The authors find that most parents are relieved to hear that the EMDR approach addresses underlying traumas and helps integrate the child's brain. The therapist might explain EMDR to the parent in this general way:

> "We know that trauma is stored differently in the brain than other experiences. It is stored in an unprocessed form in the emotional part of the brain—encapsulated along with the feelings, body sensations, and beliefs present at the time of the trauma. EMDR is a method that we use to jump-start your child's natural information processing system in the brain. By stimulating the right and left portions of the brain, EMDR helps your child work through the traumatic memories and any present-day re-

minders of those memories. The bilateral stimulation helps connect his [her] upsetting feelings and thoughts to more helpful, left-brain information. Before we start working with any upsetting feelings or memories, we will use EMDR to increase positive feelings of safety and connection with you."

The therapist may wish to demonstrate the various methods for implementing bilateral stimulation to the parent.

The therapist might explain EMDR to the child in this general way:

"I'm going to show you some of the fun little gadgets we use here." *(If the EMDR therapist has the equipment, he or she encourages the child to briefly follow the lights on the eye scan machine and to hold the tactile pulsars. The therapist may go on to demonstrate all the possible methods of bilateral stimulation.)* When upsetting things happen, they get stuck in the right side of your brain. Really upsetting feelings and thoughts get stuck there, too. *(Here the therapist may choose to draw a simple picture, looking down at a brain. The therapist can draw a little circle in the right hemisphere and write: stuck memories, stuck feelings, and stuck thoughts.)* When we use these buzzers or these lights during EMDR, we are lighting up very important areas in the right and the left sides of your brain. This is good for you, because it helps the upset pictures, feelings, and thoughts get all connected up to the helpful ideas you have stored there in your left brain. *(The therapist can draw numerous lines connecting the two hemispheres.)* EMDR helps upset feelings become smaller, and it also helps good feelings become bigger. Every time we use EMDR, we are helping you to have a stronger, happier brain."

This last statement is really all that needs to be said to very young children, or to children with developmental delay.

Choice of Bilateral Stimulation

Before the child is ready for trauma work, EMDR is used to strengthen a positive inner state and positive feelings of connection with parents. During this preparation phase, we favor use of bilateral hand taps, electronic tactile pulsars ("tappers"), or audio stimulation through headphones, rather than the use of eye movements, as these forms of stimulation seem to slow associations and create a greater relaxation effect for more effective strengthening of positive affect.

Later, when children begin EMDR reprocessing of recent triggers and past traumas, we encourage them to participate in bilateral eye movements if they are able to do so. Shapiro (2005) suggests implementing eye movements as rapidly as the client can sustain and still remain comfortable.

General EMDR Suggestions Related to Age Groups

Careful observation and attunement to children's cognitive and emotional development is crucial to successful EMDR. Same-age children can vary widely in their ability to focus and sit still, cooperate, manage their impulses, comprehend abstract ideas or difficult vocabulary, and express themselves with words. Following are some general guidelines related to age groups.

Children Age 5 and Younger

In general, very young children respond positively to the EMDR therapist who is gentle, patient, and attentive. The therapist should be curious about everything the child does or says, and should sit fairly close without invading the child's space, catching his or her gaze, perhaps pulling the chair up close to keep the child's attention. Of course, with young children the EMDR therapist should be willing to get on the floor as needed, move about, and be silly, all the while remaining cognizant of the child's shorter attention span, cognitive limitations, limited self-awareness, and limited capacity to verbalize thoughts and feelings. The therapist should avoid the use of metaphors or abstract ideas, and use "concrete" vocabulary the very young child can understand.

Because of their size and age, younger children generally can be enticed into sitting on their parent's lap, snuggling close, or sitting with their parent's arm around them for short periods of time to begin with, extending the time as treatment progresses. They usually can be enticed into participating in EMDR by saying, "First we'll do our work, and then you and I and your mom (or dad) can play." A game, sand-tray time, or floor time with toys is a nice reward and also helps extend the positive feelings of connection with the parent.

Many young children enjoy the tactile pulsars and willingly hold them or keep them in their pockets or shoes. Our colleague, Kris Walpus, makes pillows with pockets to hold the tactile pulsars and tucks the pillows on either side of the child, who sits cuddled up with the parent. Children who are overly sensitive to the pulsars are soothed by the vibrating pillows. Sensory tools can also be helpful. A colleague, Jennifer Anderson, places younger children and parents in big beanbag chairs and covers them with a weighted blanket throughout the session. Some children prefer to sit on the parent's lap while the parent strokes or gently squeezes one arm and then the other, or they prefer to lie on the couch while the parent strokes their legs or feet. Other children will sit on their parent's lap facing the therapist while the parent sways them from side to side. During EMDR trauma desensitization, many young children can be enticed into moving their eyes bilaterally by encouraging them to follow a toy or puppet held in the therapist's hand, or by turning on the bilateral moving lights on an eye scan machine. Some children willingly settle down on the parent's lap and cooperate with either eye movements or tactile stimulation while sucking on a lollipop or holding a stuffed animal. Gomez (2012) suggests offering the use of a "shy blanket," a loosely woven blanket such as an afghan that the younger child can put over his or her head to feel safe and less vulnerable during therapy; the child can see out but cannot be seen.

Elementary School-Age Children

Early experiences of neglect and attachment trauma can result in cognitive, emotional, and social deficits so that elementary school children with a traumatic history may be functioning in some ways like children who are much younger. No two children with a history of attachment trauma are identical, and the successful EMDR therapist should observe the child carefully to adapt to his or her individual needs. A 9-year-old with a history of attachment trauma may be functioning intellectually at age level but have the attention span of a younger child, requiring adaptations that are usually implemented with much younger children.

Adolescents

By adolescence, children who have spent their previous years avoiding and repressing emotions and needs for closeness may be fully entrenched in an identity built on a view of self as independent and strong. Furthermore, the avoidant method of minimizing anxiety is now compounded by the adolescent developmental task of separation and autonomy, which is expected at this age. The older the child, the more the independent self-view is integral to self-worth. It is important not to threaten that self-view with avoidant adolescents, but to accept it and work with it.

It can be helpful with avoidant adolescents to use language that does not threaten their independent self-view. An adolescent being seen by one of us (DW) exclaimed, "I hate it when you use your warm, fuzzy voice!" The therapist eliminated any warmth or softness from her tone and the adolescent became more cooperative.

The family therapist can help the EMDR therapist by educating the parents regarding the need to work "with" instead of "against" the child's avoidant style. For example, avoidant adolescents may reject the goal of learning to trust and depend upon their parents, but they may cooperate with the goal of learning that their parents are on their side. Physical closeness can be encouraged to some extent with avoidant adolescents, but not forced. The EMDR therapist can acknowledge adolescents' independence by providing some therapy, one-on-one, without the parents in the room. However, no serious trauma work should take place without a parent present unless the child is an older adolescent and there is an agreement to connect with his or her parent immediately after EMDR trauma work. This adaptation should be fully explained to the parents.

Dissociation

There is some measure of dissociation in most children who suffer from attachment trauma. A traumatic history combined with a lack of felt emotional connection and support leaves children in a chronic state of high stress that reinforces dissociative defenses and interferes with the development of an integrated sense of self.

Excessive dissociation in children may indicate a need for increasing the number of EMDR preparation therapy sessions as well as mindfulness and self-regulation family therapy work. When children are highly dissociative, the parents' emotional attunement and use of integrative parenting strategies on a consistent basis are crucial. Children's symptoms of dissociation typically improve through increased attunement on the part of the current caregiver. The secure holding environment, along with the child's use of new skills, helps "hold" the child's personality together. Emotional attunement from parents helps integrate the child's brain before, during, and after EMDR reprocessing. However, the therapist should be prepared to assist the child who easily dissociates or gets "stuck" in emotions from the past with the EMDR adaptations described in this manual.

Various forms of dissociation are observed in traumatized children. A common defense in traumatized children, as well as the general population, is "shutting down" when anxiety is high. Most of us have had difficulty staying focused during highly stressful situations, and many traumatized children are wired for mild dissociation that leaves them with attention and concentration problems. Repeated traumatic experiences interfere with the normal development of a cohesive sense of self, leaving children vulnerable to extreme mood and state fluctuations, a sense of disconnection from the body, fluctuating access to certain memories, or feelings of depersonalization or derealization, especially related to memories. More rarely, children may adopt new personas as part of an unconscious need to dissociate from unwanted memories or emotions, or they may project dissociated emotions onto imaginary friends. Strengthening self-regulation skills and the security of the child's attachments with the strategies outlined in this chapter and reprocessing past trauma with sensitive parental support will help to gradually decrease the child's dissociative symptoms throughout the course of treatment.

Careful listening to both the parent and child reports and observation of the child's behaviors during therapy often bring to light dissociative processes that are present in the child. See Appendix B for screening tools that can provide additional information regarding the dissociative processes that may be present.

The therapist should explain the symptoms to both parents and children as a normal and common response to distressing conditions. Child and adolescent therapists should not implement the kind of parts work that is utilized with dissociative adult clients. The International Society for the Study of Dissociation Task Force on Child and Adolescents (2003) cautions that "simplistic application of treatment approaches for adult dissociation to children may be potentially dangerous to children." Any approach that reinforces separateness of parts will exacerbate dissociation in children. The therapist should never encourage naming of parts of self or emphasizing or delineating separate personalities, and should discourage the parents from doing so as well. Consistent with the task force guidelines, the child who enters treatment with a sense of having alternate selves should be given hope for developing a more integrated sense of self with appropriate trauma work and the development of healthy attachments.

We find "inner child" work to be a safe approach with traumatized children who experience varying levels of dissociation. The Integrative Team Treatment model utilizes the inner child activities with every child in the treatment, and normalizes the concept of the "child within" as something to which every individual can relate. Inner child work should always focus on helping all younger parts of the child's self inside feel safe and loved, while simultaneously strengthening the competent, most mature self. Sometimes parents refer to younger parts of the child's self in a derogatory way (e.g., "the mad one" or "the evil twin"). Younger parts of self should never be shamed or devalued—the therapist should model only compassion, respect, and appreciation for how the "younger child part" survived or coped with traumatic circumstances.

TRADITIONAL RESOURCE DEVELOPMENT AND INSTALLATION

During the preparation phase, resource development and installation (RDI) (Korn & Leeds, 2002) can be used to give the child greater access to positive affect, which increases the child's ability to self-regulate at home and in the therapy office. This section outlines 1) RDI for reinforcing a safe state, 2) RDI for reinforcing a "big girl" or "big boy" affect state, and 3) the butterfly hug method.

Safe Place/Safe State

Most EMDR therapists utilize the development of a safe or calm inner place to increase the client's access to feelings of safety (Shapiro, 2001). This practice may be challenging with severely traumatized children who have never experienced safety. The child can be encouraged to think of a place that is completely imaginary, a place out of a book, a television show, a movie, or a place the child has visited—a real place in the child's life. Children need direction when they describe a place that the therapist suspects may be connected to something disturbing, such as a house where the child lived when he or she was abused. If simply thinking of a "safe place" is difficult for the child, it may be because the word *safe* itself triggers thoughts of *unsafe*. The word *calm* or *relaxing* may be more readily accepted. The therapist, child, and current caregivers can work together to create a picture of the safe or calm place through a drawing or painting or by cutting out pictures from a magazine. To lessen the chances of triggering a negative association during reinforcement of a safe place, we find it useful to implement slow bilateral stimulation, and to do so only while the therapist is verbally guiding the child's thoughts and images. Following is a sample script for safe place development and installation.

> *Karen:* My safe place is my room.
>
> *EMDR Therapist:* Can you describe it to me? *(Listens to a detailed description of the child's room and then implements slow hand taps throughout the safe place guided imagery.)* Put yourself there now. Notice the flowers on the wallpaper, the yellow curtains at the window, your polka-dot bedspread, and the big, fuzzy pillows. Relax on the bed with your favorite stuffed bear, and play some of your favorite music. Feel the soft mattress, the fluffy pillows under your head, and listen to the sound of your grandma making dinner in the kitchen. As you relax there, just notice the calm feelings in your body, notice the feelings of safety inside of you, in your safe

room, in your safe house, in your safe neighborhood. *(Stops bilateral stimulation.)* How did that go?

If the child's report is positive, the therapist can repeat the exercise. If the child reports a problem, the therapist should change or alter the safe place as needed, before repeating.

Competency Memory/Power Memory/Big Boy/Girl Self

A child's sense of self is created by looking at him- or herself through the eyes of attachment figures. Children impacted by attachment trauma typically lack a sense of competency and self-efficacy and instead believe themselves to be incompetent and bad. RDI can be implemented to develop and reinforce a memory of feeling competent, strong, or powerful (in a healthy way) to access and strengthen a positive state within the child. RDI can also be used to strengthen a "big boy" or "big girl" memory to assist the child in recognizing and finding a positive affect state that is associated with responsible behavior. Similarly, an adolescent can be assisted in reinforcing a memory of feeling "mature" or "competent." Following is a sample transcript for reinforcing the "big-girl" self.

EMDR Therapist: Jane, I would like you to think of a situation or something you did that made you feel kind of grown-up, like a really big girl.

Jane: Yesterday, Mom asked me to pick up my shoes and my backpack and I did it without whining.

EMDR Therapist: That is really great.

Mom: Yes, I was shocked.

EMDR Therapist: (Applies slow hand taps while guiding the child in thinking about the entire scenario.) Put yourself back in that situation now. Think about what your mom asked you to do, and how you just walked right over there and picked those things up without one word, and how mature and grown-up you were. Picture your mom's face when she felt surprised and happy. Notice how your body feels right now as you remember back to yesterday. *(Stops the hand taps.)* How did that go? *(The child gives a positive answer, and the therapist reinforces the positive big-girl feeling one more time.)*

Butterfly Hug

The EMDR therapist can instruct the child to think about good feelings related to a recent positive situation or to his or her safe place, and then to give him- or herself "a big hug" and tap his or her own shoulders back and forth, bilaterally (Shapiro, 2001, p. 284). The child can be empowered in this way to reinforce positive affect for him- or herself, at home or at school. Do present this as an optional idea that the child can choose, or not choose, to use, however, and caution the parents in this regard. We have learned that if parents think that children are *supposed* to practice the butterfly hug at home, they may command children to do so, turning it into a power struggle. Following is a sample script with which the EMDR therapist might describe the butterfly hug exercise:

> "I'd like you to bring your safe place to mind. Let me know when you have it. Put yourself there, in your safe place. *(Shows the child how to cross his or her arms and tap them anywhere between the elbow and shoulder.)* Now give yourself a nice hug, like this, and move your hands like a butterfly to make those relaxed, safe feelings even stronger inside. *(Allows the child to practice and makes sure the child has a positive experience.)* "You can try this at home or even on the way to school. A good time to do the butterfly hug is in bed, to help you fall asleep and have good dreams."

COMMENCING ATTACHMENT RESOURCE DEVELOPMENT

Attachment resource development (ARD) involves exercises that create experiences of closeness in session and slow tactile or audio stimulation to enhance the child's feelings of trust, safety, and connection with his or her parents (Attachment and Trauma Center of Nebraska, 2011; Wesselmann, 2006, 2007). Strengthening the child's sense of security with his or her parent during the preparation phase helps the child open up emotionally during EMDR memory work.

ARD may be the sole focus of the EMDR sessions for 3 or 4 weeks, or even more, in some cases. Once EMDR reprocessing of memories and triggers commences, some ARD should be conducted at the beginning or end of each session ongoing. During ARD, children are developing new positive memory networks associated with secure and safe attachments, but repetition is needed to maintain and strengthen these completely new neural connections.

Preparing Parents for Attachment Resource Development

It is important to prepare parents without the child present. The therapist should explain that ARD enhances positive feelings of closeness and trust, and that the role of the parents is to describe positive traits they enjoy in their child, activities they enjoy doing with their child, traits they share, the positive feelings they felt the first time they saw their child, and their positive early memories. Discuss with parents some ideas regarding things they might say. Explain that you will encourage physical closeness during ARD and explore any concerns the parents may have. (See Appendix C for a parent preparation handout.) If parents feel a little awkward or self-conscious, create a written list of positive ideas (a "cheat sheet") to which parents can refer during the ARD.

Some parents have a harsh or loud tone of voice, or rapid or pressured speech that may be very triggering to the traumatized child. Some parents need to be coached to use a soft and soothing voice. For some parents who struggle with voice tone, speaking in a whisper is helpful. Other parents have a habit of furrowing their brow, pursing their lips, or clenching their jaw. Parents can be coached to slightly lift their brow and soften their facial expression.

Naturally, it is imperative to be sensitive to the parents' "performance anxiety." The therapist should not expect perfection from the parent. Stay lighthearted, warm, positive, and encouraging with the parent. Avoid using an authoritarian or judgmental tone. Parents who had little nurturing when young will likely have difficulty with the "Messages of Love" and "Playing Baby" exercises. Be prepared to provide assistance by coaching the parent and possibly helping the parent write down ideas for the "Messages of Love" exercise.

Occasionally, a parent will object to ARD. The objection may be related to a feeling that the child hasn't "earned" positive time with the parent, and that the child should change before being "rewarded" with ARD. In this case, more psychoeducation may be needed to help the parent make the important shift from the "old school" thinking to the "new view" from the AIP model lens. The following example illustrates how to speak to a parent, Jan, who is resistant to ARD.

Jan: So during these first two or three EMDR sessions, the plan is to give Susan positive messages and feelings of closeness? That's really backwards, isn't it? It's not the way life works! I don't want Susan to learn that she can act up and be mean to people and then get rewarded with all kinds of warm fuzzies. When we misbehave, it is a natural consequence that people don't want to be close to us!

EMDR Therapist: I understand your concern, Jan. A lot of parents come in feeling this way. But remember, Susan is functioning with a survival brain, and that changes everything. Susan's brain is stuck in hyperarousal probably 90% of the time. The hyperaroused brain is unable to learn. That is why all of the behavioral modification techniques you have already tried have not created any change in Susan's behaviors. We have to calm her brain before any kind of learning can take place. The best way we know to accomplish this calming is to wrap Susan in a cocoon of safe and nurturing messages and to create in her brain a feeling of loving connection to you. Using bilateral stimulation to create new positive memory networks of love and safety will begin to calm her firing brain.

Jan: OK, what you are saying makes sense. But I might have to fake it a little bit, is that OK?

EMDR Therapist: That's OK, Jan. A lot of parents have to "fake it" 'til they make it.

Potential Rebound

The child usually feels more feelings of affection for the parent during and immediately following the nurturing attachment work. Some children experience a "rebound" effect afterwards, however, because the resulting closeness and intimacy lead to heightened fear of rejection later. A stern look or a redirection from the parent in the week following attachment resource work may trigger a huge reaction in the child. Some children have a rebound effect because when the exercise is over, it feels like the closeness is over and will never return. An analogy that can be used to help parents better understand the child's reaction is the feeling of disappointment we have all experienced when a holiday has ended and it is time to return to the day-to-day reality of work and school.

Implementing Attachment Resource Development with Resistant Children

A helpful way to disarm the resistant child of any age is to begin ARD by saying something like the following: "You are lucky today, because you get to just settle back and relax. You won't have to do a thing. Your parent [supportive adult] has to do all the work today." With a child who is still refusing to listen and cooperate, it can be helpful to coach the parent to speak lovingly about the child to the therapist, even while the child is acting out. Allowing the child to "listen in" as others speak positively about him or her helps lower the child's anxiety. Sucking on a sweet lollipop can also calm the dysregulated younger child. Offering a snack of any type, bringing out clay or paper and markers, or getting down on the floor with toys may calm the child, allowing him or her to "listen in" to the positive, loving dialogue. Another option is to begin with the fun activities described at the end of this chapter. Initially, the activities can be implemented without bilateral stimulation, with a gradual addition of the stimulation as the child's anxiety begins settling down.

The EMDR therapist may wish to collaborate with the child's parents to work out a reward system. For example, two of us (CS, DW) worked with a young boy who had a meltdown whenever he entered either the family or EMDR therapist's office. We spoke to the mother by phone after a session, and the mother mentioned that the boy really liked gum and playing with small soldiers. Thereafter, at the beginning of each session we offered gum and rewarded the boy with 20 minutes of play at the end of each session for remaining cooperative. This intervention allowed both of us to conduct successful sessions with the little boy. The playtime at the end of the sessions was gradually decreased.

At no time should a therapist use force, intimidation, or threat, nor should the parent be allowed to engage in those tactics. Clearly, a child should never be held down and forced to utilize bilateral stimulation.

Implementing Attachment Resource Development with Biological Children

ARD is completely appropriate for strengthening attachment between biological children and their parents. When early separations, illnesses, temporary foster care, or other traumas interfere with the development of a secure attachment, ARD can help heal and repair the relationship damage. If attachment insecurity is related to a generational issue of discomfort with closeness or a harsh parenting style, parents should be required to participate in individual therapy, preferably EMDR, to address their own memories. (See more about helping parents in Chapter 8.)

Creating Physical Closeness during Attachment Resource Development

Coach the parent and younger or elementary school-age child to cuddle together during these exercises, in whatever way is comfortable. Some older children and adolescents are quite comfortable with closeness, but those who are avoidant can be encouraged to sit as close as possible while still feeling comfortable. Forced holding of children or forced physical contact can be traumatizing. Be patient, and over time, the avoidant or older child may become more comfortable with contact. The child may only be willing to sit on the opposite end of the couch with the parent in early sessions, but slowly inch closer as treatment progresses, allowing the parent's arm around his or her shoulders in the end.

Gomez (2010) describes a way to help parents become more empathic in response to the child's discomfort with closeness. She asks parents to think about how the stomach shrinks in response to starvation. The person who has starved is later unable to take in what would be considered normal amounts of food; at first, normal intake causes sickness and discomfort. Similarly, the child who has been deprived of closeness and affection naturally has a reduced capacity and tolerance for both.

THE ATTACHMENT RESOURCE DEVELOPMENT EXERCISES

During ARD, the EMDR therapist creates an experience of closeness between the parent and child and implements relatively slow tactile or audio bilateral stimulation (slower than the typical speed implemented for memory reprocessing), while the therapist (or parent, under the therapist's direction) guides the child's thoughts with positive statements (Wesselmann, 2006; 2007; Attachment and Trauma Center of Nebraska, 2011). In our experience, many children experience a calming effect from the alternating vibrations of the tactile pulsars during the ARD exercises, and children like having the option to hold the pulsars or place them in their pockets, socks, or shoes. It is also helpful to ask children if they want the pulsars to be set at a slightly higher or lower speed. Alternately, children may be comfortable wearing headphones with alternating tones or sitting on their parent's lap and swaying gently from side to side.

The ARD exercises include (1) the "Messages of Love" exercise, (2) the "Playing Baby" exercise, (3) the "Lollipop Game" exercise, (4) the "Magical Cord of Love" exercise, (5) the "Circle of Love" exercise, and (6) the "Safe Place for the Little One" exercise.

The "Messages of Love" Exercise

While encouraging as much physical closeness as the child and parent can comfortably manage, the therapist asks the parent to describe enjoyable memories, positive traits of the child, and his or her emotions that allow the child to experience at least rudimentary feelings of belonging and safety within the attachment relationship. As long as the parent is speaking positively, the child's experience is reinforced with relatively slow bilateral stimulation. Occasionally, throughout this exercise, the therapist brings the child's attention to his or her feelings of calm or connection by saying, "Notice how good it feels to snuggle up with Mom/Dad today," or "Notice the good feeling inside, knowing that Mom/Dad loves you, and that you belong."

The parent is prompted to speak these messages of love by the following statements and questions from the EMDR therapist:

- "Tell me about the first time you met your child. What do you remember thinking? What do you remember feeling?" In the case of biological children, the therapist asks about the parent's memories of the pregnancy and the birth.
- "Let's hear about some of the other fun memories of the early days." The therapist can ask the parent to bring photos and other mementos to the session to spark positive early memories about the child.
- "I would love to hear more fun memories about the child's first words [first steps/first friends/funny moments/first trips/first holidays/favorite activities, etc.]."
- "Can you describe the things you most enjoy doing with your child?"
- "Tell me about the traits and potential traits you see in your child that you most appreciate."
- "What things make you feel proud of your child today?"
- "Describe the traits or habits the two of you have in common."
- "What things do you hope to share with your child in the future, or do you hope to watch your child do in the future?"

In the case of children who are wards of the state in foster care, group homes, or residential treatment, a committed foster parent, relative, or staff member can provide warm messages of positive regard for the child, noting positive traits, positive behaviors, and other things the individual feels proud of regarding the child, while the therapist reinforces the child's feelings of connection, safety, and pride with bilateral stimulation. For children in residential care, this exercise can be conducted almost daily, strengthening the child's sense of self and connectedness to others at the facility.

The parent who cannot guarantee a future with the child might remind him or her that "I will always have you in my heart," instead of, "I will be your parent forever." Relatives can reassure the child, "I will always be a part of your life," if they are committed to an ongoing relationship, even if they are not the final, permanent placement for the child.

The "Playing Baby" Exercise

The child may enjoy "playing baby" by curling up on the parent's lap and pretending to take a bottle or even using a real bottle in the play. A lollipop can be used to simulate the sucking and sweet feeling related to sucking on a baby bottle. The parent can be encouraged to talk playfully about how fun it is to care for the baby and act out rocking, feeding, and singing to the baby, and so on. The child can also be encouraged to place his or her ear over the mom's heart. The therapist can describe how the child's heart is synching up with the mother's heart, like two musical instruments playing in rhythm together. The therapist can also put on lullaby music or other soft music and dim the lights to encourage the child to relax and enjoy the closeness. The child may enjoy cuddling up with his or her old baby blanket or stuffed animal or a borrowed cozy item while playing baby.

During any part of this exercise, the therapist can place pulsars in the child's socks or shoes or tap slowly and rhythmically on the child's legs or feet to create bilateral stimulation while calling attention to the child's sensations and emotions: "Notice how safe and secure you feel curled up in your mom's lap. Notice how relaxed your body feels while Mom is in charge of taking care of you." The age at which children participate in the "Playing Baby" exercise varies in relation to developmental maturity. We have discovered that many middle school children enjoy the activity when their early needs for nurturing and closeness were left unmet. At the end of the session the EMDR therapist should say something like this:

> "Let's tuck the baby away in his [her] safe place now. Can you picture him [her] there? Now we want the 'big boy'

['big girl'] back. Tell me about some of the 'big boy' ['big girl'] things you did this week."

This transitional message helps ground the child back into his or her more mature state before going home. Nevertheless, after the "Playing Baby" exercise, the therapist should caution parents that their child may temporarily have periods of speaking more baby talk and asking for more baby-like attention at home. The therapist should explain that this is only temporary, and that these periods of regression provide a wonderful window of opportunity to make up for some of the child's earlier unmet needs.

The "Lollipop Game" Exercise

This adaptation to "Playing Baby," developed by Joan Lovett (2009), enhances the child's feelings of closeness and trust, and most children love the game. The age at which the game is appropriate is really dependent upon the child's developmental level. Following is a sample script for the EMDR therapist:

> "Sally, you and your mom [dad] are going to play the lollipop game. You get to lie across your mom's lap while she holds the lollipop. Your job is to use your eyes and mouth to signal when you want the lollipop in your mouth and when you want the lollipop out of your mouth. Mom, your job is to watch your child's face and read her signals. Sally, it may be difficult, but try not to crunch the lollipop, because then we have no more lollipop and the game has to end."

If the child crunches the lollipop, just commend him or her for how long he or she resisted the urge and reassure the child, "It's OK, we will play again another time."

Children tend to regress and become very "little" during this game, as they give up all control and allow their mother to be in charge. At any point during the lollipop game, the therapist can tap or place tactile pulsars in the child's pockets or socks and call the child's attention to feelings of closeness and safety. Following is a sample script for the EMDR therapist:

> "Just notice how comfy you feel in Mom's [Dad's] arms. It's fun to let Mom be in charge and feed you and take care of you. It's good to know you can trust her to know just what you need. Notice how you can depend on your mom to take good care of you."

If an older child is uncomfortable with the lollipop exercise, he or she may still enjoy sucking on a lollipop (reminiscent of the sweetness of a baby bottle) while listening to the parent's messages of love.

The "Magical Cord of Love" Exercise

Children who have not developed secure attachments tend to have very little object constancy when it comes to their parents' love for them. They seem unable to carry the feeling of love or believe the connection exists when parents are not present and focusing attention on them. Developing a "magical cord of love" directly creates this sense of constancy (Attachment and Trauma Center of Nebraska, 2011; Wesselmann, 2006). This magical cord of love is not magical, however; it needs to be reinforced a number of times and referred to throughout therapy. Relatively slow bilateral stimulation (through tapping or tactile pulsars) is implemented while the child cuddles with the parent and the therapist guides the child's thoughts with the visualization. Following is a sample script.

> *EMDR Therapist:* Susie, I would like to invite you to close your eyes and picture the magic invisible cord that connects you to your mom and dad, heart to heart. The cord is made of a beautiful light, the light of love. Susie, what color do you think love is?
>
> *Susie:* Red.

EMDR Therapist: Red is a wonderful color for your cord of love. Imagine this beautiful red cord, like a shimmery red light, connecting you heart to heart. This cord is magical because it can stretch, so no matter how far away you go, and no matter how far away your mother or father goes, it can stretch and stretch so you are always connected. Right now, the love is pouring into your heart from your mom's heart and from your dad's heart. And no matter how much love they send you, there is always more. Just notice the good feelings as you lay back comfortably with your mom and dad. *(With the parent's permission, the therapist may also tap slowly on the parent's shoulders, while calling the parent's attention to feelings of comfort and closeness.)* Mom, just notice how comfortable and close you feel to Susie right now.

The therapist and child can draw pictures of the magical cord between the child and parents in situations in which the child typically feels insecure, rejected, or unloved (e.g., when the parent is giving attention to a sibling or is disciplining the child). Ask the parents to talk about how they still love the child in these situations while the child looks at the picture and the therapist reinforces the parents' words with slow tapping on the child's shoulders or knees.

For resistant adolescents or children who are wards of the state with no stable placement, the "cord of love" can be reframed as the "cord of caring." The Cord of Caring exercise can be conducted with the help of a committed foster parent, a court-appointed special advocate (CASA) worker, or residential facility staff member who is willing to describe feelings of care and commitment to the child without a placement. The child can visualize a beautiful cord of caring, connecting him or her heart to heart, to the adult who is committed to the child's well-being. For the adolescent who might find the words *magical cord* to be childish, the therapist can conduct a guided imagery of a simple *cord of light.*

The "Brain Cord" Variation

Deanna, the child described in Chapter 7, invented a variation of the Cord of Love exercise that we have found useful with other children. One day when her therapist asked her to look at her mother's calm face as a way to calm herself, she smiled broadly and said, "brain cord!" After that day, whenever she began to feel anxious she would think of the "brain cord" between her mother's calm brain and her brain as a way to calm herself.

The "Circle of Love" Exercise

In order to expand the child's sense of safety and belongingness in the world, the therapist can ask the child to list all the people who care about him or her (Wesselmann, 2006). These individuals can include relatives, caseworkers, teachers, siblings, friends, and so on. With children who have no stable placement, this exercise can be conducted as the "Circle of Caring," if they are able to name friends or professionals who are concerned for their welfare.

The EMDR therapist might say: "Let's make a list of all the people you have in your life who care about you." The therapist may wish to ask the child to draw a very simple picture of all the people surrounding him or her. After adding bilateral stimulation while guiding the child's thoughts, the therapist continues:

> "Picture all these people in this room with you. Think about how crowded this room is right now. Imagine the love of all of these people surrounding you. Picture their love as a beautiful light filling the room."

The "Safe Place for the Inner Child" Exercise

The family therapist usually introduces the concept of the inner child during a family session, fairly early in the treatment (see Chapter 4). The EMDR therapist creates a sense of safety for the "younger self within" by collaborating with the child and the parents to create a "special" or "safe" place for the baby or younger self within (Attachment and Trauma Center of Nebraska, 2011; Wesselmann, 2006).

Most children enjoy drawing a picture of their safe place, which helps make the baby place more concrete. Invite the parent to participate in thinking about what the baby might need or want. The parent can participate in drawing the picture if the child wants this help. If the child wants to take the drawing home, the therapist should first make a copy for the file, so that he or she can bring it out during future therapy sessions. The safe place for the smaller hurt baby or child should be revisited and reinforced again and again. In the sample script for the EMDR therapist, we have incorporated some language used by Sandra Paulsen (2012) in her treatment for adults with preverbal trauma:

> "I know that you and Cathy [the family therapist] have talked about the hurt smaller child and the hurt baby who lives inside your heart. I think we should all work together to help those littler parts of you to feel safe and loved. To start with, let's imagine a safe place for the baby you. Let's think about a place that would be comfortable and cozy and fun. Now is the time to give that baby everything he could possibly need. Let's really go for the gusto. Let's help that baby live it up now."

Involve the parent in the fun of creating an ideal place for the baby. Don't worry about what is or is not age-appropriate. If the parent says, "A baby isn't old enough to jump on a trampoline," reassure him or her that babies can do anything they want and have anything they want when they live in the mind's eye.

Ten-year-old Tommy, who now lives with his grandmother, was severely neglected as an infant. Figure 5.1 is a picture of a safe place drawn by Tommy for his infant self. When Tommy's drawing was completed, the therapist used bilateral stimulation

FIGURE 5.1. The Safe Place for the Baby Tommy.

to reinforce Tommy's positive emotions and sensations as he described the details of the safe place. Tactile pulsars were placed inside Tommy's pockets and set to a relatively slow speed.

The next part of the exercise is a crucial step for healing preverbal trauma and abuse and increasing the sense of trust from the child toward the parents. Invite the parents, one at a time, to talk about what they will do for the baby in the safe place. While the child's thoughts are focused on the healing imagery, implement slow bilateral stimulation. The child can also be invited to talk about what he would like his or her present-day parent to do for the child within, as illustrated by the following transcript, in which Tommy's grandmother is present as his attachment figure.

EMDR Therapist: Tommy, can you close your eyes now and picture the baby you, comfy and cozy inside this special place, within your heart?

Tommy: Yes, I see him—he is in his special bed.

EMDR Therapist: Tell me more about that special bed.

Tommy: (Pointing to the drawing) I can sit in my bed and watch whatever television show I want. All I have to do is press the special button and any kid show will come on. The bed also has tons of blankets to keep me warm.

EMDR Therapist: I bet Baby Tommy loves watching all those favorite shows and feeling warm. *(Turning on the tactile pulsars)* Close your eyes again, and see if you can just notice the warm, comfy feeling of Baby Tommy in his special bed.

EMDR Therapist: (Turning off the pulsars and pointing to another button) What is this button for, Tommy?

Tommy: This is the button that sends me my food though the catapult [drawn near the bottom of the picture]. When I push this button, it throws me whatever food I want and plenty of milk. The catapult is attached to a conveyor belt, and the food never runs out.

EMDR Therapist: That is so cool. Baby Tommy never even has to leave his bed for food or milk. *(Turning on the tactile pulsars again)* Notice what Baby Tommy feels like when he knows he has enough food.

Tommy: It feels good, I'm never hungry.

EMDR Therapist: I bet that is such a good feeling—always satisfied. *(Turning the pulsars off)* Tell me more about who is sitting in the rocking chair.

Tommy: That's Grandma.

EMDR Therapist: Why is Grandma there?

Tommy: She is there to keep me safe and play with me.

EMDR Therapist: Wow, that is great. *(Turning on the pulsars)* Let's notice the feeling of Grandma always keeping you safe and never letting you be alone.

Tommy: (Pointing to the picture) This is the button for the library.

EMDR Therapist: Tell me more. *(pulsars off)*

Tommy: I push this button and whenever I want Grandma to read a book to me, she comes right into my room.

EMDR Therapist: You love stories. *(Turning on the pulsars again)*

What is the feeling when Baby Tommy is listening to the story while sitting in Grandma's lap?

Tommy: Happy.

EMDR Therapist: Let's just notice that happy feeling, and how you feel when Grandma's arms are around you, while you are looking at the book.

Tommy: I also have plenty of toys and clothes that match.

EMDR Therapist: (Pulsars off) With plenty of toys there is always something for Baby Tommy to do, and even Grandma could play toys with you in this room. Let's notice the feeling of always having something and someone to play with. What is that feeling, Tommy?"

Tommy: Happy and excited, not bored!

EMDR Therapist: I bet. Let's notice that happy, excited, not bored feeling. (*Turning on the pulsars and continuing to discuss the rest of the picture, including the bright sunshine coming through the windows and the fun football curtains that Tommy put on the windows. Later, Tommy's grandmother is asked to picture "Baby Tommy" and talk about caring for Baby Tommy in the safe place.*)

Grandmother: (Pulsars on) I love being inside the safe place with Baby Tommy. We rock, and I sing lullabies and funny little songs I learned when I was a child. Today, I am singing "This Little Light of Mine" to Baby Tommy, and we rock and rock. Next, we get down on the floor, and we roll a little car back and forth, and we make little car noises together.

Tommy's grandmother continued to describe playing with Baby Tommy, feeding him, and tucking him in bed, while the therapist ran the tactile pulsars in Tommy's pockets to reinforce the happy pictures and Tommy's feelings of closeness to his grandmother. This safe place was used many times for Baby Tommy as the therapist, Tommy, and his grandmother worked through current-day triggers and early experiences of neglect. Again and again, Baby Tommy was visualized in his safe place, and relatively slow bilateral stimulation was used to reinforce Tommy's feelings of inner safety.

Meeting the Needs of the Inner Child at Various Ages and Stages

If there was serious trauma during the time in utero, the birth, or postbirth, the "Safe Place for Baby" can be conducted as an exercise to give the baby an ideal situation in utero as well as at various ages throughout the first 3 years of life; this is an adaptation to the early trauma protocol as described by Paulsen (2012). Chapter 7 of this book describes the use of the Safe Place for Baby exercise at several ages of infancy and toddlerhood for Justin, a child who was adopted after being hospitalized for the first 2 years of his life.

We frequently create a safe place for various ages of younger parts of a child's self, depending upon what ages the child believes he or she was most hurt. For example, 10-year-old Darlene developed a safe place for her "inner baby" because she suffered early neglect in her biological home, and also for her "inner 3-year-old" who suffered the loss of her biological family when she was moved to foster care. Later, when Darlene revealed abuse in her second foster home, she developed a safe place for the "inner 5-year-old." Darlene's adoptive parents participated in providing loving care through guided imagery to each of Darlene's hurt little ones inside. Bilateral stimulation reinforced Darlene's experience of inner safety and love for these vulnerable, wounded little parts of herself.

Ongoing Care for the Baby Inside

Once the safe place has been established for the baby or smaller child within, the child and parents together can continue nurturing the younger part of the child through dialoguing and caring for the littler self in session. The therapist might invite the parents and child to picture an imaginary baby or toddler in the arms of the parents, or a doll can be used to represent the baby. Relatively slow bilateral stimulation is implemented through hand taps or tactile pulsars to reinforce the nurturing words spoken by the therapist, parents, or the child throughout the session and to reinforce the child's feelings of connection.

Following is a transcript of a session introducing the "Safe Place for Baby" and "Caring for the Baby Inside" exercises to 8-year-old Bella and her adoptive mother and father. A baby doll was used to represent Baby Bella.

EMDR Therapist: Bella, today you talked with Deb [the family therapist] about your timeline, is that right?

Bella: Yes.

EMDR Therapist: (The timeline that was drawn in family therapy is used by the EMDR therapist now, as a visual aid.) Bella, can you tell me about your timeline?

Bella: It shows the time before I came to live with Mommy and Daddy, and then when I came to live with them, and now. It shows how scared I was before.

EMDR Therapist: Dad, what do you remember about this timeline?

Dad: I remember us learning that Bella didn't feel safe before, and now, there are times when the baby who lives inside her heart still doesn't feel safe. Then, big Bella doesn't feel safe either.

EMDR Therapist: (Checks for understanding from prior family therapy sessions before continuing with the intervention.) Well, today we are going to take care of that little Baby Bella who lives in your heart. Do you remember when Deb talked with you, Bella, about how we all have a little baby who lives inside our heart?

Bella: Yes, we used those red China dolls [referring to the nesting dolls], and the baby was very little. We put the baby back inside, nice and safe.

EMDR Therapist: Well, today all of us are going to take care of Baby Bella. I have a baby right here, and we are going to pretend that she is Baby Bella! *(Brings out the baby doll, wrapped in a blanket.)* We are going to hold her and rock her. We will talk to her and tell her how safe she is now. *(Cradles the baby doll and rocks the baby as she speaks.)*

EMDR Therapist: Mom, would you like to hold Baby Bella first?

Mom: Yes, I would love to hold Baby Bella. *(The therapist gently hands the baby over to the mother.)*

EMDR Therapist: Mom, what do you want to say to Baby Bella? *(Bella sits between her adoptive mother and father on the couch. The tactile pulsars are placed in Bella's hands and turned to a slow rhythm to reinforce the child's feelings of safety and closeness as each individual speaks, throughout the rest of the session.)*

Mom: I love you, Baby Bella. You are safe now. No one is going to hurt you ever again. We keep you safe. *(Cradles and rocks the baby doll gently as Bella looks up at her mother and then back at the baby doll again and again.)*

Mom: If you are hungry, we will make sure you have a bottle. If you are wet, we will change you. If you are scared, we will help you. The scary time is over now, and you are safe, Baby Bella. You are safe.

Bella: *(Reaches up and touches the doll's head.)* You are safe now, Baby Bella. Mom and Dad will keep you safe. *(The mother begins to cry.)* We have a safe house and good dogs to protect us. Mom makes good food, too.

Dad: Yes, Baby Bella, it's all OK now. We are so sorry you were so scared. You have a safe place now inside Bella's heart, where Mom and Dad are rocking you and taking care of all that you need.

Bella: *(to therapist)* Can I give Baby Bella the tappers?

EMDR Therapist: Yes, you can hold the tappers on Baby Bella's hands.

Bella: *(Holds the pulsars on the doll's hands.)* Baby Bella likes the tappers. They help her feel better. Shhh, Baby Bella, it's OK now. You won't have any more bad dreams. Mom and Dad are here now to keep you safe.

Mom: Yes, we are here, Baby Bella. We will be here forever, and we will never leave you.

Dad: That's right, we will never leave you.

EMDR Therapist: Gosh, I wonder how Baby Bella feels on the inside right now?

Mom: I bet she is calm . . . she seems calm.

Dad: Yes, she seems calm and relaxed.

Bella: She's calm, but still worried about the nightmares. Mom, could you tell her that she doesn't have to have the nightmares anymore?

Mom: Yes. Bella, it's OK now. All the scary stuff is over and you can relax and be calm. You don't have to worry anymore about the scary stuff. We will help Bella with all of that.

EMDR Therapist: If Baby Bella could talk, what do you think she would say?

Dad: I think she would tell us that she feels comfortable and warm and safe right now.

Bella: I think she would say, the bad dreams are over.

For about 8–10 more minutes, the three sat on the couch and continued to nurture and comfort Baby Bella. The therapist continued to use interweaves to reinforce Bella's safety and to assist Bella in healing the hurt inner baby. This exercise helped Bella begin feeling the safe, holding environment of her new life with her new parents. The parents benefited from this exercise because they learned just how scared Baby Bella was. At closure, Bella was guided in visualizing Baby Bella in her safe place, and the picture was reinforced with tactile pulsars. Then the therapist engaged her mother and father in talking about "big-girl" things Bella had done the previous week, while Bella held the tactile pulsars to reinforce the "big-girl" state.

CREATING INNER SAFETY FOR ADOLESCENTS WHO ARE NOT IN A PERMANENT PLACEMENT

When it is likely that a permanent placement will not be located for an older adolescent, the Safe Place for the Inner Child exercise can be conducted, but with an imaginary ideal parent figure or spiritual figure taking the role of the nurturing parent (Wesselmann, 2006). The ideal caregiver figure can be an individual who has been a positive support in the adolescent's life (e.g., a grandparent, childhood neighbor, or teacher) or a spiritual figure (e.g., an angel, Jesus, Buddha). Additionally, the entire circle of caring individuals/figures can be invited to encircle the younger baby or child part of self. Following is a transcript of an EMDR therapist's work with 16-year-old Annette.

EMDR Therapist: Would you be willing to do a little imagery exercise that can help the younger, scared child in your heart to feel calmer and safer?

Annette: (Nods.)

EMDR Therapist: We are not going back in time—we are working with the younger child self who is a part of you today. You said that things were especially tough when you were 6, is that right?

Annette: (Nods.)

EMDR Therapist: Let's talk about a place that might feel comfortable and secure to your 6-year-old self. It will also be important to find a caregiver to watch over your 6-year-old self in the comfortable place. This could be someone who has been in your life, or it could be a spiritual figure.

Annette: (Develops an image of her 6-year-old self in a cabin in the woods, surrounded by flowers. Her caregiver is a beautiful angel.)

EMDR Therapist: Stay in your 16-year-old self now, and picture this wonderful cabin in the woods, surrounded by tall trees, flowers, and wildlife. Your angel is there with your 6-year-old self, picking flowers.

EMDR Therapist: (Continues adding detail about the cabin in the woods and the angel caring for the 6-year-old self while implementing relatively slow bilateral stimulation through hand tapping.)

Annette reported only positive emotions and sensations associated with the imagery, so in the following session, the therapist asked Annette if she thought she could dialogue a little with her younger self. Annette was willing to try. The EMDR therapist explained this activity to Annette in the following way:

> "Remember, Annette, that at any point, if you are having difficulty, just hold up your hand to give me a stop signal and we will stop and regroup. *(Recreates the safe place with the angel and the 6-year-old and adds bilateral hand taps.)* Now, I would like you to imagine that you are walking into this beautiful scene as your 16-year-old self. I wonder if you might be able to reach out to the 6-year-old in some way, or just talk to her with words. Let her know that she is being taken care of, that she is safe, that she can relax here and play, and just be a child. *(Pauses and implements 9–10 slow hand taps)* I would like to check in with you now, and find out how this is going for you."

ATTACHMENT RESOURCE DEVELOPMENT VIA MOVEMENT, SONG, AND RHYTHM FOR YOUNGER CHILDREN

Bilateral stimulation can be implemented with toddlers and preschoolers in a fun way through rhythm, song, and bilateral swaying along with tapping if possible. Infants and toddlers who are in a nurturing environment naturally experience a great deal of bilateral stimulation through bilateral swaying. The infant who is held lying in the parent's arms and rocked in a rocking chair is experiencing bilateral stimulation through side-to-side movement. Pay attention the next time you see a mother holding her infant upon her shoulder. She naturally sways her body from side to side, providing her infant with bilateral stimulation. In the 1950s, during Harlow's famous experiments with monkeys, it was discovered that the functioning of infant monkeys raised with wire mothers could be enhanced by placing them on contraptions that swayed them from side to side. As a form of ARD, toddlers and preschoolers can sit on the parent's lap facing the therapist, while the parent and therapist sway from side-to-side, rhythmically chanting or singing nurturing messages and positive ideas to enhance the child's trust and feelings of safety (Wesselmann, 2006). The following songs were developed by Stefanie Armstrong (2011):

Sung to the tune of "Hush Little Baby":
Hush little Isaac, we love you.
Mommy and Daddy keep you safe.
You are always safe with us.
Learning everyday that you can trust.

Sung to the tune of "Frère Jacques," a traditional French song (English version, "Brother John"):
Cali is safe, Cali is safe.
Yes she is, yes she is.
Her mommy and daddy, her mommy and daddy,
Keep her safe, keep her safe.
Cali is loved, Cali is loved.
Yes she is, yes she is.
Her mommy and daddy, her mommy and daddy,
Love her very much, love her very much.

Sung to the tune of "The Wheels on the Bus":
The love in mommy's heart never stops, never stops, never stops.
The love in mommy's heart never stops, even when she's at work.
The love in mommy's heart stays forever and ever, ever and ever, ever and ever.
The love in mommy's heart stays forever and ever, even when she says No!
Mommy whispers to Isaac, "I'll keep you safe, I'll keep you safe, I'll keep you safe."
Mommy whispers to Isaac, "I'll keep you safe, forever and ever."

Before the next song begins, the caregiver asks, "How much of Jacob does Mommy love? She loves him from his . . . " sung to the tune of "Head, Shoulders, Knees, and Toes":

Head, shoulders, knees, and toes, knees and toes. Head, shoulders, knees, and toes, knees and toes. Eyes and ears and mouth and nose . . . head, shoulders, knees, and toes, knees and toes.

The caregiver can also ask, "How much of Jacob will Mommy keep safe? She will keep him safe from his. . . ."

Two-year-old Amy sat on her mother's lap, while her mother sat on the couch, facing the therapist. The therapist sat on the floor in front of Amy while her mother swayed side to side, and the therapist tapped on Amy's knees in synchrony with the swaying. The therapist led Mother in singing "Amy is safe" to the tune of "Frère Jacques." Amy loved the singing and swaying and tried to join in the singing. Amy and her mother continued singing and swaying as a nightly ritual, which appeared to calm Amy and help her feel safe and more securely connected to her mother. Amy's mother was also encouraged to stand and sway to music on a CD player while whispering nurturing and loving messages to her daughter.

SELF-REGULATION DEVELOPMENT
AND INSTALLATION

Children with a history of attachment trauma have feelings of anxiety about feelings. The layers of feelings upon feelings can spiral quickly into panic and meltdowns. Chapter 4 describes the role of the family therapist member of the team in teaching and coaching children to self-regulate. Self-regulation development and installation (S-RDI) reinforces the child's experience of moving from a dysregulated to a regulated state and reinforces the child's use of skills for doing so. The protocols decrease children's panic related to their own affect and widens their window of tolerance (Siegel, 2010).

The EMDR therapist should make good use of opportunities to reinforce the child's experience of self-regulation "in vivo." When a child feels impatient to get to the end of the session or becomes upset with his or her parent during the session, the S-RDI protocols can be utilized to help the child manage the "I can't wait" feeling or the annoyed feeling right in the moment, while it is happening. This is the most powerful way to implement the S-RDI exercises, which should be repeated frequently to gradually widen the child's window of tolerance for his or her emotions. Portions of the therapist's words can be used during reprocessing, to help keep the child from dissociating or becoming overwhelmed.

S-RDI includes the following components: (1) mindfulness coaching, (2) mindfulness coaching with photographs, (3) talking to the brain, (4) talking to the body, (5) "cooked noodle" and "belly breath" exercises, and (6) speaking to the inner child.

Mindfulness Coaching

Bilateral stimulation can be used to reinforce children's experience of mindfulness through the coaching they receive from the EMDR therapist. The exercise in mindfulness helps children decrease their fear of their own inner emotional states, decrease their judgments regarding their emotions, and increase their level of self-awareness.

The therapist should move his or her chair close to the child's chair to keep the child's attention—but without overwhelming him or her or appearing threatening in any way. The exercise can be implemented when the child has noted an emotion during the session, or without any present emotional disturbance. Following is a sample script of what the EMDR therapist might say. The tactile pulsars are implemented, on a relatively slow speed, as the therapist speaks:

"You know, Johnny, all your feelings are normal and OK. We all have all kinds of feelings throughout the day. A whole bunch of feelings may wash up on top of us all at once like a big ocean wave, but that is normal. We can have the feelings and still be OK. We can ride out the feelings, and after a bit, the waves of feelings will wash back out to sea. The feelings will pass. Feelings are just feelings. Feelings are not right or wrong, good or bad. They just *are*. You can have your feelings and be OK."

Mindfulness Coaching with Photographs

To conduct this S-RDI exercise, the therapist finds photographs through Google Images or another website showing various faces with emotions, animals showing emotions, or situations in which people are exhibiting emotions. Alternatively, the therapist can ask the child to draw a picture that represents a certain feeling or a symbolic representation of the feeling. Next, the therapist implements mindfulness coaching while the child looks at the picture, allowing the child to externalize the emotion and view the emotion without "taking on" the emotion. The EMDR therapist might say the following:

"The feeling in the picture is temporary. This feeling comes, and then it will go. The feeling this person is having is very normal. He [she] can have this feeling and be OK. The feeling is OK. The feeling won't hurt him [her]. The feeling will pass."

After 2 or 3 short sets of slow BLS hand taps while focusing on the picture and the emotion, the child is asked to change the picture in some way. As the child imagines it changing, slow, short sets of taps are added. For example, while looking at a picture of a lion looking sad, the child creates a story of the lion moving to a different emotion. If this shift does not occur spontaneously, the therapist might say the following:

"Remember, feelings come and feelings go. No feeling lasts forever. Just think of the feeling coming and going in the picture."

This exercise is an adaptation of the early trauma protocol step, "Resetting of the Affective Circuits," as described by Paulsen (2012).

Talking to the Brain

Coach children in "talking" to their feeling brain about a challenging topic or situation. Often we ask a child to use the "thinking brain" to "talk" to the "feeling brain." Reinforce the child's experience of self-regulation with bilateral stimulation. The EMDR therapist might say the following:

"Johnny, I can tell that the back part of your brain is firing a little bit. Let's see if you can use your smart thinking brain right now and talk to that feeling brain. Tell the back of your brain, 'It's OK. This session won't last long. I'll be at the skating rink before I know it. I can handle this. I can be in my 11-year-old, mature self today. I can do it.' OK? Now you try. You can talk out loud, or you can talk in your head." *(The therapist implements relatively slow bilateral stimulation through hand taps or tactile pulsars while the child speaks to his brain.)*

Talking to the Body

Children with a history of attachment trauma are typically not connected to their bodies and have little control over the dysregulation experienced within their bodies. We often explain to parents that the children are like "little floating heads" without bodies to help parents understand this concept. The therapist can describe self-talk directed to parts of the child's body (Schweitzer, 2011), reinforcing the awareness and connection, providing a tool for regulating the somatic responses to emotion. Following is a sample excerpt.

EMDR Therapist: Sarah, I notice your body is full of big feelings today, and your body is having a hard time sitting here. Maybe you could hold the tappers, and then let's see if we can calm those feelings down a bit, OK? What part of your body would you like to start with? Do you want to talk to your feet? What do you want to say to your feet?

Sarah: I want to tell my feet, "Be calm, feet. There's nothing to be nervous about, feet." *(The therapist implements bilateral stimulation while the child talks to her feet.)*

"Cooked Noodle" and "Belly Breath"

This exercise is designed to bring the child's awareness to his or her body and reinforce the actual experience of becoming physically calm.

Seven-year-old Kaya entered the EMDR session in an agitated state after another child had mocked her in the waiting room. She sat down next to her mother, bumping her mother's sore shoulder with her head. When her mother asked her to stop, she became increasingly tense and irritated, kicking, hitting the couch, and growling. Following is a sample script of what the therapist said to Kaya:

"Kaya, right now, I think you are feeling like you need to 'get the anger out' by hitting or kicking." *(Kaya nods and begins hitting the arm of the couch with her fist.)* But Kaya, you are not really getting the anger out of your brain and body. You are actually getting yourself worked up and putting more lightning bolts in your brain [Gomez, 2010], making you feel yucky. Let's see if we can calm you body and your brain and help you feel better. *(Invites Kaya to lie down and places a small toy on her belly.)*

"Let's see if you can breathe air into your belly and make the doll move up, and then breathe it out and watch the doll go down. That's right, up and down, as you breathe, that's right. Just like you learned in Stefanie's office. Let's see if you can make your arms and legs floppy like cooked spaghetti noodles. I'm going to do the cooked noodle test and see if your arms and legs are floppy noodles. *(One by one, she tests Kaya's limbs to see if they are relaxed.)* Wow, Kaya, that's impressive. Would it be OK for me to gently tap on your shoulders? *(Gently taps on Kaya's shoulders as she continues to belly breathe.)* Just notice how good this feels inside your body, and inside your brain. Notice the calmness, and the heaviness, in your body, and just think—inside your brain, all the lightning bolts are disappearing, one by one. It's all peaceful in your brain now. That feels better, doesn't it?"

Speaking to the Inner Child

Once a safe place has been created for the "inner child," the child can be coached to visualize his or her child part in the safe place and to dialogue with the younger self as a way to self-regulate.

For Derek in the following example, learning to speak to the younger part of himself was a way for him to develop the skill of positive self-talk. This experience of self-regulation was reinforced with bilateral stimulation. Ten-year-old Derek was very triggered each time his adoptive mother paid attention to others or talked on the phone. Derek had experienced a great deal of neglect and being left alone for lengthy periods of time when he was 3 years old. Following is a transcript of this portion of the session.

EMDR Therapist: Do you think that "alone feeling" you were having when Mom was on the phone was coming from little "3-year-old Derek" who lives in your heart? Take a moment to think of the feeling.

Derek: (Nods.)

EMDR Therapist: What do you suppose big Derek can say to 3-year-old Derek to help him right now?

Derek: Tell him we're not really alone? Mom loves me too?

EMDR Therapist: Yes, great idea. Why don't you hold the tappers and talk to little Derek about that right now. You can talk out loud or in your mind, whichever you want. *(Implements the bilateral stimulation while Derek speaks to the little Derek inside his heart.)* Now, I wonder if you can visualize little Derek in his safe place with Mom and Dad. *(Bilateral stimulation is applied to reinforce the safe, nurturing image.)*

Reinforce Positive Experiences of Self-Regulation from the Week

When the parent reports that the child used skills to calm him- or herself down during the previous week, we give the child a "high-five," hand him or her the tactile pulsars, and then ask the child to think about how it felt to calm him- or herself down while the EMDR therapist reinforces the memory with bilateral stimulation. Encourage the child to remember the sensation of his or her body moving from high alert to low alert and to notice how good the child feels about when he or she uses these newly acquired skills.

Tumbling Towers—Optional Resource Development Activity

This fun, optional activity was developed by Stefanie Armstrong (2011), who also gives credit to Joan Lovett (2009) for the idea of using bilateral stimulation to reinforce positive cooperation in play. Children who have experienced attachment trauma commonly have difficulty relying on caregivers and trusting them to be in charge. For example, they have difficulty asking for help or tolerating "no." The following games help the child practice tolerating these situations in a less threatening way. The EMDR therapist can use these exercises for resource development as well as future template work.

Prior to implementing the following activities, children should have completed some "detective work" in family sessions so that they have some insight into their triggers and their feelings. They also should have experienced some family and EMDR therapy to develop self-regulation through "self-talk."

The "Tumbling Towers" activities can be played with any small blocks or a Jenga game. Follow the general rules of the game (stacking the blocks, taking a block from the stack, and putting the block on top of the tower) while adding the intervention below. Explain the games to the parent before introducing the games to the child. As the therapist, parent, and child talk, they can sit on the floor and build a tower with the blocks together. Following is a transcript for the Tumbling Towers activity.

> *EMDR Therapist:* Today we are going to play Tumbling Towers. However, we will play it differently than you have probably played it before. Kiya, I know it is hard for you to rely on Mom and Dad and trust them, so we are going to play a game today that will help you practice. That way, you will have less upsetting things happen during your week. To show you how to play, I will role-play with your mom's help. I will pretend to be you. OK, let's get started. Mom, you will tell me which block to take by pointing to that block. I will then take that block and put it on top while saying, "OK, Mom." *(Mom points to a block; the therapist takes the block, saying, "OK," and positions it on top of another block to begin building the tower.)*
>
> *Mom:* Thank you, Kiya, for doing exactly what I asked you to do, exactly the way I asked you to do it. [This phrase was borrowed from work by Joan Lovett (2009).]

At this point, the parent and therapist model it one or two more times, building the tower a little taller each time. Next, it is the child's turn. Before the child and parent begin, place the tactile pulsars in the child's shoes or pockets. It is important to tell the child and the parent the two main "rules": (1) The child practices saying, "OK, Mom," and (2) the parent practices saying, "Thank you for doing exactly what I asked, exactly the way I asked you to do it." The therapist can motivate the child by saying, "Let's see how tall you and your mom can make your tower, as you cooperate together."

Tumbling Towers Interweaves

Staying very present and attuned to the child's emotional state, the therapist should use the interweaves below to help the child notice and strengthen any positive feelings associated with cooperation and success, and to practice tolerating any discomfort related to letting his or her parent be in charge. The therapist can run the tactile pulsars in the child's shoes or pockets for a short time after each interweave to reinforce the child's positive internal state or reinforce the experience of tolerating discomfort and self-regulating. It is important not to run the pulsars continually, as the child will become desensitized to the bilateral stimulation.

- "Remind your brain that you can trust your mom to be in charge."
- "Just notice the feeling inside as you have success with saying OK."
- "Just notice the uncomfortable feeling and remind your brain, 'It's safe to let Mom be in charge.' Remember, feelings come and feelings go."
- "Just notice how it feels inside to relax and let Mom be charge."
- "Mom, tell me how you feel when Kiya says, 'OK, mom.'" (Here the caregiver can give a feeling word, such as *proud* or *calm*.)
- "Just notice how connected you and your mom are right now."
- "Notice how connected you and your mom are when you are working together."
- "It's safe to trust your mom and rely on her."

After approximately 10–15 minutes, the therapist can stop the activity and ask the child and parent to get comfortable and sit close to one another. At this time, the therapist can ask the child to remember and "just notice" the good feelings of trusting and being close to Mom as the tactile pulsars run.

To close, the therapist can ask the parent or child to identify a situation that will come up during the week in which the child will need to trust the mom to be in charge. The therapist can run the pulsars as the child and parent role-play the situation to reinforce their interaction as a future template.

Tumbling Towers: Asking for Help and Tolerating "No"

This activity is set up the same way as the previous activity and follows the same process. It is important, again, to prepare the parent first. Then, explain to the child that this activity will help build "emotional muscle" and help him or her tolerate it when Mom says "no." This game is different in that the child asks if he or she can take a block, and every three to five times the parent says, "No, I don't want you to take that piece. I'd like you to choose a different one." After the parent gives this answer, the child is instructed to say "OK," and then choose a different piece. After choosing the new piece, the child again asks if he or she can take it, and the parent replies, "Yes, you may take that piece. Thank you for asking." The child then places the block on top to continue building the tower.

Following are interweaves that can be used during this activity. The therapist again runs the tactile pulsars in the child's shoes or pockets for a short time after each interweave, to reinforce the child's positive internal state associated with cooperating or to reinforce the experience of tolerating "no" and self-regulating.

- "Just notice the sensation inside when your mom says 'no.' You can let the feeling come and then go."
- "Good moms and dads say 'no' sometimes, and it's OK."
- "Talk to your brain and tell your brain, 'I can handle it when mom says, 'no.'"
- "Tell your brain, 'This is a want, not a need.'"

- "Things are still safe, even when your mom says 'no.'"
- "Just notice the sensations/feelings you get on the inside. It's OK to ask."
- "You can trust your mom to say 'yes' to some things."
- "Just notice how connected you and your mom are right now, in this moment."
- "Just notice how good it feels to stay calm and relaxed when your mom says 'no.'"

It is imperative to take it slowly. The child will want to rush through the game and get to the "yes" and build the tower as fast as he or she can. It is important to let the child sit with the "no" and experience it and learn that he or she can cope with it. It is also imperative to allow the child to really notice and tolerate the feelings associated with asking for a block.

Again, after about 10–15 minutes, the EMDR therapist can ask the parent and child to sit back and relax and then run the pulsars for a slow, short set to reinforce this positive experience of connection between them. Finally, the EMDR therapist can ask the child or parent to identify a situation that might come up during the week in which the child will ask for something and the parent will likely say "no." The parent and child can role-play the situation, and the therapist can reinforce the child's actions with the pulsars as a future template.

Both of these interventions can be quite triggering for children, and some of them have great difficulty participating in the game the first few times. Take it slowly. The therapist may have to introduce the game a few times before the child is even willing to play it.

Tumbling Towers for Teens

This tumbling towers activity works well with avoidant teens who like to engage in hands-on activities. Sometimes the ARD process can be difficult with resistant teens. The following activity is a way to implement ARD while creating a game-like, matter-of-fact, nonthreatening atmosphere. Play almost always gets the caregiver and the teen working as a team, rather than working against one another, thereby creating a positive experience between the youth and caregiver that can be resourced later in session or in coming sessions. It places the child within his or her window of tolerance so that he or she is able to take in the experience.

Before the game gets started, say, "Now, this tower is going to get tall, and it's going to wobble. One of you will be responsible for the last block causing it to fall. However, let's make a pact now, not to be upset about it falling. It's just a game." This usually prevents the teen from becoming angry when the parent's unintentionally unsteady hands make the tower fall.

During these activities, the bilateral tactile pulsars are placed in the teen's shoes or pants pockets, and are run at a relatively slow pace. The therapist should be mindful not to leave the pulsars running through the entire game. Shut them off and turn them back on during positive, affirming conversation only.

Tumbling Towers for Teens: Paying Attention to Positive Experiences, Thoughts, and Feelings

Explain to the parent and teen that they are a team, and that their goal is to get the tower as high as possible. The therapist might say something like, "I know of a mom and son who reached 24 levels. Let's see if you can beat that." This usually makes the parent and adolescent want to work harder. Then explain that for each block that is placed on the tower (taking turns, of course), they are to share one positive experience from the week or a positive feeling, thought, or body sensation. So, for example, the mom might share this as she places a block: "I noticed how well Dimitry got up for school and did all of his morning chores, with time left to spare. I really appreciated this and felt proud of his maturity." Dimitry can share something he did well or a positive feeling about what his mom said while he places the next block. For example, he might say, "I think my mom was proud of me when I got my morning stuff done," or "I feel happy that Mom noticed when I did well this morning."

As the activity progresses, the therapist can ask further questions to encourage the teen to notice positive thoughts related to what his mother said, or to scan his body searching for where he feels the "happy" sensation. Many teens are unaware of the thoughts that drive them to do both healthy and unhealthy behaviors. This activity encourages self-awareness.

Tumbling Towers for Teens: Positive Future Hopes and Dreams

This activity encourages teens to tolerate listening to the hopes and dreams of their parents. This time, with each block that is pulled and placed, the parent expresses a future hope and/or dream for the teen. Initially, as the parent and teen take turns, the teen isn't required to do anything except listen. However, as the activity goes on, the therapist may begin to ask the teen to comment or reflect on what the parent has said.

Positive Movie Exercise for Teens

This optional activity is based on one by Ricky Greenwald (2009). The Positive Movie exercise is very helpful for motivating children toward change. Children who tend to live in their "survival brain" do not tend to think about personal goals or plan steps to achieve their goals. The survival brain lives in the moment, hypervigilant to possible threats and dangers. Planning for the future and problem-solving steps to get there are thought processes that take place only when children are feeling safe and secure in the present. The Positive Movie exercise helps children experience a sense of efficacy in determining their future life. Following is our version of the script, which we reinforce throughout with relatively slow bilateral stimulation, noting the positive emotions and sensations:

> "Think about where you would like to be and what you would like to be doing 10 years from now [or whatever time seems appropriate]. Now, let's fill in the steps you will want to take between now and then to make sure you get that positive ending to your real-life movie. *(Write down the steps together.)* I would like you to run a movie in your mind now, as I read the steps, and then picture the good ending. *(Runs pulsars)* Let's do it again, and this time, hold in mind the words 'I can do it.' *(Runs pulsars)* Now, let's think about what the ending will be to your movie if you continue making choices that are similar to the choices you have made recently. *(Discuss what this movie will look like.)* Now, visualize this ending and hold in mind the words, 'It's not worth it.'"

The therapist then guides the child back to visualizing the positive movie one more time, with relatively slow bilateral stimulation throughout the visualization.

CONCLUSION

EMDR consists of eight distinct phases. The activities and exercises in this chapter are part of the second phase, preparation. However, the word *preparation* does not suggest the transformative power of EMDR in Phase 2, as children experience real healing through strengthening bonds with caregivers, as well as increased feelings of safety and competency, self-awareness, and capacity for self-regulation through the resource development exercises.

As illustrated by the flow chart in Chapter 2 (Figure 2.1, p. 30), the EMDR therapist does not work in a linear fashion when treating the traumatized child. Once EMDR reprocessing has been initiated in Phases 3–8, the ARD and self-regulation activities remain integral to the treatment. The EMDR therapist returns to the various activities throughout the duration of the child's treatment to help maintain stability and continue improving the quality of the child's relationships. The flow chart also illustrates the work taking place simultaneously in the family therapy sessions, including strengthening of parent attunement and child mindfulness. The work accomplished by the family therapist supports the Phase 2 work of the EMDR therapist.

Following is a reference list for the Phase 2 strategies described in Chapter 5:

Traditional Resource Development and Installation (RDI)
1) Safe place/safe state
2) Competency/power/big boy/big girl
3) Butterfly hug

Attachment Resource Development (ARD)
1) "Messages of Love" exercise
2) "Playing Baby" exercise
3) "Lollipop" game
4) "Magical Cord of Love" exercise
5) "Circle of Love" exercise
6) "Safe Place for the Little One" exercise
7) Songs for younger children

Self-Regulation Development and Installation (S-RDI)
1) Mindfulness coaching
2) Mindfulness coaching with photographs
3) Talking to the brain
4) Talking to the body
5) "Cooked Noodle" and "Belly Breath" exercises
6) Speaking to the inner child

Optional Activities
1) Tumbling Towers game
2) "Positive Future Movie" exercise

Chapter 6

ADAPTATIONS FOR EMDR REPROCESSING OF ATTACHMENT TRAUMA WITH CHILDREN

FOLLOWING HISTORY-TAKING and preparation, EMDR Phases 3–8 involve identification of the target image and associated cognitions, emotions, sensations, and baseline ratings (Phase 3); desensitization of the past event or present trigger (Phase 4); installation of the positive cognition (Phase 5); scanning of the body (Phase 6); closure (Phase 7); and the follow-up at the next session (Phase 8). The ARD exercises that are officially part of Phase 2 are repeated throughout the duration of the child's treatment to ensure that the child's sense of security and safety with the parent remains strong.

PARENT AND PLACEMENT ISSUES IMPACTING READINESS FOR TRAUMA WORK

Typically, EMDR preparation work with a child may consist of four or more sessions prior to beginning trauma work. The length of the preparation phase depends largely upon the challenges related to the child's environment. Addressing traumatic memories in EMDR therapy requires children to tolerate feelings of vulnerability, which requires support from a nurturing and stable environment. When a parent or caregiver retains a highly critical attitude toward the child despite the beginning work of the family therapist, it is necessary to hold back on trauma work and allow more time for parents to understand the child's behaviors through the trauma lens. When parents appear to be stuck in their own reactivity, the EMDR therapist or family therapist should refer the parents to individual EMDR therapy, remaining sensitive to their shame and anxiety about looking at their own emotions and experiences (see Chapter 8).

When a child resides with a non-adoptive foster parent or guardian, this does not preclude implementation of trauma work, as long as the caregiver is willing and able to commit to being an ongoing part of the child's life and providing emotional support during therapy. Implementation of the team protocol in the circumstance of long-term residential care depends upon the available emotional support both within and outside of the residential center. If there are committed adults involved in the child's life, they should be encouraged to participate in the child's therapy in an ongoing way in order to implement the model as true to form as possible. In a residential setting, the child's willingness, motivation, ability to utilize available emotional support, and capacity for self-regulation are all important factors to consider in determining the child's ability to participate in EMDR trauma work.

MOTIVATION THROUGH METAPHORS

One component of readiness for memory reprocessing is the child's willingness. Metaphors can be used to help motivate children to participate in reprocessing their traumatic material. Following is a sample script the EMDR therapist can use to present the Monster in the Closet metaphor:

> "Imagine that you are lying in bed and you hear a sound in your closet. You say, 'Mom, come here. I think there is

a monster in my closet!' How would you feel if your mom came in and said, 'So you heard a sound in the closet? I'm not opening that closet if there's a monster in there. Just forget about it and go back to sleep.' Now, you're sure there really IS a monster in your closet, right? But what if you call your mom in and she throws open the closet door and says, 'Look, there's just a bunch of old junk in here. There is no monster.' Now you feel a lot better, right? Well, it's the same thing with your old upsetting memories. You think you have to keep the closet door shut because you have a bunch of monsters in there. But if we open the door and take a look—and use a little EMDR—you will come to see, as I do, that there's just a bunch of old junk in your closet and then it will no longer have power over you."

Following is a sample script the EMDR therapist can use to present the Quest metaphor:

"Just like a character in one of your video games, you are on a quest. You are beginning a very important journey to conquer your memories. EMDR is your special power, and it will help you find the other special powers you need to zap each one of your memories, and then to put each of them inside a special, powerful container."

You can have fun with this one. Interweaves might include, "What special power can you find to help you with this memory?" and "What special power can you use to put this into your container today?"

DEVELOPING A CONTAINER

Prior to trauma reprocessing, the child can be helped to develop a container. It can be an imaginary container that exists only in the mind's eye, such as a magic box or treasure chest, or it can be an actual container in the office or something that the therapist, parent, and child craft together. Following is a sample script.

> *EMDR Therapist:* Let's create a container so you have a place to put all the yucky memories and feelings when you don't want to carry them around with you. You can use an imaginary container in your mind, or you can use something in my office, like my desk drawer or my filing cabinet.
>
> *Lori:* I want to use your filing cabinet.
>
> *EMDR Therapist:* OK, good choice. Notice how solid this filing cabinet is, and how strong and secure. Let's send all the memories and feelings to this filing cabinet right now. When we work, we will just take one thing out of here, like one file folder, and leave the rest inside here. When we are done, we'll put everything back in. Anytime something comes up in between our sessions that you don't want to think about, you can send it right here.

UTILIZING THE PARENTS FOR EMOTIONAL SUPPORT DURING EMDR REPROCESSING

It is vital to provide complete emotional safety, warmth, and acceptance for the child during EMDR reprocessing of past events or present-day triggers. One of the primary roles of the family therapist is to help the parent make the "paradigm shift" from viewing the child as rage-filled and controlling to viewing the child as traumatized. The majority of parents who have a full understanding of the traumatic roots driving the child's behaviors can provide an attuned and compassionate presence. If the child is willing, suggest that he or she snuggle up next to the parent or sit near the parent during the EMDR, so the child can physically feel the parent's presence but not be distracted visually by the parent. The parent's compassion and presence provide emotional regulation, grounding, and the connection the child requires to open up emotionally.

Prior to beginning the EMDR reprocessing, it is very important to prepare the parent to be a compassionate but silent presence to the child. If the parent is not prepared adequately with an explanation regarding the importance of silence, he or she will likely interfere with the child's processing by interjecting unwanted comments. Following is a sample explanation for parents:

> "Before we begin, Mom, I want to explain that there may be some long silences during the EMDR. First, there is a lot of silence during the bilateral stimulation because this is the time that the child is making associations internally and processing, both at a conscious and subconscious level. Then, as your child attempts to put words to her thoughts and feelings, there may still be a lot of silence, because this does not come easily for her. So you and I will want to provide a mostly silent, supportive presence. There may be times when I interject what is called a 'cognitive interweave,' which is a nugget of needed information or a brief question for your child to focus on, such as 'How is your adoptive mom different from your birth mom?' Sometimes I will turn to you to provide a bit of information or for a little 'imaginary cognitive interweave.' For example, sometimes we ask parents to describe what they would do to help the child if they could travel back in time. But just wait for my cue—I will let you know when I need you."

PHASE 3: ASSESSMENT

Phase 3, the assessment phase, involves setting up the memory or trigger prior to reprocessing with bilateral stimulation (although in the Integrative Team Treatment model, the family therapist may accomplish identification of the target and NC prior to the EMDR session). Traditionally, the EMDR therapist begins by asking the client to describe the picture that represents the worst part of the event or trigger. This picture is the target. Next, the EMDR therapist asks the client to describe the negative words that go with the picture (NC), and then helps the client identify the desired PC. The client is asked to rate the validity of the positive cognition on a 7-point scale (1–7) and then to identify the emotion, where the disturbance is felt in the body, and to rate the level of disturbance in the body on an 11-point scale (0–10).

The child with a history of attachment trauma usually requires a great deal of assistance during this phase of assessment. Because the capacity to self-reflect develops through early healthy attachment relationships (Fonagy et al., 1997), the child with poor early attachments naturally struggles with self-awareness and with finding appropriate words to describe his or her thoughts and feelings. These children require more assistance than other children in identifying thoughts, feelings, and body sensations. The therapist should also be prepared to adapt his or her language to the child's developmental level (Adler-Tapia & Settle, 2008).

The family therapist often helps the child identify targets for EMDR during the family sessions, along with NCs and desired PCs. When the family therapist is able to provide the EMDR therapist with this information, the EMDR therapist may need only to obtain ratings for the validity of cognition (VOC) and subjective units of distress (SUD) and perhaps identify body sensations. This allows the EMDR therapist to begin the EMDR reprocessing of difficult triggers much earlier in the session.

To avoid overwhelming the child during the assessment phase, it is important to allow the child freedom to give as much or as little description of the traumatic event as desired. Remember that effective EMDR is not dependent upon the client giving detailed information.

Instead of becoming overwhelmed, some children with attachment trauma have difficulty accessing the memory or its associated emotions. They may be very concrete, or they may have an avoidant coping style. The therapist can ask the child to draw a picture of the memory or show what happened with figures in a sand tray or dollhouse to assist the child with accessing and identifying the image, cognitions, emotion, and sensation.

Identifying the NC and the PC

If the EMDR therapist needs to identify an NC, he or she may ask, "What is the upset thought or belief that goes along with that event/memory/trigger?" The therapist may provide assistance by suggesting, "I think I would have believed. . . . Do you suppose you had a similar belief?" We find that children are not shy about letting us know when we are incorrect.

It can be helpful to identify the emotion first, and then ask, "And what is the mad/scared/confused/sad thought?" or "What do you suppose that you believed at the time this happened? What do you think the younger child inside believes?"

To help the child identify the desired PC, the therapist can ask: "What would you like to be able to say to yourself when you remember this event?" or "What would be a helpful thought?" If the child has difficulty imagining any desired PC and shows irritation, skip this step and look for PCs later, during the desensitization phase. Belaboring the issue is not worth it if you lose the child's cooperation.

Avoid setting the child up for failure by identifying a PC that is unrealistic for the child to achieve early on in treatment. For example, the PC "I am worthwhile," although an elegant PC because it is general and self-referencing, may be far too big of a reach. Choose a more specific, achievable PC such as, "I didn't deserve to be abused" or a "process cognition" such as, "I am learning that I am worthwhile."

Identification of PCs and NCs is too complex for many children age five and younger (Tinker & Wilson, 1999, p. 87). However, the EMDR therapist may be able to identify a simple "upsetting thought" and a simple "happy thought" or "helpful thought" if the child approves. The EMDR therapist can simply repeat the happy thought aloud to the child during the installation phase. The collaborating family therapist can save the EMDR therapist a great deal of valuable time by conducting the ongoing "detective work" in which thoughts, feelings, memories, and triggers are identified.

Identifying Emotions

It can be helpful to have a poster or handout available showing faces with various emotions as a visual aid. The therapist can make suggestions such as, "I can imagine myself when I was little in that situation, and I think I would have felt sad and mad." The therapist should stay attuned to the child's reactions and notice what seems to resonate for him or her. Children will often deny that they currently have feelings about an earlier trauma. It can be helpful to ask, "What do you suppose you did feel when you were in that situation?" Then ask, "Do you suppose you have a little bit of those feelings inside you now?" or "Do you suppose the littler you inside your heart still has some of the feelings?"

If a child has extreme difficulty identifying emotions connected to a current or past incident, the therapist can ask the child to think of the target and to just notice any feelings that come up while implementing relatively fast hand taps or eye movements. Remind the child that he or she can have a feeling and be OK because "feelings come and go."

For example, 12-year-old Ted agreed to work on a memory of being left alone in an apartment at age 3. He was able to identify the "worst picture" as sitting in the middle of a small room alone. The NC was "I'm unwanted" and the PC was "I'm wanted." Following is the transcript from part of the assessment session:

EMDR Therapist: What emotions are associated with this picture in your mind, Ted?

Ted: (Shrugging his shoulders) I don't really have any feelings about it.

EMDR Therapist: Ted, maybe you could just sit with the picture and the upset thought for a little bit. And then while you are thinking about that memory, would it be OK if I turn on the eye scan machine and you could watch the lights, too?

Ted: (Watches the eye scan machine for about 15 eye movements, back and forth, and then becomes a little teary.) OK, I've got it. I'm sad.

EMDR Therapist: (Asks Ted to identify a SUD and observe where he feels the sadness in his body, and then commences the desensitization phase.)

When a child has great difficulty accessing and verbalizing emotions, the therapist should assume that there is a self-regulation issue and be prepared to use the interweaves described later in this chapter. Frequent repetition of the S-RDI protocols from Chapter 5 will help the child feel more comfortable and confident with managing emotions over time.

Subjective Units of Distress Scale and Validity of Cognition

The laminated scale with faces provided by the Humanitarian Assistance Program (HAP) is quite useful with children. Otherwise, the therapist can ask children to gesture with their hands to show how upset they feel (SUD) or how true (VOC) the PC feels "right now." The important point is to make this step fast and easy. If the child is irritated and impatient with the rating scales, the therapist can rely more on his or her powers of observation to estimate the ratings.

Identifying Disturbance in the Body

Children with attachment trauma typically lack connection to their body and their sensations due to poor self-reflective capacities and dissociative tendencies. Children may identify body sensations as only in the head in the beginning of treatment, but connection to the body may improve as they make progress in therapy. It may be helpful to ask, "If this feeling had a certain place in your body, where would it hang out? Where do you guess it might be?"

When a child has difficulty identifying body sensations, ask the family therapist for assistance. The family therapist can create various "practice" situations in which the child is able to feel sensations. For example, the family therapist can encourage the child to observe the sensation of various items against his or her skin, the body sensations associated with drinking hot chocolate or cold milk, and the sensations related to holding a rock versus holding a feather. The family therapist can teach the child about all five senses and how the body experiences each of them. The family therapist's work will enhance the success of the EMDR.

PHASE 4: DESENSITIZATION

Desensitization of past traumas and recent triggers is important to overall treatment success with children affected by attachment trauma. Chapter 5 describes suggestions related to choice of bilateral stimulation and also EMDR suggestions related to various age groups. The EMDR therapist should be prepared to assist the children with grounding, emotional regulation, and helpful associations during desensization and reprocessing, due to the possible deficits in their capacity to process information and regulate emotions.

Grounding Prior to Commencement of Reprocessing

If the therapist is concerned about the possibility of dissociation or overwhelming emotions, he or she can ground the child in present time before reprocessing trauma by asking the child what day it is, how old he or she is, and to name his or her favorite holiday, color, movie, book, and so on, prior to starting. The therapist can also ground the child by inviting the child to picture the younger part of self in the safe place and think about a recent "big-boy" or "big-girl" memory (or a memory of competency or maturity for an older child). In the following example, the EMDR therapist grounds Vince prior to commencing EMDR reprocessing:

> "Vince, before we work on that memory, I would like you to remember the picture we made of little Vince in the safe playroom. Remember how Mom said she was reading to little Vince and playing with him? Can you think about that now? Let's tell little Vince to stay in the playroom and have fun and let big Vince watch the lights today, OK? That's great. Now, I would like you to think about how you helped Mom when she had the flu last week. Think about that 'big-boy' feeling! Do you have it? I am going to turn on the buzzers *(turning on tactile pulsars)* while you think about that."

When working on memories of the past, the goal is for the child to keep one foot in the present while one foot is in the past. Beginning this process with *both* feet in the present helps keep the child from regressing or dissociating during the memory work.

The DVD Metaphor

The DVD metaphor is a helpful way to separate the past from present time prior to commencement of EMDR desensitization. Following is a sample script of how an EMDR therapist might explain the metaphor in this context:

> "Picture yourself watching a DVD. You have the remote in your hand. You can push play, pause, fast forward, fast rewind, and you can push the off button whenever you choose. Remember, this is an old memory, so the DVD may be a little scratchy and fuzzy. You can watch the memory from the safety of your favorite chair, with your favorite blanket and pillow."

Photograph Metaphor

The photograph metaphor is a helpful way to lower intensity with especially painful memories. Ask the child to put the mental "picture" on a sticky note, then crumple it up, press it flat again, and stick it on the wall across the room from the child. The EMDR therapist might say:

> "This memory is like an old photograph. Picture the photograph on this sticky note. It's old, so it's all crumpled up and faded."

USE OF COGNITIVE INTERWEAVES

Cognitive interweaves insert a little bit of information or a question during EMDR reprocessing to help the child through a "stuck" place. A cognitive interweave is completed with as much brevity as possible to avoid interrupting the flow of the child's processing. The use of cognitive interweave is a bit of an art form, in which the therapist balances the importance of providing assistance when it is needed with the importance of staying out of the child's way as much as possible. The EMDR therapist who works with children who have a history of attachment trauma does need to be prepared to utilize interweaves, and in some cases needs to use very frequent interweaves. On the other hand, many children process very slowly, but when given enough time—despite long silences—they do process on their own, without the use of frequent interweaves. Don't rush into the use of interweaves; instead facilitate the child's own internal processing system as much as possible.

The following sections describe several types of helpful cognitive interweaves to implement when children do need assistance. Notice that many interweaves are actually provided by the parent, through a prompt from the therapist. In the team model, the parent is present during EMDR to provide the child with emotional support, and inviting the parent to contribute interweaves reinforces the parent's role as the expert and the child's supporter. However, it is very important to remind the parent prior to each EMDR session to remain completely quiet until prompted, so as not to interfere with the child's processing.

Whatever the response is to the cognitive interweave, simply say, "Go with that." If the child requires an interweave after every set, don't be alarmed. We have observed that children who require assistance after each set of eye movements benefit from the reprocessing nevertheless.

Interweaves for Accessing and Verbalizing Thoughts, Feelings, and Words

The difficulty with self-reflection typical of children with attachment disorders is a frequent cause of "getting stuck" during EMDR reprocessing. Due to poor self-awareness and feelings of anxiety about their memories and emotions, these children may respond to the therapist query, "And what is there now?" with "I don't know," or "Nothing." The worst thing the EMDR therapist can do in this situation is to try to use coercion or intimidation to "force" an answer from a child. Instead, the EMDR therapist should be prepared to offer interweaves that help children observe and verbalize their thoughts and feelings. The interweaves are effective only when children sense emotional presence and support from both the parent and the therapist. The following interweaves help the child access and verbalize thoughts, feelings, and words:

- "I will continue the eye movements, and you can just look up or signal me when you have a thought, feeling, or picture that you want to share."
- "Any changes in memory, thoughts, feelings, or in your body?"
- "Can you tell me a little more about this memory? And then what happened?"

- "You say 'nothing' right now, but what do you guess you felt at the time? What do you guess you believed at the time?"
- "How about the little boy who still lives inside your heart? What would you guess he is feeling right now? What might he believe?"
- "Wow, just thinking about what happened to you makes me feel sad [mad, anxious]."
- "Mom (Dad), if this had happened to you, what would you be feeling?"
- "Mom (Dad), how do you feel right now, just knowing what happened?"
- "I am imagining that this is me in the picture. Here is what I am getting right now. . . . "
- "What is the most upsetting thing about this right now?"

Interweaves That Help Children Tolerate Emotions and Stay Regulated

During EMDR basic training, therapists learn to be emotionally present and supportive through brief comments during the eye movements (e.g., "You're doing fine, that's right"). Severely traumatized children feel extremely vulnerable when it is time to address traumatic memories, and additional interweaves for self-regulation may be needed.

Children who become emotionally dysregulated during EMDR may exhibit atypical behaviors such as agitation, excessive silliness and giggling, or hiding behind a pillow or blanket. These behaviors signal a need for additional reassurance, grounding, compassion, and connection. It may be necessary to return to RDI, ARD, and the self-regulating exercises, but the therapist may be able to help the child become regulated enough through interweaves to continue the reprocessing. The following interweaves help regulate the child by grounding him or her in present-day safety:

- "Tell me where you are right now."
- "Name three things in my office you haven't seen before."

- "What is your favorite color?"
- "Tell me about your bedroom."
- "Feel the couch cushion with one hand and your shirt with the other. How are they different?"
- "You're safe here in this office."
- "Notice your mom's arms around you."
- "Mom, I wonder if you could pull Laura closer to you, so she can feel your connection right now."
- "Dad, I am thinking that if you could hold John close to you as we continue the eye movements, it might help John remember that he is safe."

The following interweaves help regulate the child by reinforcing his or her mindfulness skills:

- "You know, you can have these feelings and still be OK."
- "By feeling your feelings, you can heal your feelings."
- "These feelings are temporary. They are like waves—they wash up on shore for a while, and then they subside."
- "Let your feelings move on through your body."
- "You can have these upset feelings and still know inside that you are loved, you are safe, and you are comfortable."

Empowerment Interweaves

When adult clients reprocess traumatic childhood events, there is quite a distance of time between the traumatic past and the present. Adult clients have reached a life state in which they naturally have more power, independence, and control. Because children remain vulnerable and dependent upon adults, their present-day self may feel no more powerful than the younger self who was victimized. For this reason, they may get stuck and loop in feelings of powerlessness during EMDR reprocessing of past trauma.

The difference between the past and present for children who are reprocessing past trauma is that someone has intervened to protect them at this point and their life circumstances have changed. The following interweaves empower the "bigger child" by encouraging him or her to help the "younger child within."

The child must identify with his or her present-day self in order to address his younger self. The EMDR therapist might say:

- "What do you think the little David inside your heart felt when Mom had to go on her business trip?"
- "Mom [Dad], the littler David who lives inside David's heart believes that all moms leave. Mom [Dad], could you talk through big David's eyes to the littler David inside and reassure him?"
- "David, what could you say to the littler David in your heart about that?"
- "What does the littler you who lives inside your heart need to hear right now?"
- "What could you do for the littler David inside your heart right now?"
- "Mom [Dad], what would you wish to do for the littler David who lives inside David's heart?"

The following interweaves can be used to empower traumatized children through "rescue" imagery. Children have wonderful imaginations, and these interweaves give them permission to enlist their imaginations for healing:

- "If you could get in a little car that flies back and forth through time, and you could fly back in time and bring along anyone or anything to help you, who and what might you bring along?"
- "Mom, Dad, if you could travel back in time, what would you do? How would you care for the little one?"
- "Could you take the little one to the safe place? What would you do for him [her] there?"

Empowerment Through Action

Interweaves can encourage a child to physically express and release urges and emotions that are stuck in the body (Paulsen, 2010). Allowing the body to release what has been held somatically is another way of empowering the child who is emotionally "stuck" in anger, fear, or sadness. Implementing the use of somatic movements involves temporarily stopping the eye movements while inviting children to move their body in a way that helps them feel better. Use simple language that the child can understand.

A simple way to utilize movements is to ask children if there is something they would like to do with their hands or feet. However, many traumatized children will respond, "I don't know." With these children, it is more effective to suggest that it would be helpful to *push out* a mad, sad, or scared feeling or *push away* the "yucky picture," and to explain how they can use either their hands or feet to do so. We caution against an overt role play of the traumatic experience or coercing children to participate in somatic movement. Either of these approaches would risk overwhelming children with intense emotions. Even without referencing it overtly, children may be mentally pushing away their perpetrator. Children should be allowed to repeat the somatic movements for as long as they want to do so, and then eye movements can be resumed after asking them to "notice what is there now." The EMRD therapist might use the following sample script to encourage somatic movements:

> "It might feel good to push that mad and scared feeling right out of your body, what do you think? Do you want to use arms or feet? I can hold up this pillow and you can push, push, until your arms are all the way out straight in front of you. In fact, you can push me all the way out this door, if you want! You will need to push hard, but go really slowly at the same time, OK? We can stop anytime you want to."

By giving the child a choice of pushing with feet or hands, the therapist is tapping into whatever urge the child is holding in his body.

177

The following interweaves encourage traumatized children to enlist their imaginations through drawing and to empower themselves to change the picture "stuck in the brain":

- "Can you draw the upsetting picture that is stuck in your mind?"
- "Now you can draw the picture again, but this time, change the picture in any way you wish."
- "Now you have permission to change the picture in your mind the same way." *(Resume eye movements.)*

Alternatively, a sand tray could be utilized:

- "Can you arrange some things in the sand tray to represent the upsetting picture in your mind?"
- "Now you have permission to move the figures around and decide how you want the picture in the sand tray to look."
- Now you have permission to change the picture in your mind the same way." *(Resume eye movements.)*

The child may need to continue reprocessing following the empowerment interweave to eliminate all emotional charge related to the memory. However, this type of interweave gives the child newfound power over the pictures in his or her mind, and when time is running out in the session, these interweaves may help the child leave in an empowered state.

Interweaves to Provide Children with Critical Information

Because EMDR allows unprocessed traumatic material stored in separate neural networks in the brain to integrate with stored adaptive information, appropriate adaptive information is required for the child to form adequate new associations unassisted during EMDR. One reason for the frequent need of interweaves is simply that children still have much to learn and have a limited amount of stored useful, adaptive information. In fact, children tend to hold a great deal of erroneous information and ideas; they are not yet aware how much they don't know and how much misinformation they carry. For example, children commonly accept their own magical ideas as quite factual. Common magical beliefs held by children, along with beliefs about Santa and the Easter Bunny, are the beliefs that they can cause someone else's misfortune by their own thoughts, that they are evil or inherently bad if they act out or make poor choices, and that they are to blame for the actions of their caregivers. Therefore, informational interweaves are frequently required. Following are interweaves that can provide children with critical information:

- "I'll bet you didn't know that children are never responsible for the actions of adults." *(Turning to parent)* "Mom [Dad], do you think a child is ever responsible for abusive behavior by adults?"
- *(Turning to parent)* "Mom [Dad], do you believe that children who are relinquished for adoption are unlovable?"

Helping Children Overcome Memories of Their Own Past Behaviors

Memories of their own behaviors can often be as troubling for children as memories of abuse. Memories of acting out sexually toward other children or hurting children or animals are especially troubling and reinforcing for NCs such as "I'm bad" and "Something is wrong with me." Children typically do not volunteer these memories. Identification of the memories usually requires detective work on the part of the family therapist or EMDR therapist. Furthermore, children working through these memories usually require interweaves to assist them. Common NCs related to memories of past behaviors include:

- "I'm bad."
- "I'm evil."
- "I'm shameful."
- "I don't deserve to be loved."
- "I don't deserve good things."

Helpful PCs related to memories of past behaviors include:

- "I'm good in my heart, because I don't want to do those things anymore."
- "My heart is healing and I don't do those things anymore."
- "I know how to make better choices now."
- "I have better control of myself as my heart heals."
- "It is OK to make mistakes."

Helpful interweaves related to memories of past behaviors include:

- "I wonder if you knew that a lot of kids do what you did to cope with the hurt they carry in their hearts."
- "I wonder if you knew that this kind of behavior is common in kids with hurt hearts."
- "I wonder if you knew that kids who feel sad inside often try to fix their sad feelings with anything that they think will make them feel good or powerful."
- "You feel guilty about what you did. Do you think someone who was evil would feel guilty?"
- "Knights in the Middle Ages would often do some kind of special good deed to atone for something they did that hurt someone. Can you think of a special good deed you could do to make up for that past mistake?"

EMDR Reprocessing of a Traumatic Memory with Joan

Following is part of a transcript from a session with 13-year-old Joan during EMDR trauma reprocessing. Joan was adopted at age 4, but she had lived with her adoptive parents since she was removed from her biological parents for abuse and neglect at age 2. Joan was exhibiting violent anger explosions and was referred to treatment as her parents were completing paperwork to have her placed in residential care. Joan and her parents had been participating in the Integrative Team Treatment for approximately 4 months when she spontaneously recounted a memory of her parents bringing her to court-ordered visits with her biological father when she was only 2 years of age.

During the assessment phase, the therapist checked Joan's cognitive understanding of the memory and found that Joan did understand that her parents had no choice regarding the visits to the biological father. Joan knew, intellectually, that the visits had been court-ordered. However, at an emotional level, Joan could not get past the feelings of rejection and the stuck "2-year-old" belief that her adoptive parents actually did not want her.

- Target = Adoptive mother (who was her foster mother at the time) placing Joan into the arms of her biological father.
- NC = "My [adoptive] parents don't want me."
- PC = "My [adoptive] parents had to leave me there, but they didn't want to."
- VOC = 3
- Feelings = rejection, fear, anger
- Body = sensations in chest
- SUD = 8.

This memory was actually processed over two separate therapy sessions. Joan's adoptive father sat with Joan and supported her through the first session. Her adoptive mother supported Joan through the second processing of this memory. To shorten the transcript, the symbols >>> substitute for the therapist's words, "Go with that," and then, "Take a breath, what is there now?"; EM = eye movements. This transcript begins partway into the EMDR reprocessing session.

EMDR Therapist: >>>EM>>>
Joan: Scared . . .
EMDR Therapist: OK . . . where do you notice that in your body?
Joan: Ummm . . . in my hands.
EMDR Therapist: >>>EM>>>
Joan: Confused.
EMDR Therapist: Anything in your body?
Joan: Confused why we had to . . . uh . . . why we had to go back and forth.

EMDR Therapist: >>>EM>>>

Joan: Disruption.

EMDR Therapist: Disruption? Can you say any more about that?

Joan: Like when . . . when I was with Mom and Dad, I was . . . it was all good, and then I went back to the place, it wasn't very good.

EMDR Therapist: >>>EM>>> *(Joan is crying through the eye movements.)* OK, let me ask Mom a question. Mom, when Joan was visiting her bio dad, and you were at home, how were you feeling and how was Dad feeling? [Informational interweave]

Mom: Well, first of all, we were scared. *(Turning to Joan)* We were scared for you, because we didn't know how well they were taking care of you. These were the very same people they had taken you away from because they weren't taking care of you, and we were worried about you, and we missed you.

EMDR Therapist: So while she was over there, you were thinking about her . . .

Mom: All the time.

EMDR Therapist: She was in your heart and mind the whole time she was there.

Mom: All the time. Dad and I both were. *(Joan nods.)*

EMDR Therapist: Is it OK if Mom puts her arm around you? [Coaching for emotional regulation]

Joan: Yeah.

EMDR Therapist: OK. All those feelings are OK, Joan. [Coaching for emotional regulation] *(Slightly later in session)* >>>EM>>> Mmmm. Where do you feel it?

Joan: In my heart.

EMDR Therapist: OK. Yes. Just let yourself feel it. [Coaching] Joan, what would you say to that little girl, that little Joan? What would you want to say to her? [Use of inner child interweave]

Joan: Sorry.

EMDR Therapist: Mom, What would you say to little Joan?

Mom: *(Speaking to the inner child)* It wasn't fair. I'm sorry you got stuck in this. *(Joan looks at Mom with tears in her eyes.)*

EMDR Therapist: Just let those feelings out, Joan, that's the best thing you can do. It's so healing. Just let them out. [Coaching for emotional regulation]

EMDR Therapist: >>>EM>>>

Joan: Sad.

EMDR Therapist: Can you picture in your mind, little Joan here? *(Joan nods.)* What do you want to do for her? [Inner child interweave]

Joan: Love her.

EMDR Therapist: Love her? Can you give her a big hug? *(Joan nods.)* Mom, what can you do for her? [Using the inner child interweave]

Mom: Same thing we always do. We can be happy you're home. We can make sure you've got everything you need . . . and that you know that we love you.

EMDR Therapist: (Joan is crying more.) Just let those feelings out, Joan. [Coaching] >>>EM>>>

Joan: I feel sad and happy at the same time.

EMDR Therapist: OK, yes. What do you notice in your body?

Joan: You mean, where in my body?

EMDR Therapist: Yes, where in your body? Yes, like is the sad in one place, the happy in another?

Joan: The happy is in my head, the sad is in my heart.

EMDR Therapist: >>>EM>>>

Joan: I feel happy.

EMDR Therapist: OK. Any more than that?

Joan: Just happy.

EMDR Therapist: OK. You want to take your headphones off so you can get more comfy? Yeah. Just notice Mom's arms around you. Feel that feeling of connection? Do you feel comfortable? You don't look that comfortable. Why don't you scooch over close to Mom a little more, get comfy?

Joan: (Begins watching the lights while getting a big hug from Mom.)

EMDR Therapist: >>>EM>>> What's there?

Joan: Relieved.

EMDR Therapist: Ah, yeah . . . what do you notice in your body?

Joan: That I'm not as tense. . . .

EMDR Therapist: Oh, good, yes, just notice that relieved feeling
. . . that relaxed feeling. >>>EM>>>

Joan: That . . . a little bit of sadness. . . .

EMDR Therapist: How much?

Joan: Probably a 2 or 3.

EMDR Therapist: >>>EM>>>

Joan: Happy.

EMDR Therapist: Happy? And what's that happy part about?

Joan: That I'm good enough . . . I'm in a safe and happy place.
(Slightly later in the session . . .) They didn't want to leave me
there, but they had to.

EMDR Therapist: Yes, yes . . . just hold that, OK. Hold that in your
mind with the memory.

By the end of the session, Joan's SUD = 0 and her VOC = 7. This
work was a turning point for Joan in letting go of her anger and
opening her heart to trusting her adoptive parents.

ADDRESSING PREVERBAL TRAUMA

There was a time when it was commonly believed that trauma
prior to age 2½ was not consciously remembered and therefore
had no long-term impact. Research into the implicit memory system and the storage of preverbal trauma within the limbic brain
(e.g., van der Kolk & Fisler, 1992) changed all that. Our observa-
tions are consistent with the research: Children who are placed
in permanent, safe homes prior to age 2½ frequently exhibit the
same intense emotional and behavioral dysregulation as children
who are placed later. The question then becomes: How do we reprocess trauma that is not consciously remembered?

Some children will spontaneously associate to pictures of preverbal trauma (whether they are actual memories or pictures of
what they have imagined) during EMDR or outside of EMDR.

Other children can be helped to reprocess preverbal trauma through the therapeutic narrative.

Example of Spontaneous Reprocessing of Preverbal Trauma

Five-year-old Danielle had been removed from a situation of abuse and neglect by drug-abusing biological parents just before she turned 2. The therapist had initiated EMDR with Danielle to help calm her fears related to bedtime. In the middle of reprocessing, Danielle stated, "I woke up and I was all by myself in my crib. I could see out the window. Mommy and Daddy were at a party across the street." The EMDR therapist continued the bilateral stimulation to reprocess this very early traumatic memory. Through EMDR Danielle was able to separate her current situation from her early life, and the therapist was able to install the PC, "My forever mommy and daddy will keep me safe through the night."

Another route to EMDR reprocessing is through the imagined pictures related to distressing early experiences that children know about but don't consciously remember. Sometimes the pictures are erroneous, and supplying the appropriate information is an important part of the reprocessing.

Example of the Use of the Client's Mental Images of Preverbal Trauma

Eleven-year-old Lori was adopted from overseas at 9 months of age. She had been placed in an orphanage by her birth mother when she was just 2 days old. When discussing her history with her family therapist, she said, "I can see my birth mother's face when she left me at the orphanage. It is a mad face, because she didn't like me. I think I must have been bad, and that is why she left me there."

This information was brought to the EMDR therapist for reprocessing. The preverbal incident was reprocessed by targeting the imagined face of the birth mother and the NC, "She left me because I was bad."

During EMDR reprocessing, the EMDR therapist created an informational interweave by asking Lori's adoptive mother, "What do you know about Lori's birth mother?" The adoptive mother replied, "I was told that she loved Lori very much, but she was too poor to take care of Lori herself." Lori was able to utilize the EMDR to reprocess her hurt, anger, and sadness related to the preverbal loss of her birth mother.

USING THE THERAPEUTIC STORY AS A ROADMAP AND A TOOL

The EMDR therapist can effectively utilize the therapeutic story (Lovett, 1999, 2009) as a roadmap for any level (implicit to explicit) of travel, ensuring that important traumas and losses are targeted and reprocessed. In the Integrative Team Treatment model, the family therapist writes the therapeutic story with the child. (See Chapter 4 and Appendices E and F for instructions on writing the therapeutic story.)

Because the therapeutic story includes the PCs and children's positive, present-day situation in addition to earlier traumatic events, it provides what Lovett (2009) has referred to as "the light at the end of the tunnel" for the child. Children can begin to make sense of the events of their lives and to organize those events chronologically.

The first full reading of the story can be done by the therapist or the parent, while the child sits comfortably with the parent; bilateral hand taps or tactile pulsars are applied through the reading of the entire story. Children can choose the speed of bilateral stimulation with which they are most comfortable (Lovett, 2009).

In subsequent sessions, after the first full reading of the story, the therapist can reread the entire story or just a portion of the story and then ask, "What part of the story did you like? And what part of the story was hard for you to hear today?" That section of the story can then be used as a target for EMDR reprocessing. Even if the child has no conscious memory of the event, the therapist can reread that part of the story and then ask, "When you heard that part of the story just now, what picture did you have in your mind?" The picture becomes the target, and the therapist continues with the assessment phase, identifying the negative words that go with the picture, the desired positive thought, and so forth, followed by desensitization, installation, and closure.

On subsequent readings, the therapist can engage the child to describe more about the child's thoughts and feelings with a series of questions: "What do you imagine the girl thought? What did she feel? What did she want? What did she need?" As the child imagines the wants and needs of her younger self in the story, the therapist can invite the parent and child to imagine giving the child what she wanted and needed. For example, if the child identified that she needed food, the therapist can ask the adoptive parent what he would have done if he had been there and had known that the child was hungry. Then alternating bilateral stimulation can be used for resource enhancement as the child imagines her adoptive parent giving her the food she needed.

Using Stuffed Animals to Tell the Child's Story

For younger children (or developmentally young children), a simplified story can be effectively told "off-the-cuff" by the EMDR therapist using puppets or dolls to "play out" the story during the telling. The child can listen and watch from the parent's lap, while the parent sways the child side to side or gently taps. If the child wants to be down on the floor participating with the puppets or dolls during the story, the bilateral stimulation can be added at the end of the story through swaying or tapping while the therapist reinforces the PCs from the story.

Following is a transcript involving the use of stuffed bears and a tiger to tell a therapeutic story to a 30-month-old boy adopted from overseas. The boy was exhibiting excessive aggression and fears. The adoptive parents had picked him up from a foster home, which was the only home the boy knew or remembered. The parents and therapist theorized that the event of being removed from his foster home had been a very traumatic experience for the boy. The therapist and Evan were sitting on the floor with the stuffed animal during the stories. The adoptive parents were watching from the sofa. Here is how the EMDR therapist told Evan's story with bears:

> "I have a story about this little baby bear, OK? *(Evan nods.)* When this baby bear was just little, he was taken care of by this tiger, Sarah. Sarah was such a good caregiver. Sarah rocked the little bear. And Sarah fed a bottle to the little bear. Sarah told the little bear, 'Everything is OK. You are such a good little baby.' Sarah said to the little bear, 'I am taking care of you until your forever mommy and your forever daddy can get here. Then they will be able to take care of you forever and forever.' And then, the forever mommy and the forever daddy arrived. They were so happy to finally get to hold their little boy bear. The mama bear and daddy bear loved their little boy bear so much. They said, 'We will never let you go. We will take care of you forever and ever. We will feed you every day. We will hug you every day. We will love you every day. We will keep you safe every day.'"

Following the story, the adoptive mother sat Evan on her lap facing the therapist, who sat on the floor. The therapist directed Evan's mother to sway Evan rhythmically side to side while the therapist repeated PCs from the story: "The new mommy and daddy loved their little bear every day. They gave him kisses and hugs. They tucked him in at night and woke him in the morning. They fed him and loved him and kept him safe. They were a forever family, every day and every day."

The EMDR therapist saw the family for 10 sessions over a span of 8 months. Through the story work, ARD, and the use of songs along with rhythmic swaying, as described in Chapter 5, Evan's concerning symptoms were eliminated.

WORKING THROUGH TRAUMATIC GRIEF

Children with a history of attachment trauma are typically suffering from traumatic grief related to the loss of attachment figures in their life, as well as the loss of a normal lifestyle, losses of friends, homes, pets, and more. Reading the part of the child's therapeutic story that addresses caregiver losses or other losses can help the child access his grief and reprocess with EMDR. The NC related to grief can be as simple as "My sad feelings are not OK" or "I can't be happy." The PC may be simply "I can have these feelings and be OK" or "I have room inside for my sad feelings and my happy feelings all at the same time."

The parent should be coached to provide warm, sensitive attunement to the child's grief. It is important that both the therapist and parent avoid denigrating the biological parents who were lost. EMDR reprocessing of the child's traumatic grief is a wonderful window of opportunity for bonding between the current parent and the child. Emotional support from the parents along with the bilateral stimulation can remove obstacles to the natural grieving process and reduce acute pain and acting out related to unprocessed grief. However, EMDR does not magically remove appropriate feelings of grief related to significant loss. Avoid overly focusing on the SUD when processing children's grief. They may perceive the therapist as invalidating the significance of their first attachments and the enormity of the losses they have experienced.

Example of EMDR Reprocessing with Grief

Carl, age 10, had been removed from a mentally ill mother for neglect as a toddler and placed with his grandmother for 1 year. The grandmother was also quite neglectful of Carl, and she eventually placed Carl voluntarily in state care. Carl was placed with his adoptive parents at age 3. His parents stated that he had never shown sadness, but that he had been extremely controlling, oppositional, and aggressive. His parents reported that all of his behaviors had improved over the first month of therapy through ARD and family therapy. However, he was still guarded, especially with his adoptive mother, and he became tearful when discussing the biological grandmother. He was able to identify the NC, "I was unwanted." It was clear that in addition to believing that he was unwanted, he felt a mountain of grief. Following is a transcript of the first EMDR reprocessing of both feelings of grief and feelings of rejection related to Carl's memory of leaving his grandmother's home at age 3.

- Target = Picture of driving away from Grandma's house
- Feeling = Sad and scared (in Carl's heart)
- NC = "I'm unwanted."
- PC = "Grandma loved me, but she just couldn't take care of me."
- VOC = 2
- SUD =9

Carl's adoptive parents sat closely on either side of him while he held a sheet of feelings faces as a reference to help him identify his emotions during the reprocessing.

After Carl shared between sets, the therapist asked him to "think of that" and resumed eye movements. After each set, the therapist asked Carl to "take a breath" and share what he was thinking, feeling, or noticing. The standard therapist prompts are represented with >>>, and EM = eye movements.

EMDR Therapist: OK, Carl, just let yourself think of the picture of leaving Grandma's home along with that upset thought, "I'm unwanted," and the sad and scared feelings in your heart. We will all be quiet for a few moments while you watch my fingers and notice any other thoughts, feelings, or pictures that come up. >>>EM>>>

Carl: She wasn't able to take care of me, but she wanted the best for me. *(Repeating what he had been told.)*

EMDR Therapist: >>>EM>>>

Carl: Worry. I think Grandma didn't really like me.

EMDR Therapist: >>>EM>>>

Carl: Confused. I thought that she liked me, but then it seemed like she didn't.

EMDR Therapist: >>>EM>>>

Carl: Hurt. Disappointed. *(Very tearful now)*

EMDR Therapist: >>>EM>>>

Carl: Sad. Hurt. In my heart.

EMDR Therapist: Let's pretend little Carl is right here sitting next to me. [Adaptive information is provided through an inner child interweave.] Let's take turns speaking to him. I'll start. "Little Carl, I want you to know that you are special and lovable. Your grandma loved you, but she was a much older lady. She didn't feel she could keep up with a little boy. She didn't feel she could do a good job."

Mom: (Pretending to take little Carl from the therapist) "Little Carl, your grandma did a very hard thing. She loved you, but she knew she wasn't the best person to raise you. You are a wonderful boy." *(The therapist now taps on Carl's knees while Mom and Carl look in each other's eyes.)*

Dad: (Taking his turn) "Little Carl, your grandma loved you so much that she wanted only the very best for you. She knew she couldn't give you what you needed." *(The therapist taps on Carl's knees while Dad speaks.)*

EMDR Therapist: Just notice those feelings, Carl, let them out, it's so healing for you. Feelings come and feelings go. These feelings are normal. *(Taps on Carl's knees)* Mom? Could Carl come to you any time with his feelings?

Mom: (Turning to Carl) I want you to come to me with your feelings. I want to help. When you cry, I feel sad because I love you. *(The therapist taps on Carl's knees.)*

Carl: (With tears) I love you, Mom.

Mom: (Through her tears) I love you, Carl.

Dad: (Reassures Carl he can come to him and says, "I love you.")

EMDR Therapist: >>>EM>>>

Carl: Happy and sad at the same time. She had to give me away, but she wanted me. And happy I was able to be with her for a while.

EMDR Therapist: >>>EM>>>

Carl: Happy and sad.

EMDR Therapist: What would you say to her?

Carl: I miss you *(tearful).*

EMDR Therapist: Just notice the "missing" feelings. Feeling your feelings is healing your feelings. >>>EM>>>

At the end of the session, Carl reported a SUD of 5. The session was closed by talking about the fun things they were going to do the rest of the day.

Carl's Follow-Up Session

The following week, the EMDR therapist asked Carl what he noticed when he brought up in his mind the picture of leaving Grandma's home. Carl's face immediately crumpled. He said he no longer believed that Grandma had abandoned him. He understood why Grandma couldn't keep him. "But," Carl said, "I just miss her." Mom and Dad snuggled on either side while the therapist commenced the EMDR.

EMDR Therapist: Just bring up that memory of leaving Grandma and notice the missing feeling . . . in your heart. >>>EM>>>

Carl: Just sad. Just missing her *(tearful).*

EMDR Therapist: >>>EM>>>

Carl: Still the same *(tearful)*.

EMDR Therapist: (To Mom and Dad) Let's each take turns looking at Carl and letting him know how truly sorry we feel. Carl, I am so, so sorry. I am so sorry that that happened to you. *(Tapping on Carl's knees while looking in Carl's eyes.)*

Mom: (Tearful, and looking at Carl) Carl, I am so, so sorry that that happened to you. I feel so sad that you had to experience such a loss. *(The therapist is tapping on Carl's knees.)*

Dad: (Looking at Carl) I am real sorry that you had to go through that, Carl.

EMDR Therapist: Why don't you snuggle with Mom, and let yourself feel whatever you are feeling right now, Carl. *(Taps on Carl's knees, while Carl cries with Mom. Dad has a hand on his shoulder.)* What is there now, Carl?

Carl: I feel better, happier.

EMDR Therapist: And I hope you are remembering that what happened was not your fault. You didn't do anything to cause it. >>>EM>>>

Carl: (Turning to smile at each of his parents) I feel happy.

The positive feelings were reinforced further with the eye movements. Then the therapist asked Carl and his parents to practice sitting close every single day during the upcoming week, and they all agreed. The therapist asked to talk with Carl's parents alone, and she suggested to his parents that whenever they noticed Carl feeling mad or sad, they give him a hug and tell him how sorry they felt.

Whereas prior to treatment when Carl had suppressed his grief and it had caused him to be shut down and angry, his natural feelings of grief were now freed to surface and be processed normally. So naturally Carl continued to experience sad feelings about his grandma from time to time, and now he was open about his feelings and receptive to comfort.

INVERTED PROTOCOL AND WEAVING BACK AND FORTH BETWEEN PAST, PRESENT, AND FUTURE

EMDR is a three-pronged approach involving targeting of past events, current triggers, and then developing and reinforcing future templates. Although targeting past memories first is a standard and sensible order with which to proceed with EMDR generally, it requires the client to have a fairly solid foundation and good regulation skills. A safer way to begin the work with children who are easily dysregulated is to use EMDR initially to reinforce positive resources and future templates, followed by reprocessing of one or more present-day triggers. The memories are addressed after the child has successfully utilized EMDR in the work with some of his or her present-day challenges.

Hofmann (2009) makes the same recommendation for any EMDR clients who are easily overwhelmed by emotions related to complex trauma. Hofmann's "inverted EMDR standard protocol" involves starting with the resource development needed to handle current challenges. Following the development of three or four resources, a future template related to positive handling of the current challenges is developed, and clients are asked to imagine bringing their newfound resources with them into the positive future template. The resource and future template work are followed by reprocessing of current triggers, and lastly, reprocessing of past traumatic memories.

Over the duration of therapy, we typically weave back and forth between present-day material and past events. This "weaving" more effectively ties the past to the present, providing insight to the child and the observing parent. The EMDR reprocessing of present-day triggers often leads naturally to EMDR reprocessing of related touchstone memories. Reprocessing of past events is always followed by reprocessing of present-day triggers or reinforcing of future templates.

Weaving back and forth between past and present also helps

prevent children from becoming overwhelmed by successive sessions focused on serious trauma. Just as a surgeon allows a patient time after one surgery before starting another surgery, the EMDR therapist must allow the child time to regroup following serious trauma work before commencing more trauma work.

ADDRESSING CURRENT TRIGGERS

Both the family therapist and the EMDR therapist regularly speak with the child and parents about the child's triggers. Following is a sample script for the EMDR therapist:

> "A trigger is anything that your eyes or ears pick up that causes automatic big feelings. A trigger might be something someone does or something someone says to you, a look on someone's face, a tone in a voice, or a challenging situation of any kind. A trigger can be a sight, a smell, a sound, or a taste. It can be a time of year, or a time of day. A trigger can even be something that seems like it should be a happy thing, like a compliment or a holiday."

Each week, the therapist should ask the child and parent, "What were the triggers this week?"

Contained Reprocessing of Current Triggers

When targeting current triggers prior to reprocessing of past events, EMDR can help stop the past events and emotions from driving the current emotional responses even before fully reprocessing those past events. There are two important steps to doing this:

1. Implement contained reprocessing.
2. Use interweaves to separate the past from the present.

Contained reprocessing of current triggers is a way of putting some controls on the EMDR to prevent opening up past material before the traumatized child is ready. Longer sets of bilateral stimulation increase the associations that are made. Therefore, reducing the number of back-and-forth round trips helps keep the focus on the current trigger. Although it differs with each child, some children tend to associate and reprocess more quickly than adults. Other children have processing problems and need more time and longer sets to achieve any type of shift. The therapist should observe the speed with which the child seems to reprocess. Contained reprocessing may consist of around 8 round trips for a fast processor, or up to 15 round trips for a child with slow processing.

In addition to shorter sets, the therapist can also ensure containment of the present trigger by suggesting that the child return to the target event or the upsetting picture very frequently, even after every set if the therapist senses that past memories might surface quite easily.

Separating the Past from the Present

Because of the stored, unprocessed traumas, children with a history of attachment trauma are often stuck in "trauma time." In other words, it feels like the past is present because they are stuck in the fear, anxiety, and negative beliefs about their safety. They are easily triggered, time and time again, by current triggers, because the past subjectively "feels" present-day. Cognitive interweaves can be used during EMDR reprocessing of current triggers to help separate out the past events without fully opening up the memories when the child isn't ready for them. These interweaves keep the past in the past and help draw a firm dividing line between then and now.

Following are examples of cognitive interweaves to help separate past from present:

- "Even though it may feel the same, how is this situation now actually different from the past situation of _____?"

- "But how is your new mom actually different from you birth mom?"
- "When you think about the food that your mom and dad put on the table at mealtime, does it seem different from the way you were fed in your first home?"
- "When your forever dad is angry, how does his behavior compare to the way your foster dad acted when he was angry?"
- "I know your biological mom left because she was on drugs. Are there any important ways that your grandma is different from your biological mom?"

The therapist should not allow the child to give too much information in response to the interweave question, or the child may become flooded with memories. The therapist should limit the child's answer and then simply say, "Think of that" (meaning, think of the difference between the past and present), followed by bilateral stimulation. If the child associates to a past memory on his or her own while doing EMDR on a current trigger, and he or she is not ready to reprocess the past, the therapist can respond with one of the interweaves to separate the past from the present before resuming bilateral stimulation. The therapist should continue to bring the child back to the present target frequently, until the associated emotions are reduced, and then move to Phase 5, installation. Additional interweaves for helping children get unstuck from present-day triggers include:

- "What feels most upsetting about this present-day situation?"
- "What feels unsafe about this?"
- "What is the worst thing that could happen in this present-day situation?"
- "What would be scary about letting go of trying to control this situation?"
- "Why wouldn't you deserve this good thing?"
- "What would be most helpful to say to yourself?"

- "What does the little boy [little girl] inside your heart feel about this present-day situation?"
- "What could the big you say to the little girl [little boy] about that?"

Current triggers should be targeted repeatedly and consistently—until the child is no longer triggered by situations in his or her present-day life.

Following is an example of the use of interweaves to separate past trauma from a current situation with Eugene, age 11, who is frequently triggered by his teacher at school. (Therapist prompts are indicated with >>>; EM = eye movements.)

EMDR Therapist: Just think of the way your teacher looked when she was angry yesterday, and the upset thought, "She is mean." >>>EM>>>

Eugene: She's scary. I think she hates me.

EMDR Therapist: >>>EM>>>

Eugene: She thinks I'm bad. It reminds me of my first foster mom, and she used to hit me.

EMDR Therapist: And what is different about this situation, Eugene? [Interweave to separate the past from the present situation]

Eugene: Well, my teacher doesn't hit me. She's all bark and no bite.

EMDR Therapist: >>>EM>>>

Targeting Current Triggers for Compulsive, Habitual Behaviors

We often utilize a simplified version of the addictions protocol developed by A. J. Popky (2009), when addressing children's compulsive, habitual behaviors with EMDR. Compulsive behaviors treated with the addictions protocol can include stealing, lying, anger explosions, sexualized behaviors, and avoidance, to name a few. It is important that, before implementing the addictions protocol, the therapist have an established relationship with the child and a level of cooperation and motivation.

The simple version of the addictions protocol that we utilize with children involves the following steps:

1. With the child, the therapist writes down how life would look if the child were free of the compulsive behavior.
2. The therapist guides the child in creating a mental movie, observing him- or herself in the future, free of the compulsive behaviors, with all the positive effects in his or her life. The therapist reinforces the mental movie with relatively slow bilateral stimulation.
3. The therapist guides the child to put him- or herself into the mental movie, thinking about how it feels as a future self, free of the addiction or compulsions. The child notices how his or her body feels, how his or her voice sounds, and how he or she moves about and interacts with others. This is reinforced with relatively slow bilateral stimulation.
4. The therapist and child make a list of current situations, people, thoughts, or feelings that trigger the child's compulsive behavior.
5. Starting with the biggest trigger, the therapist implements EMDR to target and reprocess each trigger, one by one. We utilize level of urge (LOU) on a scale of 0 to10, with 10 representing the strongest urge and 0 representing no urge. The LOU can be utilized in place of the SUD.

Following is a transcript utilizing the addictions protocol with 13-year-old Don.

> *EMDR Therapist:* Don, your anger explosions have really decreased a lot, but as long as they occur occasionally, the quality of your life is not as good as it can be. And you continue to reinforce the anger pathways in your brain, keeping your brain more reactive to stress than it needs to be. Let's do some work on this anger habit, would that be all right with you?"
>
> *Don: (Nods.)*
>
> *EMDR Therapist:* What would be good about your life if you were

explosion-free? *(Makes list, hands Don the pulsars, and turns them on.)* Don, see if you can picture yourself explosion-free. Pretend you are watching a movie of your future self on a movie screen. See your future self acting confident and happy. Notice how your face looks, and how you are holding your body. See yourself with all your privileges, your parents trusting you, happy with you. See yourself hanging out with friends. See yourself at school, talking with teachers, happy and confident. See your teachers smiling, trusting you. *(Stopping tactile pulsars)* How did that go?

Don: (Nodding) Good.

EMDR Therapist: Great. *(Turning sensors back on)* Now put yourself right in the movie, and think about how it feels to be in your body, at home, feeling confident and mature, with your parents smiling and happy. Think about how it feels to be relaxing, hanging out with friends. Now you are at school, notice how it feels to interact with teachers when they are happy and smiling, and notice how you are standing, walking, holding your body.

Don: I feel tall. I feel relaxed, happy.

Don and the therapist identified several situations that triggered Don's reactions in the past, including being criticized or redirected, being teased, and being touched when he was already feeling angry. Don and the therapist decided to begin with the experience of being redirected, and Don identified a recent situation when this had happened at school and he had exploded. The therapist followed the standard protocol for the assessment phase. Instead of a SUD, the therapist asked Don to think about how difficult it would be for him to stay calm if he were in this situation today. The therapist asked Don to identify his LOU to explode if he were back in this situation "right now." Don rated his LOU as a 5. EMDR was implemented to reprocess the recent event, and Don was able to reduce the LOU to 0. In follow-up sessions, the positive future state was reinforced again, and

EMDR was implemented with each of Don's triggers to reduce the LOU to 0.

COMPLETION OF DESENSITIZATION PHASE

Standard EMDR procedure involves installation of the PC after the client has reported a SUD of 0 or 1. If the SUD is higher, asking "What keeps it from being a 0?" can be a very useful interweave, uncovering blocks or obstacles that were not previously identified. EMDR therapists generally find a SUD of 1 or 2 to be acceptable if deemed "ecological" in the situation.

Due to the impairment in their self-reflective capacity, many traumatized children have difficulty judging change in a SUD. Some children actually become quite distressed with the rating questions, both because they find them difficult and also because the questions may remind them of being quizzed at school. It can be helpful to have them show ratings very simply with a gesture of the hands, such as holding both hands close together to indicate a small rating and wider apart for a larger rating. The laminated rating scales sold through the Humanitarian Assistance Program (HAP) can also be helpful. In some cases, it is more helpful for the therapist to observe the child's body language and facial expression as a way to judge change in SUD.

Occasionally, a child will report a high SUD despite clearly observable relaxation and relief. In this case, the child may be interpreting a low SUD as equivalent to admission that the trauma or loss was unimportant. Traumatized children who experienced a lack of validation from caregivers early in life need clear validation regarding the enormity of what they have suffered. The therapist might say, "What happened to you was a very terrible thing. It should never ever have happened. But I am just wondering, you used to get really anxious inside when you thought about it, and now it looks like you are able to stay calmer inside when you think about it. What do you think? There is no right or wrong answer."

The therapist should avoid becoming overly focused on the SUD rating. We worked with an adolescent female who was resistant to EMDR because of her prior experience with EMDR in another city. She said, "I can't stand those number ratings—they pressure me. The therapist kept asking, 'What keeps it from being a zero now? What keeps it from being a zero now?' I finally told her it was a zero to make her stop!" The young woman was willing to participate in EMDR when it was agreed that the SUD would not be utilized. She was then able to successfully reprocess memories of sexual abuse.

PHASES 5–8: INSTALLATION, BODY SCAN, CLOSURE, AND REEVALUATION

Phase 5: Installation

When the emotional charge related to the incident has been eliminated or has reached a level that is ecological, it is standard procedure to check as to whether or not the original PC is still a fit. For children who were not able to identify a PC during the assessment phase, the shifts that took place for them during desensitization now should allow them to think about what they would like to be able to believe. Standard EMDR protocol involves asking the child to hold the PC in mind along with the original picture and then reinforcing the PC until it feels completely true. If it is not completely true, the therapist can ask, "And what keeps it from being completely true?" to identify the blocks.

Phase 6: Body Scan

The last step in the reprocessing session is scanning the body for any remaining disturbance. This is an important step in work with children affected by attachment trauma, although there may be limited feedback from children who have not yet developed awareness of their body sensations. Throughout the course of therapy, children typically develop increased body awareness.

Phase 7: Closure

If time has run out and the session is incomplete, the therapist can ask, "What would be most helpful for you to keep in mind about this memory right now?" Add a short, slow set of eye movements or alternate form of bilateral stimulation to reinforce the child's positive response. Because children's thinking tends to shift throughout the reprocessing, most can identify a helpful thought that has occurred to them as a result of reprocessing: for example, "It's all over now"; "My new parents/foster parents/ grandparents will keep me safe"; "I do have people in my life now who care about me"; "It wasn't my fault"; "I'm good in my heart."

Whether reprocessing is complete or incomplete, it is helpful to remind children to put the day's work in the container at the end of the session. The therapist can ask the imaginative child, "What magic or special power can you use to zap the memories into the container?"

Remind parents that processing may continue, and that temporarily, the child may be more sensitive and need extra attunement and support throughout the week. Ask the parents to note anything unusual in the child's words or behaviors, and to call if there is a serious escalation in behaviors.

Phase 8: Reevaluation

At the beginning of the following session, check with the parent first, and ask what behaviors he or she observed following the EMDR. Interpret the behaviors in terms of the issues with which the child is dealing. The therapist can then ask the child, "When you think about what we worked on last time, how upset do you feel inside, right this minute?" Or, "What is the most up-setting part about it now?" Or, "Is there anything else related to this event that is bothering you?"

DEVELOPING AND REINFORCING FUTURE TEMPLATES

For every situation that has been a trigger to a child, there is potential for a future template. Once that trigger has been processed, talk with the child about how he or she would hope to handle the situation. The child, the therapist, and the parent can all participate in role-playing the situation while the child practices the desired response and holds the tappers to reinforce the positive behavior. Often, future template work involves reinforcing behavioral skills that the child was taught during the family session. If the family therapist taught the child how to share, take turns, or speak politely, the EMDR therapist role-plays the new skill with the child and reinforces the skill with bilateral stimulation. The therapist may also guide the child in a mental movie of the desired response, while adding the bilateral stimulation.

When a child reports difficulty, assess what part of the template was difficult. The therapist may need to repeat the role play or the visualization with bilateral stimulation until the disturbance is gone. If the disturbance is too high, target the "worst part" of the role play or visualization and reprocess with EMDR.

Future Template for Positive Self-Talk

After the child has learned self-regulation through self-talk in the family sessions, the EMDR therapist can reinforce the skill through a positive future template. Implement relatively slow bilateral stimulation while guiding the child in a mental movie of a challenging future situation. Ask the child to state prepared positive messages aloud. It's a very simple yet extremely effective exercise, and can be repeated frequently for use with various situations.

For example, the therapist may guide the child in visualizing his or her teacher at school raising her voice. The child states aloud the following preplanned statements to him- herself: "Her voice is loud, but it's not dangerous. I'm fine. She's not going to hurt me. She's a pretty nice person. She won't be loud for long." Reinforce the child's use of the self-talk throughout the mental movie with relatively slow hand taps or use the tactile pulsars.

OPTIONAL EMDR ACTIVITY: THE TALE OF THE HAMSTER AND THE PORCUPINE COAT

The Tale of the Hamster and the Porcupine Coat is found in Appendix H. The story is helpful for children who learned to keep themselves safe by pushing people away. The therapist can change the gender of the hamster or reword the story to better match the particular details of a child's life. In the tale, a hamster that experiences trauma in his (for male children) early life finds a spiky porcupine coat that he wears for self-protection. The hamster continues to wear the coat despite a new, safe life, and it becomes clear to the child listening to the story that the coat keeps the hamster from experiencing the closeness and warmth that are available to him. The child is asked to hold the tactile pulsars, which are run throughout the reading of the story. Then, the child is asked to choose from two endings to the story—both endings are positive, but one is even more positive than the other. The chosen ending is reread while the child holds the tactile pulsars to reinforce the positive feelings associated with the "hamster's" new choices. The EMDR therapist can also use the positive ending of the story to help the child develop and reinforce a positive future template based on a decision to "throw off the porcupine coat."

Following is a script of a session utilizing the porcupine coat story to create a positive future template for Sue Ann.

EMDR Therapist: Sue Ann, can you tell me how you would be able to get along at school and at home if you were able to toss your porcupine coat in the closet?

Sue Ann: I would be able to stay in my classroom all day. My teacher would be really happy with me. The kids would want to play with me at recess. My mom and dad would be happy with me too, and they would let me have all my privileges at home. It would be more fun.

EMDR Therapist: I want you to hold the buzzers in your hands. *(Runs the tactile pulsars.)* Now watch a movie of yourself at school without your porcupine coat. See yourself sitting at your desk doing your work; you are relaxed, and you have a smile on your face. Your teacher is smiling at you as she walks by your desk. . . . *(Continues describing the positive future state movie while running the pulsars.)* How did that go?

Sue Ann: Good. I like this movie.

EMDR Therapist: Now I would like you to put yourself right in the future movie and imagine how it feels in your body to be sitting in the classroom without your porcupine coat. Imagine how it feels to be smiling and relaxed while sitting at your desk; imagine how it feels to look up and see your teacher smiling. . . . *(Continues describing the positive future state while running the pulsars.)*

Following the future template, Sue Ann and the therapist developed a list of situations that made Sue Ann want to put on the porcupine coat. Each trigger was reprocessed until her LOU to use the porcupine coat went to 0.

ONGOING EMDR THROUGHOUT THE EMDR INTEGRATIVE TEAM TREATMENT

1. Begin each EMDR session by asking the parent, "What did you appreciate about _____ this week?" Reinforce the parent's positive words with slow bilateral stimulation.
2. Continue reinforcing positive experiences of connection

and positive affect by returning again and again, however briefly, to ARD, RDI, and S-RDI.

3. Continue reprocessing triggers week after week until there are no major triggers left (utilizing the "detective work" of the family therapist).

4. Continue developing and reinforcing positive future templates (utilizing skills the child has been taught in the family therapy sessions).

5. Continue reprocessing any traumatic experiences that are identified (during EMDR or family therapy).

6. Continue returning to and reading aloud the therapeutic story. Reprocess the next worst part of the story by asking, "What part of the story is most upsetting to you now?"

Chapter 7

COMPLICATED CASES

Cases involving children affected by attachment trauma can be quite complicated due to the severity of the effects of early attachment trauma. In addition, problems may arise related to the child's present family supports and to decisions that sometimes need to be made regarding the placement. The following cases consider challenges related to case management as well as extreme behaviors.

WORKING WITH BEN, AGE 14

Complications

Ben presented the following complications:

- Resistant to closeness.
- Engaged in self-harming, burning, and cutting behaviors
- Referred with a diagnosis of dissociative identify disorder (DID)

Ben and his mother had recently moved to the area and were referred by her previous therapist. During history-taking, Ben's mother stated that Ben had a habit of self-harming, and that he had been given a diagnosis of DID from his previous therapist.

Ben later confirmed that he had a habit of self-burning and also that when he was triggered by something in his environment, he occasionally experienced a period of time loss lasting for a few minutes up to a couple of hours.

As a young child, Ben had become a "pseudo-adult," monitoring his parents' drug use and hiding their drugs in an attempt to help them. He had also been sexually molested by his great-uncle. Ben had been removed from the biological family at age 8 and adopted by a single mother when he was age 9. He had a very strong, aggressive personality, whereas his mother was reserved. Ben made it very clear that he wanted to be in charge and that he was not interested in physical or emotional closeness with his adoptive mother. On the other hand, he was forthcoming about his distress, and he wanted to feel better.

Adaptations/Interventions

Ben's treatment included several adaptations and interventions, for example:

- His participation in a skills group
- Allowance for his need to feel independent
- Creation of safe places for all his young parts
- A longer preparation phase and use of the inverse protocol (Hoffman, 2009)

A plan was made for longer Phase 2 preparation involving family therapy mindfulness work, extra focus on skill development, a longer period of EMDR resource development, development of safety for inner parts, and an extended period of relationship building between Ben and his adoptive mother in family sessions and through attachment resource development.

Skills Group

Ben began with an EMDR and family therapist team, but in addition, he attended an adolescent DBT skills class (Linehan,

1993) for 15 weeks. Ben complained about the class, but it none-theless gave him a jump-start on learning a broad set of coping skills.

Allowance for Child's Need to Feel Independent

The EMDR integrative team protocol was modified by allow-ing for Ben's strong need for autonomy and independence. The therapist and mother discussed ahead of time the importance of acknowledging Ben's characteristics of strength and indepen-dence, knowing that this would be important to him. Ben was allowed to meet with the EMDR therapist and the family thera-pist without his mother present for part of every session, and Ben's mother was supportive of this decision. In the therapy ses-sions with his mother, Ben was asked to sit next to her on the sofa, but as with most adolescents, emphasis was not put on "snuggling together" out of respect for his age-appropriate desire to feel independent.

The family therapist helped Ben's mother develop integrative parenting skills and also helped Ben apply the expanded set of coping skills to specific situations in his present-day life, espe-cially those situations that normally triggered the self-harming behaviors. She facilitated the communication exercise described in the family therapy chapter (Chapter 4) during several sessions to help both Ben and his mother learn to both express them-selves and to listen to the other without becoming dysregulated.

During the EMDR ARD exercises, care was taken to acknowledge Ben as a mature young man and to avoid anything that he would reject as "childish." For example, during the Messages of Love exer-cise (as part of the ARD described in Chapter 5), Ben's mother talked about feeling proud of the mature parts of Ben while Ben held the tactile pulsars and noticed the feelings inside as she spoke. This was repeated at the beginning of many of the EMDR preparation ses-sions, due to Ben's positive response to the intervention. The EMDR therapist believed that Ben would be more accepting of the "Circle of Caring" exercise imagery over the "Cord of Love" exercise, and Ben and his mother were able to identify many people in his life who cared about him, including his adoptive mother, but also his friends, biological relatives, teachers, and so on. Ben cooperated in holding the tactile pulsars while visualizing the caring group of people surrounding him. The EMDR therapist used a matter-of-fact voice during the ARD exercises instead of the soft, nurturing voice that Ben might find irritating.

Safe Places for All Young Parts

The family therapist explained the DID diagnosis Ben had received and the presence of dissociated parts in a way that made sense and reduced the anxiety around the diagnosis for both Ben and his mother. This is how she worded her explanation, careful to use inclusive first-person pronouns until the very last sentence, when she finally switches to second person and a direct, though brief, focus on Ben:

> "We all carry younger parts of ourselves inside—thoughts and feelings from earlier in our lives that stay tucked away inside. However, when intense trauma occurs, it is overwhelming to the whole self. So the memory and the feelings around it are pushed way to the back of the brain. It is like that younger part of ourselves that is holding the pictures and the feelings is placed behind a little protective barrier. This protects us, sort of, but at the same time, it is not a solution that works forever. When that memory gets triggered and that barrier comes down for a few minutes or hours, the little part is in charge and we lose our bigger self. So we need to strengthen your bigger self and also work with those younger parts of yourself and make them feel safe."

Ben worked with his family therapist to identify the ages of the parts he sensed inside. Using the family therapist's laptop, they accessed a website for designing rooms, and Ben used the website to design a special safe room for each of his inner child parts. A mental picture of each safe room was reinforced with the tactile pulsars set on a relatively slow speed. Ben rejected the idea of using his adoptive mother as caregiver for the younger parts of self, but instead created an ideal "nanny" figure to care for these parts. The EMDR therapist guided Ben through a visualized "mental movie" of each part of self being safely cared for by the nanny figure, and this imagery was reinforced with slow tactile pulsars.

Inverse Protocol

The inverse protocol was used, beginning with development and reinforcement of inner resources and future templates in which Ben visualized positive future coping behaviors, followed by EMDR to reprocess recent triggers (Hofmann, 2009). Participation in EMDR reprocessing of trauma was negotiated with Ben, one small piece of memory at a time, incorporating interweaves for grounding and current safety. Ben was not pushed to tackle anything for which he did not feel ready. After 1½ years of therapy, Ben's mother stated that the therapy had created a remarkable change in Ben, which Ben also acknowledged. Ben had ceased all self-harming behaviors, and he was an A and B student with many friends. Ben and his mother were discharged from the family therapy, but Ben attends EMDR therapy twice per month and continues to process individual memories at a very slow, comfortable pace. His mother continues to attend part of each session to demonstrate her ongoing positive support.

Conclusion

One therapist would clearly have become overwhelmed trying to implement the many types of interventions Ben required to stabilize and prepare for EMDR memory work. Without the communication and relationship work with his adoptive mother, the development of coping skills, and the "detective work" identification of parts, triggers, and memories—all accomplished in family therapy—EMDR would have been put on a "back burner" and Ben's progress would have been severely delayed.

WORKING WITH TONY, AGE 8

Complication

Tony's complication was his need for adoptive placement. Shy and clearly anxious, Tony had been in care since he was 18 months old. His troublesome behaviors included lying, aggression, enuresis, encopresis, and a strong need to be in control. His biological father was very low functioning, and according to reports, his mother had been diagnosed with schizophrenia. Tony was also born several weeks prematurely and had suffered as an infant with ear infections, upper respiratory issues, failure to thrive, and allergies. At 6 months, his biological father had left him in the care of his biological mother. He was removed from her care due to neglect at 18 months of age.

Tony was placed in a foster home with a couple who fell in love with him. He remained with the same foster family until he was 5 years old. During this time, he had court-ordered visits with his biological mother. During the 4 years of visits, both supervised and unsupervised, the foster parents expressed serious concern that Tony's biological mother might be sexually and physically abusing him. Even though the foster parents continued to report their concerns, the state workers only relied on the documentation provided by the visitation workers. This documentation did not include any of the foster family's concerns. Tony's biological mother was able to present with acceptable behaviors from the perspective of the state workers. However, Tony continued to display serious self-harming behaviors, constipation, smearing of his feces, uncontrollable fits upon leaving for a visit with his mother, fear of adults, nightmares, and urinary infections.

Because the biological mother was completing the tasks that were required of her, the court decided to place 5-year-old Tony back in his biological home. After 2 months, due to serious concerns regarding the mother's erratic behavior, unwillingness to cooperate with state workers, and a cut on Tony's nose, the state removed Tony from her care once again and pursued terminating the mother's rights. Due to the conflict between the first foster home and the biological mother, however, the court concluded that it was not in Tony's best interest to be placed in the same foster home. The first foster parents had been vigilant in trying to protect Tony, so from the perspective of the state workers, they had appeared over-involved and sabotaging of the goal of reunification. From the age of 5 to age 8, Tony was moved from one foster home to another. His behaviors were so critical that the foster families could not handle him.

At age 8, Tony was placed in a foster–adopt home and began Integrative Team Treatment. His behaviors had calmed somewhat after his mother's rights were terminated, but he still struggled with lying, aggression, control issues, and toileting issues. The foster parents struggled with parenting Tony from a place of attunement and mindfulness. They preferred a more punitive style of parenting and disagreed with the integrative parenting strategies recommended by the therapists. Tony was repeatedly punished by spending time in the corner, losing the privilege of participating in family activities, and completing extra chores. His behaviors began escalating.

The therapists reported to the workers that the placement was a poor fit and that it was unlikely that Tony would improve. During some sessions in which Tony was seen alone, he talked about the people who took care of him when he lived with his mother. The therapist observed comfort in his eyes and calmer affect. The therapist did a little more investigation and discovered that this was the family that took care of Tony from 18 months to age 5. The therapist communicated with the workers that Tony had an attachment to this family and that it may be helpful for both families to have a relationship, but her recommendations were dismissed. After 18 therapy sessions, the foster parents refused to continue, stating that the recommended integrative parenting approach was "equivalent to coddling of naughty children." A few months later, the foster family requested that Tony be removed from their home. Without any preparation, Tony was suddenly and unexpectedly moved again. As one can imagine, Tony's behaviors escalated severely, and his spirit was broken.

Adaptations/Interventions

Tony's treatment included two key elements:

- Peer consultation and support
- Advocating for the appropriate placement

Peer Consultation and Support

The therapists in this case disagreed with the caseworkers, who did not understand the level of attachment that Tony had with the previous foster family. The caseworkers stated that they were unwilling to consider placement with the first foster family because the first family had been "too involved" and "advocated too much for the child." The caseworkers asked for hard evidence that the first family should be again considered as a possible adoptive family for Tony.

The team peer consultation component of the Integrative Team Treatment model was vital to this case. The situation was discussed in consult over the course of several weeks, and the consultation group was able to identify significant reasons for reconsidering the first family for placement and to strategize the presentation of their case.

Advocating for the Appropriate Placement

Over time, the therapists were able to communicate their point of view effectively regarding the nature of Tony's attachment trauma and why he had a yearning for the previous foster family. Without the team consultation, it would have been difficult to persuade a team of "nontherapists" to consider the first family for placement.

The therapists were allowed to have a meeting with the first family. When they met, it was clear that the family loved Tony as if he were their own. After 4 years, the father still carried a picture of Tony on his phone. The family therapist began educating the family, explaining Tony's current behaviors and history, as well as the Integrative Team Treatment model and the recommended integrative parenting methods. The parents were more than willing to do whatever they could to help Tony.

Tony was placed with the family just before he turned 9, and he was adopted 6 months later. Over the first year in his adoptive home, Tony made tremendous progress in all of his behaviors. As of this writing, the therapists are working with Tony to help him with his remaining anxiety related to the long separation from the family and the accompanying fear of having to leave again.

Conclusion

This case illustrates the importance of finding an appropriate placement, especially for a child with a traumatic history, and the need for the therapist to attune to the child's needs and at times, to advocate for what is best. A team can advocate much more effectively than a solo practitioner. By helping this little boy reunite with a family with whom he had once found love and security, Tony was able to utilize his therapy to help him heal.

WORKING WITH ABIGAIL, AGE 14

Complications

Abigail presented for treatment with the following complications:

- Substance abuse and other behaviors masking deep emotional pain
- Refusal to participate in court-ordered treatment or to stop using substances
- Several months of probation and intense court involvement

Abigail's parents had both died within the same year, when she was 11, from alcohol and drug overdoses. She had lived with her father in an environment of neglect throughout most of her younger years. Abigail had experienced frequent verbal abuse and emotional rejection from her mother before her death. Abigail's paternal grandmother was now her guardian, but Abigail was disrespectful and angry toward her. Abigail had begun abusing marijuana and alcohol by age 12 and was frequently truant from school. She was court-ordered to Integrative Team Treatment because she was not complying with probation or the drug and alcohol treatment program. Abigail presented for therapy with an attitude that vacillated between irritation and indifference.

Adaptations/Interventions

Abigail's treatment included the following adaptations:

- Extra education, support, and coaching for her grandmother to let go of a punitive style of parenting and increase emotional support
- Expression of gratitude to Abigail's younger part of self for using a tough demeanor to manage her feelings after the death of her parents

- Very intense attunement and empathy for the feelings of grief and sadness underlying Abigail's behaviors

Extra Education, Support, and Coaching for the Grandmother

At the beginning of treatment, Abigail's grandmother presented as angry and overwhelmed. She was surprised when she was told that she would be participating in Abigail's treatment. Both therapists took extra care to help the grandmother understand Abigail's substance use and other behaviors as methods she employed to avoid deep emotional pain, and that her supportive presence would be critical to helping Abigail open up emotionally.

Expression of Gratitude to Abigail's Younger Part of Self

Both therapists emphasized gratitude to the smaller, hurt Abigail for developing the protective, tough shell that helped her to survive emotionally during the traumatic events of her life.

Intense Attunement and Empathy

The family therapist did not directly address the substance abuse, but instead educated Abigail and her grandmother about the stages of grief and the importance of validating her feelings in order to heal, while the EMDR therapist began initial resource work. Both therapists repeatedly attuned to and empathized with Abigail's underlying feelings of grief, hurt, and anger.

Abigail soon began verbalizing her emotions and sharing painful memories of her past with her therapists and grandmother; these memories were then processed with EMDR. Abigail and her grandmother were asked to begin practicing hugs each day and communicating emotions with each other. Within 5 months, Abigail and her grandmother were becoming closer and more affectionate. Abigail had stopped abusing drugs and alcohol, was attending school, and was complying with the rules set for her by the court.

Conclusion

The challenging behaviors of traumatized children help them avoid their vulnerable emotions of hurt, fear, sadness, and grief. When the therapists honored Abigail's behaviors as strategies of self-protection coming from the younger part of self, Abigail felt understood and willing to open up emotionally, which allowed her to address her deep pain with EMDR.

WORKING WITH JUSTIN, AGE 6

Complications

Working with Justin involved addressing three major domains with significant challenges:

- Severe preverbal childhood medical trauma and abandonment
- Traumatic memories related to food
- Ongoing medical issues

As described in Chapter 3, working with Justin was complicated by trauma and attachment issues related to abandonment and severe medical problems early in life. Justin was born with problems surrounding his digestive system, and he needed a liver transplant at a very young age. His biological parents felt unable to care for his needs and left him in state care. Justin was transferred to a hospital in another state due to his medical needs. Eventually, a local family was moved when a story about Justin appeared in the local newspaper, and they sought to adopt him. When the family met Justin, they were shocked to discover that his primary emotional attachment was with an IV pole. Luckily, Justin's parents had read about the importance of attachment relationships and began holding him, talking to him, and playing with him right away.

When Justin was first allowed to live with his new family, at age 2, the parents worked extensively with an occupational therapist to help him adjust to new foods and learn to chew and swallow. The ingestion of food often caused intestinal pain, vomiting, and diarrhea. Justin sometimes found the taste of a new food enjoyable, but suffered stomach pain later—a medical situation that had not improved. His food intake had to be carefully monitored, and there were certain foods, primarily sweet carbohydrates, that were off-limits. Justin exhibited aggression and meltdowns frequently, but most often around mealtime.

Adaptations/Interventions

Two main areas were addressed in our interventions:

- Elaboration of "Safe Place for Baby" Exercise
- Extensive EMDR with food-related memories and triggers

Elaboration of the "Safe Place for Baby" Exercise

The "Safe Place for Baby" ARD exercise (see Chapter 5) was implemented in an extended fashion. First, the EMDR therapist helped Justin create a safe place that was pain-free, where touch was welcomed and safe, food did not make him sick, he was able to swallow, and his forever mom and dad were with him at all times, even while he was sleeping. This safe place was reinforced many times during his EMDR sessions. Then, because of the severity and length of the early medical trauma, the therapist created a safe place for baby Justin, month by month, from birth to age 18 months—an adaptation of the early trauma protocol presented by Paulsen (2012). Each safe place for Baby Justin was reinforced with tactile pulsars at a relatively slow speed. The goal was to give Baby Justin everything that he needed and more.

Adoptive mom and Justin also repeated the "Playing Baby" and "Lollipop Game" exercises (see Chapter 5) many times to further strengthen the relationship and help meet Justin's unmet early life needs. Justin thoroughly enjoyed snuggling in his mother's lap and playing baby with the lollipop. As therapy progressed, the clinician and Mom noticed that Mom and Justin seemed emotionally more connected, and Justin was less argumentative overall with his mother.

Repeated EMDR with Food-Related Memories and Triggers

Food intake problems presented the next big challenge in therapy. Food was a central issue that not only disrupted the relationship with Justin and his parents, but impacted the whole family at mealtime, at extended family gatherings, and even at school.

Because Justin felt more trusting and relaxed with his mom, he was willing to begin working on his fear and anger related to food. Justin had several memories in which he had experienced severe pain after eating a new food, and he was able to identify his belief, "Food is painful." These memories were targeted and reprocessed with EMDR. Over time, Justin came to believe, "There are foods that I can eat without getting sick." The therapist reinforced positive memories related to food along with the body sensation of good taste on the tongue and a good feeling of food in the stomach to reinforce Justin's newfound PC.

The EMDR therapist also helped Justin reprocess many food triggers that were experienced every day of his life, including just sitting down to a meal at home. Current triggers were associated with anger and the negative belief, "I should get to eat what I want to eat, like all the other kids." Eventually, Justin came to believe, "I just can't eat everything that other kids eat, even though some of those things taste really good on my tongue. They make my body sick and it's not worth it (even cake)." With EMDR and the help of some special foods that he could handle and special gum that he was allowed to chew at school, Justin's food behaviors began to settle down.

Conclusion

Justin's parents were relieved by his remarkable progress in dealing with and changing his feelings and behaviors related to food and his relationship with the two of them. The elaboration of the ARD followed by extensive EMDR on memories and triggers was crucial to helping Justin learn how to manage his special diet and stay healthy for life.

WORKING WITH DEANNA, AGE 13

Complications

Working with Deanna presented significant challenges in several areas:

- IQ of 68
- Most of Deanna's trauma took place prior to 7 months of age.
- Behaviors that caused Deanna to be rejected by other children, including touching of others' body parts, "pestering" and "arguing" behaviors
- Acute anxiety, panic attacks, and obsessive–compulsive symptoms
- Poor cooperation in therapy

Deanna's case was outlined in Chapter 3. Deanna was adopted at 7 months of age from a Russian orphanage by a single mother. Deanna had participated in behavioral therapy programs and occupational therapy for years but still presented with severe behaviors. For example, she panicked in the presence of dogs, children, and babies. She claimed that crying babies were trying to "argue" with her "like the babies in the orphanage." Her panic and meltdowns were very difficult for her adoptive mother to manage, especially in public situations. Deanna compulsively touched the fatty places on other people's bodies and protruding veins in their hands. She clearly had no sense of boundaries or personal space. She argued incessantly with her classmates in the special education room and with her adoptive mother. Periodically, at home, in public, at school, and in therapy, Deanna escalated into a loud, shrill, half-shriek, half-laugh that sounded quite maniacal and was difficult for others to tolerate. Her behaviors caused classmates at school to react very negatively toward her.

Initially, Deanna was uncooperative and reactive in the therapy sessions. She was obsessed with a small, plastic guinea pig that she always brought to therapy. Deanna described the guinea pig as "mad" and "wanting to lick."

Adaptations/Interventions

Five main intervention approaches were implemented with Deanna:

- Repeated coaching for connection and self-regulation
- Repeated EMDR future templates, reinforcing the low-alert state
- EMDR targeting of preverbal trauma
- Healing of Deanna's smaller child self through Joseph, the plastic guinea pig
- Use of metaphorical "porcupine coat" story

Repeated Coaching for Connection and Self-Regulation

Initially Deanna was very uncooperative in therapy sessions. She made no eye contact, didn't listen, flailed her body, and interrupted the conversation repeatedly with a maniacal laugh. The family therapist used a very calm voice and encouraged self-regulation through use of "belly breath" and "cooked noodle" (see Chapter 4) and encouraged Deanna to calm herself by imagining the "cord of love" (see Chapter 5). When the family therapist encouraged Deanna to look into her mother's eyes and use her mother's brain to calm her brain one day, Deanna herself suggested that she and her mother were also connected by a "brain cord," and this became another tool for self-calming. Deanna enjoyed these practices and slowly started to utilize them more readily.

223

The family therapist helped Deanna use the nonjudgmental/neutral words *high alert* and *low alert* (see Chapter 4) to help her become mindful of her inner state. Deanna was able to verbalize that the low-alert state felt much better than the high-alert one and gave her much more control over her behavior. Deanna also was assisted in identifying when she was thinking with her "calm brain," and she learned to "talk back to the feeling brain" to self-calm. She learned to tell herself, "Remain calm, there is no danger."

Repeated Use of EMDR Future Templates to Reinforce Low-Alert State

Repeatedly throughout treatment, the EMDR therapist guided Deanna in creating "mental movies" of challenging situations at school and home, and helped her imagine responding from a low-alert state by using self-talk and other strategies to maintain a calm brain. Deanna held the tactile pulsars, which relaxed and reinforced the calm state and positive imagery. In addition, the EMDR therapist, Deanna, and her mother role-played the situations, allowing Deanna to act out use of positive skills for self-calming and acting appropriately while holding onto the pulsars.

EMDR Targeting of Preverbal Trauma

The therapeutic story was a very important way of reaching Deanna's preverbal traumas. Following ARD, S-RDI, and reprocessing of several current triggers, the family therapist wrote a therapeutic story (see Appendix F), which was utilized repeatedly during EMDR therapy.

After the EMDR therapist read Deanna her story for the second time, she asked Deanna, "Which part of the story is most upsetting to you right now?" Deanna responded, "The babies crying in the orphanage." She claimed that she could remember crying and listening to the other babies crying. She said, "The other babies were trying to argue with me, because I was the problem." The EMDR therapist decided to target Deanna's image of herself as a baby in the orphanage, crying, along with the NC, "I am the problem." Deanna identified the feelings, "mad" and "nervous." The happier thought (PC) was, "Baby Deanna wasn't the problem, she had needs. All babies have needs, and that is OK."

In later sessions, EMDR was used to reprocess emotions related to pictures in Deanna's mind about her months in the orphanage. The therapist determined it was not necessary to know whether Deanna had actual memories or whether she was reprocessing feelings and imagined pictures related to what she knew had happened. The following is an excerpt from the session. (The symbols >>> represent the therapist prompts; EM = eye movements.)

EMDR Therapist: OK, Deanna, I just want you to think about that unhappy thought, "I am the problem" and the feeling of mad and nervous. >>>EM>>>

Deanna: (Holding a picture of herself as a baby in the orphanage) I am the problem. I have always been the problem. I'm still the problem.

EMDR Therapist: Deanna, just think about that. >>>EM>>>

Deanna: All those babies crying. I just couldn't cry loud enough. I tried to get those ladies to come. They never did. So I was the problem—the worst one. That's why they didn't come.

EMDR Therapist: (Using mom to provide an informational cognitive interweave) Mom, didn't you tell me that there were many, many babies at the orphanage who all had lots of needs, and there just weren't enough caregivers there to help all the babies?

Mom: Yes, when I went there, there were so many babies who needed things, and the caregivers were trying their best. None of the babies were a problem.

EMDR Therapist: Think about that, Deanna. >>>EM>>>

Deanna: I stopped crying. I remember that . . . I stopped crying so they would come.

EMDR Therapist: OK, let's just think about that. >>>EM>>> *(Mother whispers to therapist, "That is true. When we got her, she never cried, she had stopped.")*

225

Deanna: They didn't come even when I stopped crying, so I was still a problem. I thought that if I stopped, I wouldn't be a problem anymore. All those other babies were fighting with me.

EMDR Therapist: OK Deanna, just notice that. >>>EM>>>

Deanna: (Still looking at the picture of herself as a baby in the orphanage) Mom, was I the problem when you got there? Were all the babies fighting?

Mom: No, Deanna. You were not a problem. You were a beautiful baby. Grandpa and I picked you up and held you and fed you a bottle, and you were no problem at all. It may have seemed that the babies were fighting with you, but they weren't. They were all fighting to get their needs met. They weren't fighting with one another, though.

EMDR Therapist: Think about that, Deanna. >>>EM>>>

Deanna: So babies aren't problems? Even crying babies? They don't fight?

EMDR Therapist: No, babies are not problems. In fact, they are very smart because they know to cry. You were a very smart baby who knew to cry. It was not your fault that no one came. They were trying their best. All the babies were smart and just trying to get what they needed, right, Mom? >>>EM>>>

Mom: Yes, Deanna. When I got there, they had those pictures of you and you were in a nice warm sleeper, like the ones in the pictures. They did their best. You were never a problem.

EMDR Therapist: >>>EM>>>

Deanna: What about now? Am I a problem? Everybody still fights with me.

Mom: (Therapist signals mom to respond.) No, you aren't. Sometimes when you forget to tell yourself to "remain calm," or when you forget to let me be in charge, your behaviors can be a problem for both you and me. But, no, Deanna, you are never a problem.

EMDR Therapist: Think about what Mom just said. >>>EM>>>

Deanna: Babies just cry when they need food or when they are lonely. I was lonely.

EMDR Therapist: Yes, Deanna. You were lonely. Not the problem. >>>EM>>>

Deanna: Mom, I will try my best to "remain calm" and let you be in charge, OK?

Mom: OK, Deanna. We will keep working and working to help Baby Deanna on the inside know that she was not a problem.

EMDR Therapist: Think about that, Deanna. >>>EM>>>

Deanna: OK, I feel better now. Is it time to go?

Healing the Younger Child Self through Joseph, the Plastic Guinea Pig

One day, the family therapist heard Deanna's maniacal shriek/laugh in the waiting room and quickly entered to find her intensely searching through the coloring books. She excitedly held up the object of her search, the *Alvin and the Chipmunks* coloring book, and she pointed at the *Alvin and the Chipmunks* movie playing on the TV.

In the office, Deanna's mother stated that Alvin triggers Deanna because he reminds her of her plastic guinea pig, Joseph, who goes everywhere with Deanna. However, she explained that Deanna would not allow anyone to see Joseph except Mother and Grandmother. Joseph had a place at the dinner table each night, where he was given a little lettuce and carrot. And he rode in the car, but had to wait in the car so no one would see him, per Deanna's instructions. Deanna described Joseph, not as a comfort or a "lovey" type toy, but as a "mad, angry" guinea pig. The therapist viewed Joseph as a projection of Deanna's younger child self, a "child part" of Deanna wearing a guinea pig costume. The family therapist explained that we might be able to help Joseph feel safe and loved so that he didn't have to be mad anymore.

When Deanna moved into the EMDR therapist's office following her family therapy session, Deanna's mother went to the car to find Joseph.

"Safe Place for Joseph" Exercise. Deanna's mother brought Joseph into the EMDR session, and Deanna promptly put him in her purse. She was angry with her mother for bringing Joseph into the office because she feared that others would make fun of her little plastic animal. As the therapist tried to talk to Deanna about Joseph, Deanna repeatedly told the therapist, "Be quiet! You need to whisper. I don't want anyone to know about Joseph!" The therapist explained in a whisper that Joseph might feel very left out and lonely in her purse. Deanna responded, "Yes, that's true. He doesn't like it when I go to school." The therapist gave Deanna the tappers and asked her to hold them on Joseph (*still in her purse*). Deanna had a tapper in each hand and held them on Joseph and together, Deanna, her mother, and the therapist created a safe place for Joseph, following the "Safe Place for the Inner Child" exercise (see Chapter 5). Toward the end of the "Safe Place for Joseph" exercise, Joseph came out of Deanna's purse.

"Magical Cord of Love" Exercise for Joseph. As therapy continued, both the EMDR and family therapists got to know Joseph better. They discovered that Joseph was a toddler who "spoke" to Deanna. During one EMDR session, Joseph was licking Deanna and trying to touch body parts, and Deanna was responding by hitting Joseph. (The therapists had hypothesized that Deanna's compulsions about touching were related to unmet needs for physical touch in infancy, and Deanna's compulsion to touch body parts had actually greatly decreased from the start of therapy.) The therapist and Deanna's mother reminded Deanna about the "no hitting" rule and also reminded Joseph that it is not nice to hit, lick, or touch others' body parts. At this point in the session (still conceptualizing Joseph as Deanna's "inner child"), the therapist asked Deanna to hold the tappers on Joseph (who was now hiding in the purse) and to picture a magical cord of love between Deanna and Joseph and between Joseph and Deanna's mother. Close to the end of the exercise, Deanna said, "OK, Joseph feels better now. He wants to come back."

Targeting Preschool Memories Through Joseph. From discussions with Deanna's mother and with Deanna, it was apparent that Joseph's behaviors also mirrored the behaviors that Deanna exhibited when she was a toddler. At the beginning of treatment, Deanna talked at length about the difficulties she had experienced in preschool. She described instances when she was unable to "remain calm" and "was the problem." As the sessions continued, the EMDR therapist targeted memories that Deanna had from her preschool days, using the NC "I'm the problem" and the PC "I'm a good girl, and it's OK to make mistakes—I'm always learning new things." Joseph continued to attend therapy with Deanna. He sat in his safe place on the couch in both the family therapist's office and in the EMDR therapist's office. Continued work with Joseph included resource development exercises. Deanna also told the therapists that her grandfather didn't like Joseph. Deanna's mother confirmed that Deanna's grandmother had difficulty tolerating Deanna's voice as Joseph and would not allow Joseph to sit at the table, and so on. The therapists recommended that Deanna's mother talk to the grandmother and explain that Joseph was Deanna's "inner child." She did, and the grandfather became more accepting of Joseph.

Deanna also learned how to ask her mother for what she needed at home. When she was feeling anxious, she often asked her mother to hold her and let her drink from a straw, which helped her feel secure. Mother reported that Deanna's anxiety and her obsessions and compulsions continued to improve.

Use of the Metaphorical "Porcupine Coat" Story

During a family session with Deanna and her mother, they described a nearly perfect week at school with no incidents between Deanna and her peers, but high anxiety and combativeness nonetheless at home each morning. During the discussion, Deanna shouted, "But it's not safe to relax. Children will argue with me." Then Deanna stated that each day upon entering the classroom, she would say to herself *argument* to brace for any conflict that arose. Deanna's mother stated that it seemed like Deanna often braced for an argument at home as well, even when there was no conflict between them. The therapist said, "I think I have just the story for you today." She pulled out "The Story of the Hamster and the Porcupine Coat" (Appendix F) and read the title. (To recap the story, this is a metaphorical tale of a hamster who chooses to wear a spiky porcupine coat when he is very young due to his difficult life. He is later adopted by a forever mother. At the end of the story the child chooses from two endings, both of which involve removing the porcupine coat.) Deanna asked if the story could be changed to tell about a guinea pig named *Joseph* instead. The family therapist changed the name of the animal and some of the other story details to better match Deanna's early situation (see Deanna's guinea pig story in Appendix G). The family therapist brought the guinea pig story to the EMDR therapist, who read the story aloud to Deanna, while Deanna held the tactile pulsars in her hands, vibrating bilaterally at a medium speed.

At the end of the story, Deanna was asked to pick an ending (either ending is acceptable, but the second is better) and Deanna shouted, "I pick ending number two!" Deanna role-played the positive ending with her mother, while holding the tactile pulsars.

Conclusion

At the end of 1 year, Deanna was coming into sessions more relaxed and cooperative, making more eye contact, and communicating her feelings more directly. Deanna had started walking calmly to school, which she had not done previously, and her anger episodes became far fewer and less intense. She was much calmer in public and much more relaxed around babies and children. She stopped touching others' body parts, and other obsessive–compulsive symptoms lessened. She was much less argumentative at both school and home. Her vocabulary noticeably improved as she exhibited more of a desire to communicate. Instead of being afraid of anything new, she now became excited when anticipating a new experience.

Deanna's mother remarked, "Deanna continues to require patience and consistent attunement, but it keeps getting better. We keep peeling back the layers, and every bit of progress gives me hope for the next bit of progress."

Deanna's case illustrates how children with developmental delays can benefit from an Integrative Team Treatment approach, and how EMDR can be used to process infant trauma by utilizing therapeutic narrative as well as mental images, whether real or imagined. EMDR, inner child work, and teaching and coaching with Deanna and her mother in family sessions were all crucial ingredients to Deanna's progress in treatment.

Deanna and her mother are presently continuing the therapy past 1 year, as Deanna continues to work cooperatively in the sessions. Deanna is now working on and making progress toward achieving some new goals, including empathizing with the emotions of others, managing feelings about boys, improving her social skills, and learning how to think things through and solve problems.

Chapter 8

WHEN PARENTS HAD A DIFFICULT CHILDHOOD

Parenting any child is challenging. Even parenting well-attached children can leave parents frustrated, angry, hurt, fatigued, stressed, or disappointed. However, when the relationship is based on a foundation of attachment and trust, the challenges are interspersed with moments of connection, warmth, comfort, pride, and satisfaction, and these moments outweigh or at least help balance out the moments of heartache.

When a child exhibits severe behavioral challenges related to attachment trauma, the parent is not experiencing adequate positive moments of connection, warmth, and pride to offset the experiences of hurt and frustration. With few or no counterbalancing positive moments of closeness, it is normal for the parent raising a child with a history of attachment trauma to experience the desire to escape the situation and question his or her decision to parent the child at times. Even a parent raising a biological child affected by earlier relationship trauma may experience serious self-doubts.

All parents who bring their child to treatment, whether they are guardians, foster, adoptive, or reunifying biological parents, desperately need a trusting and supportive relationship with their child's treatment team, with whom they can honestly express their doubts, hurts, and fears without feeling judged. Through a positive relationship with a treatment team, parents can feel supported and gain hope.

THE GENERATIONAL TRANSMISSION OF ATTACHMENT STYLE

It is helpful for the therapist team to be able to observe the difficulties of the parents coming to treatment with their children through the lens of adult attachment. Although research in the area of adulthood attachment has identified discreet categories of attachment rather than the quality of attachment problems, adults as well as children certainly vary in terms of degree of attachment anxiety. Most of us fall somewhere on a continuum between totally secure and entirely insecure, and we probably all carry some upsetting childhood memories. When parents carry a very strong degree of attachment injury, however, they desperately struggle with their parenting challenges.

Adult attachment categories include secure, dismissing, and preoccupied. A third attachment designation, unresolved/disorganized, pertains solely to the adult's state of mind in regard to past losses and childhood abuse by parents (Hesse, 1999). Research shows that attachment styles of parents are transmitted to the children between 70 and 80% of the time (van IJzendoorn, 1992). The attachment styles of adoptive parents have the same influence over the attachment status of adopted children when they are placed at a young age. One study found that securely attached adoptive parents created security in 68% of adopted infants and toddlers when they were placed by 20 months old. Conversely, 81% of children placed by 20 months old with nonsecure adoptive parents exhibited a nonsecure status (Dozier, Albus, Stovall, & Bates, 2001).

Research shows that mothers with a *secure* style of attachment are attuned and responsive to their children's emotions and

233

needs, and their children learn that they can turn to them for comfort when they are distressed. The children of secure mothers are usually also found to be *secure*. These mothers become their children's secure base as they begin exploring the world. The children have positive expectations as they move out into the bigger world of relationships, and they exhibit positive attitudes and look for the most positive explanations for the behaviors of others. Their positive attitude breeds positive reactions from other people.

Parents who are uncomfortable with closeness and affection would typically be classified as *dismissing*. These parents back away from their children in the face of their children's strong emotions, and their children learn to repress their emotions to keep the parents in proximity. Children with dismissing mothers are typically classified as *avoidant*. These children do not tend to turn to their mother for comfort, but instead appear aloof. In the bigger world of relationships, avoidant children appear more aloof and less trusting.

Parents who feel unlovable, anxious, and preoccupied with their adulthood relationships would typically be classified as *preoccupied* in attachment style. Because of their own anxiety, they are poorly attuned and inconsistently responsive to their children's needs. Their expressions of affection tend to take place when they themselves need the closeness. Children of preoccupied mothers are usually classified *ambivalent/resistant*. Because these mothers are poorly attuned, the children are anxious and try to alleviate their own anxiety by crying and loudly demanding to get what they need. Ambivalent/resistant children turn to the mother for comfort but are difficult to soothe.

Parents who remain unresolved about major losses or childhood abuse experiences are designated *unresolved/disorganized*. Unresolved/disorganized parents can be easily triggered and dysregulated. Their infants or toddlers may subsequently have a *disorganized/disoriented* attachment designation. Disorganized/disoriented children are at high risk for emotional and dissociative problems and may later internalize or act out their emotions via severe behaviors (Cassidy, 1988; Lyons-Ruth et al., 1993).

The relationship between the avoidant child and dismissing parent usually functions well enough when there is a biological tie. There exists an unconscious, mutual agreement for avoiding intense closeness and a connection that began at conception. Similarly, the relationship between the ambivalent/resistant child and preoccupied biological parent may be conflicted, but their history through pregnancy and birth helps them through. The relationship between the unresolved/disorganized parent and disorganized/disoriented child is at highest risk for dysfunction, even in the case of biological families.

WHEN PARENT AND CHILD SHARE A SIMILAR PAST

The child placed outside of his biological home due to a history of early maltreatment may have one or some combination of avoidant attachment, ambivalent/resistant attachment, and attachment disorganization. The severely neglected child may be unattached (Zeanah & Boris, 2000) due to a lack of opportunity for experiencing an attachment. All children in out-of-home care have experienced traumatic attachment losses.

When the foster, adoptive, or reunifying biological parent comes from a similar past of trauma, the attachment disorganization and insecurity can be reinforced by one to the other in so many ways. When both the adoptive parent and child have a history of unresolved, untreated loss and/or trauma, the parent's "survival brain" triggers the child's "survival brain," and vice versa. The parent may have a window of tolerance (Siegel, 2010) for emotion that is as narrow as the child's window. Neither the parent nor the child can experience feelings of love and affection when operating outside of their window of tolerance. Traumatized adults need extra assistance in resolving their own traumas in order to calm their own and their child's brains. Consider the following vignettes.

Carmen was physically abused as a child. She has adopted a toddler who is emotionally dysregulated and disorganized. When he throws himself on the ground and screams, Carmen tells her husband, "Matthew is yelling at me—he hates me."

Jerry had a very authoritarian father and was punished severely if he spoke out of turn or tried to argue. His father used to say, "You will do as I say without argument. To argue with me is to disrespect me." He has recently taken in his adolescent niece, Sarah, because his sister was sentenced to 5 years in prison related to a drug charge. Sixteen-year-old Sarah is depressed and anxious following the separation from her mother. She also has a disorganized attachment resulting from the years of chaos related to her mother's drug use. As a result, Sarah is reactive and argumentative. Jerry tells Sarah's therapist, "The girl is intentionally trying to disrespect me. She is a spoiled kid who does not appreciate what I am doing for her."

Janice was sexually abused as a child by her father's brother, who lived in the family's home. She has become a foster parent to 4-year-old Sam, diagnosed with RAD, who is indiscriminately affectionate due to early neglect and many moves through foster homes. Sam demands closeness and has no sense of boundaries. He climbs on Janice's lap and tries to nuzzle into her chest for comfort. Sam also self-comforts through masturbation, without concern for privacy. Janice calls the caseworker and states, "You have to remove Sam right away. He is showing perpetrator behaviors, and the other children in this home are not safe around him."

Even parents who did not endure what would be considered "Big T" traumas such as physical or sexual abuse in childhood may be affected by chronic "small t" traumas that may include experiences of rejection, excessive criticism, or emotional neglect. If the parents did not experience affection or closeness during childhood, they may interpret their child's pleas for affection as "weak" or "needy." If the parents were criticized and shamed as children, they may have a strong need to micro-manage the child in their care. If the parents were constantly criticized as children, they may fear what others are saying about them when their child misbehaves (Wesselmann, 1998, pp. 89–107).

It is no surprise to professionals familiar with the AIP model that parents' unprocessed distressing memories are triggered by interactions with their children, consciously or subconsciously. It is easy to see how the traumatized child's behaviors can trigger big feelings and behaviors in parents, and how the parents' reactions can trigger the big feelings and behaviors in the child—in a vicious cycle that seems never-ending.

Addressing Challenges with the Dismissing Parent in Session

It is helpful for the therapist team to think about the core NCs that may be blocking parents' success with their children. When the adoptive parent is dismissing and the child is avoidant, both may hold core unspoken NCs that dictate "It's not safe to have feelings. It's not safe to be close." This might seem workable, since both parent and child are comfortable with the same amount of emotional distance. However, without a foundation of bonding through pregnancy and childbirth, the avoidant child and dismissing adult have nothing to connect them. The lack of connection will eventually lead to bigger and bigger child behaviors. The avoidant child needs to be coaxed by the parent into a relationship some way, somehow. On the other hand, when a dismissing parent is raising a child who demands closeness, the parent may be extremely triggered by the demands and automatically withdraw from the child or push the child away for self-protection.

Parents with a strongly dismissing attachment style typically have difficulty understanding attunement or "buying into" the need for attunement. Strongly dismissing adults lack awareness of emotions in themselves or others. Explaining children's emotions to strongly dismissing parents may be analogous to explaining sounds to someone who is deaf or explaining colors to someone who is blind. Furthermore, because of the constant reference to emotions, the therapeutic process itself is anxiety-provoking for dismissing adults. Being a part of the child's therapy, then, is quite challenging. Dismissing parents are the most likely to be unwilling to participate in the child's therapy or to consider seeking individual therapy for themselves.

Building a trusting relationship with strongly dismissing parents is vital to keep them and the child in therapy. The therapist should avoid appearing critical of these parents and take a practical approach to teaching them Integrative Parenting skills. Strongly dismissing parents may never be able to "attune" to the child intuitively, but may respond to a direct prescription, such as: "When your child behaves _____, he [she] is really feeling _____, and it will be most effective for you to respond by _____."

During ARD, dismissing parents may be extremely awkward in response to "warm and fuzzy" nurturing words or affectionate touch. These parents may have to be given a script and extra coaching prior to ARD. The therapist may have to accept whatever these parents are able to do to show positive regard for their child, even though it is not the attuned and affectionate approach the therapist prefers.

Addressing Challenges with the Preoccupied Parent in the Session

Parents with a preoccupied attachment style become easily overwhelmed and have poor self-worth. Both parents and traumatized children may hold core unspoken NCs that include "I cannot trust. I will be rejected. I need to be in charge of getting my own needs met." In this case, the parent's needs and the child's needs clash. Both the parent and child read rejection on the face of the other, trigger fear and anger in the other, and react accordingly. Both the parent and child try to reduce their own anxiety by taking control of the situation and making sure their own needs are met, and then feel frustrated when the other does not cooperate. The dyad is caught in a never-ending negative feedback loop, causing the child's emotions and behaviors to continue to escalate. The preoccupied parent requires a great deal of assistance in developing a clear understanding of the meaning of the child's behaviors in order to keep a mindful, attuned approach.

It is very difficult for preoccupied parents to attune to traumatized children because it is difficult for them to see past their own strong emotions. Preoccupied parents operate out of their emotions; they lack the ability to reflect upon their own thoughts and feelings with insight and tend to react with anger or fear. If the preoccupied parent is angry, he or she assumes that others will share the same viewpoint. Common interpretations of the preoccupied parent who tends toward anger include:

- "He knew exactly what he was doing—it was purposeful."
- "She is trying to push my buttons."
- "He is disrespecting me."
- "She is trying to control me."
- "I cannot let him win."

Common interpretations of the preoccupied attached parent who tends toward fear:

- "She is trying to hurt me."
- "I am not safe with my child."
- "My child is dangerous."

Preoccupied parents show such passionate conviction for their own point of view that it is difficult to know how to counter it. In this situation, the team of therapists working together can brainstorm and role-play methods for shifting a parent's thinking. Providing psychoeducation with emotional attunement is one direction that may be effective. For example:

- "I know that kind of behavior is really challenging. Let's think about it from the viewpoint of your child's negative core beliefs. . . ."
- "I can sure understand your strong feelings, but let's stop and think together about what your child learned from his early life experiences. . . ."
- "That behavior would be very triggering to any parent. Your child was certainly operating outside of her window of tolerance. Let's review what happens when the brain goes into fight or flight modes. . . ."

Finally, the therapist may say something like, "Now, considering this point of view, let's come up with a response that will be more effective in helping your child learn to view you as someone he [she] can trust and rely upon."

Parents with a preoccupied style of attachment often look to the child's therapists for emotional validation and understanding. They may be overly sensitive to the feedback from the therapists and sometimes reactive, but at the same time, they may be open to guidance if the therapists stay positive and attuned. These parents may also be open to the suggestion for individual therapy if the child's therapists have built rapport and voice the suggestion out of concern for a parent's welfare.

Addressing Challenges with the Unresolved/Disorganized Parent in the Session

Parents who carry their own unresolved trauma or loss may easily become triggered and hyperaroused in the presence of their dysregulated child. The hyperarousal in a parent further triggers the child, leading to the endless negative feedback loop.

When the family therapist is unable to shift the parent's emotional reactions through psychoeducation and integrative parenting tools, he or she should then begin gently asking questions about the parent's story. A nonjudgmental approach and a trusting therapeutic relationship is a prerequisite to asking more personal questions of the parent. Empathy and attunement regarding the hardship that the parent experienced in childhood as well as the challenge of parenting a traumatized child help the parent understand that the child's therapeutic team intends to be helpful, not hurtful or reproachful. Suggesting involvement in individual therapy, especially EMDR therapy, to the traumatized parent is vital to making progress with the child.

APPLYING THE "DOMINO EFFECT" INTERVENTION WITH A STRUGGLING PARENT

Both the EMDR and family therapist who are treating parents should have a clear understanding of the acute stress related to raising children with severe behavior problems. Despite any trauma or attachment issues that may be impacting the parent's reactions to her child, the parent's frustration, hurt, fear, and anger are all very real. The therapeutic team should be prepared to listen, empathize, and validate the stress the parent is facing. As the therapeutic relationship develops, both therapists should begin feeling more comfortable in addressing the parental behaviors that may be contributing to negative interactions in the home or perhaps in the therapy sessions.

The concept of the domino effect was introduced in Chapter 4. The family therapist helps the parent and child with "detective work" to examine the falling dominoes of thoughts, feelings, and actions that may have led to a meltdown or another problem behavior. The therapist helps both the parent and child look at the part each played as the dominoes fell and think about where each might have been able to "pull a domino." This logical, rational approach to analyzing the problematic situations and brainstorming solutions helps both parent and child adopt a more nonjudgmental and rational demeanor overall.

When the family therapist recognizes that the parent is subconsciously reacting in ways that are detrimental to the child and the relationship, the domino effect analogy can be used to help the parent examine his or her own vulnerabilities, triggers, emotions, thoughts, and actions with more detail during the one-on-one parent time at the beginning of the family session. The therapist can help the parent find ways to "pull" his or her own dominoes once the parent has been able to recognize his or her own contribution to the problematic patterns.

Dave Examines His "Dominoes"

Dave was guardian to his 14-year-old grandson Nick. Dave and Nick had gotten into a yelling match the night before after several weeks of Integrative Team Treatment in which the relationship between them had shown very encouraging signs of improvement. Dave had come into the session feeling very discouraged. Luckily, Dave had developed a trusting relationship with the family therapist and together, they examined the falling dominoes. Dave was able to recognize that both he and Nick had been highly vulnerable due to a stressful month in which the family had moved and Dave had had to place his elderly mother in a nursing home due to her failing health. Dave also noted that he was suffering from a fatigue headache when he had been triggered by some back talk from Nick. Because of his vulnerable state, he had immediately experienced some negative thoughts, such as, "Nobody appreciates me or cares about me." His thoughts led to anger, and he had reacted by yelling. Dave agreed that yelling is a big trigger for Nick, who experienced a lot of verbal abuse from his biological father as a younger child. Dave recognized that both he and Nick had entered a hyperaroused state in which they lost their ability to reason or problem-solve. Following is an excerpt from their session.

Family Therapist: Dave, where do you think you might have been able to pull some of your own dominoes last night? Remember, the point in doing this exercise after the fact is so that you might be able to change the course of things next time.

Dave: First, I should have realized that I was mentally exhausted from all that has gone on just recently. I probably should have told the family up front that I felt awful, and I should have gone to bed right after dinner with that headache.

Family Therapist: That would have stopped the dominoes from falling right there, wouldn't it?

Dave: Yes, and otherwise, as soon as Nick started talking back to me, I should have told myself to take some space. I might have said to Nick, "We're both stressed and tired. I know I'm too tired to talk rationally right now. Let's do some problem-solving in the morning."

HELPING PARENTS GAIN INSIGHT

Once the therapeutic team has developed rapport with the parents, it may be possible at times to conduct an informal "float-back" to help parents "connect the dots" between their reactions with their children and earlier events in their own lives.

Helping Marcia Gain Insight

Marcia, a single mother, had adopted her 6-year-old son James 3 years earlier. She and James had been meeting regularly with the family therapist and EMDR therapist team for approximately 2 months. At the beginning of the family therapy session, while James was still playing in the waiting room, Marcia had stated one of her worst struggles was at bath time.

Family Therapist: Would you be willing to try a little exercise with me? *(Marcia nods.)* See if you can bring up the memory of bath time last night—before you lost your cool. Take your time and notice what you feel.

Marcia: I get really anxious just thinking about it.

Family Therapist: OK, and now I wonder if you could let your mind float back to your own childhood. Just be open to whatever comes up for you.

Marcia: Hmm, what pops up in my head is something that happened when I was about 10. My dad asked me to fill the bathtub for my little brother. I didn't know what I was doing. My brother hopped into the water and started screaming because it was too hot. I got a really bad spanking that night.

Family Therapist: No wonder you have a tough time at bath time! Subconsciously, you probably believe something bad is going to happen.

Marcia: Yes, my dad was really harsh, and something bad usually did happen—because it seemed like I was always getting punished for something.

Family Therapist: I wonder if your experiences growing up have created anxiety for you in other areas related to parenting. Of course, James is also anxious and reactive, which is challenging in itself. So you and James are stuck in a negative feedback loop.

Marcia: Yes, my anxiety and reactivity trigger him, and his anxiety and reactivity trigger me.

Family Therapist: You know, Marcia, these kinds of reactions rooted in early life experiences are really hard to get a handle on without some assistance. I would really like you to consider working with one of the therapists on our adult team. Remember how we have talked about the family as a system? I would be doing you and Tim a disservice if I didn't give you the same opportunity for healing as we have given Tim. We have some wonderful therapists here who could really help you feel better.

Marcia: Maybe. . . .

Marcia needed time to digest what was discussed, but a couple of weeks later, she asked the therapist for the name of a therapist she could work with individually. EMDR was able to help Marcia reprocess trauma from childhood that was directly related to anxiety and overreactions to James. Marcia was able to calm her anxiety and become more attuned and nurturing with James—the kind of mother she really wanted to be.

COUPLES IN CRISIS

Most child therapists recognize the damage that marital conflict can cause to children in any family. The stress of raising a traumatized child can create enormous strain on couples and intensify conflict in the relationship. If there was prior tension in the relationship, the task of parenting easily creates a deeper chasm. Commonly, one partner becomes overly involved with the parenting while the other becomes resentful and withdrawn. Or partners may fight over decisions related to parenting the child. The family therapist should normalize the stress the couple is experiencing, and encourage the partners by explaining that many parents raising traumatized children need couple counseling to help them get "on the same page" and learn how to stay connected and be more supportive to one another. In addition to couple therapy, partners should be encouraged to take care of their relationship by finding some reliable respite care and scheduling regular date nights or weekend getaways.

PARENTAL GRIEF

Many parents struggle with an underlying grief related to their children. Even biological parents can experience grief for a child with disabilities or other problems. Parents of foster or adopted children with severe behavioral issues and a traumatic past may have committed to the child before recognizing the severity of the challenges they would eventually be facing. Many parents became parents unexpectedly to a grandchild, niece, or nephew who needed a placement at a time of life that they thought would be free of childrearing stress. Often adoptive parents struggle with grief related to infertility and the loss of the experience of pregnancy and childbirth. Parents may grieve for the child they had imagined raising, for the ideal family they had hoped for, and for the easy life they'd had prior to becoming a parent. They may grieve loss of control, loss of alone time, loss of time with friends, loss of time as a couple, and loss of ideal holidays, vacations, and leisure time. Parents may feel regret for the challenges faced by the other children in the family and feel envious of other families that seem to have easier situations. They may blame themselves, their spouse, or the child for their feelings.

As with grief related to any type of loss, parents may move back and forth through stages of denial, anger, bargaining, and depression (Kübler-Ross & Kessler, 2005). EMDR therapy for parents can remove the negative beliefs complicating the process of grieving and allow a healthy processing of emotions. An EMDR therapist can address negative beliefs such as, "I can't handle it," "I'm defective," "I have a bad child," and "My family is defective." The EMDR can shift parents to more helpful cognitions such as, "I can help my child heal," "I'm a good person," "My child has a good heart," and "My family is a good family." EMDR therapy can help parents find meaning in helping and parenting their hurt child, gain confidence in themselves as parents, and gradually reach a state of greater acceptance of the child as he or she is. The parents can be helped to let go of unrealistic expectations and find satisfaction in each small step of progress, find more enjoyment in the child's unique traits and assets, and find overall acceptance and peace.

When therapists recognize unresolved grief in parents who are stuck in anger, resentment, or despair, it is vital to give the parents every opportunity to work through their stuck emotions and find healing for themselves. Without such healing, one parent's grief can keep the entire family stuck in unhealthy interactions.

INVITING PARENTS TO PARTICIPATE
IN THEIR OWN THERAPY

Not every parent needs to seek personal therapy to achieve success in the child's treatment, but when a parent is so exhausted
or emotionally triggered that he or she is unable to carry out
the integrative parenting approach or be emotionally present in
therapy, individual therapy for the parent may be a prerequisite for a positive outcome. When the parent appears unable to
shift from a stuck place, the therapist can help the parent look at
the possibility of seeking individual help from a nonjudgmental
point of view. The conversation may be initiated by asking the
parent, "How can we help you find more support for yourself?
This is such a challenging situation, and we are not doing our
job if we don't address your needs as well as your child's needs."
Sometimes it is helpful to point out that many of the parents of
traumatized children are seeking their own help because of the
emotional stress and triggers associated with raising hurt children.

Parents can be referred to community supportive sources as
well, such as respite care (temporary care for the child often offered through local nonprofit family service organizations), community treatment aids (paraprofessionals trained to work with
the child in the home or school setting), and support groups for
adoptive parents, adult children of alcoholics, or adult survivors
of abuse. Following is a sample transcript of what a family therapist might say to a parent who is much in need of individual
therapeutic support:

> "You have been coping with an intensely stressful situa-
> tion on a day-to-day basis without much respite. Many
> parents raising traumatized children are also suffering
> from traumatic stress. This is no one's fault; it is just the
> situation. Sometimes when we live in a highly stressful

situation, our own window of tolerance shrinks, and we find ourselves triggered again and again. I think you would find that getting involved in your own therapy would help you feel calmer and more able to ride out the rocky moments. Remember that every family is a system, and one part of the system can't change unless every part of the system makes changes. Without changes in your part of the dynamic, your child may not be able change."

Drawing the Hard Line

When parents have their own complex past and are repeatedly reactive due to their inability to manage their own triggers, their participation in their own individual therapy may be the only way to succeed in helping their child. Although we try to encourage parents to voluntarily participate in their own therapy, occasionally it has been necessary to *require* individual therapy for parents as a condition for keeping the child in treatment.

Although it is possible for a therapist who works with the parent–child dyad to also provide individual therapy to the parent, it is not an ideal situation, especially if the parent has an extensive trauma history. It is preferable to bring an additional therapist to the team, preferably an EMDR therapist who is well versed in the integrative parenting methods and the Integrative Team Treatment for children. Adding a clinician to the team prevents a member of the child team from feeling overwhelmed and helps the parent feel more supported.

CONCLUSION

Children with a history of attachment trauma often exhibit behaviors that are aggressive and illogical. It is natural for parents to feel hurt, frustrated, and offended by oppositional or aggressive behaviors. For many parents, implementing integrative parenting strategies requires a major shift from a more punitive style to the attuned responses. The integrative parenting approach is counter-intuitive in that it requires parents to avoid more emotion-driven responses, to self-reflect, and to respond with calm attunement to interrupt the negative feedback loop. Parents are asked to set aside their frustrations and intentionally connect emotionally and physically with their children. The EMDR therapist can proceed with helping children address the past only when their parents can provide sensitive emotional support.

Psychoeducation and examination of parent "dominoes" can help many parents become more self-aware and intentional. When they become more insightful regarding their own internal states as well as their child's emotions and thoughts, many parents are able to make changes that support their child's healing.

Parents who experienced a traumatic childhood have increased challenges in this regard. The extreme behaviors of their children trigger their own stored, unprocessed traumatic memories. When parents react out of their own "survival brain," their ability to take control of their actions is limited. Staying observant regarding the parent's tendencies toward a dismissing versus preoccupied style of interacting can help the therapist work with the parent more effectively. Validation and sensitivity toward parents' stress can help them feel understood and strengthen the rapport, thereby empowering the therapeutic team to address the parents' need for individual or couple therapy.

All parts of the family system must change in order for the child to progress effectively and maintain gains. Some parents are able to achieve their own change through the psychoeducation and family therapy work, but for others, this is not enough. Directly addressing the parents' needs for individual and couple therapy can be critical to moving the child and parents toward long-term healthy functioning.

CLOSING THOUGHTS

HEALING TRAUMATIZED children is challenging work. Children who have experienced attachment trauma carry a negative view of the world and themselves. These children and their families are often stuck in reactions of anger, frustration, and misbehavior, creating a seemingly never-ending cycle of chaos and damaged relationships. The cycle often appears to be virtually unbreakable.

Many families do not know where to turn. They have searched the Internet, talked with friends, and attended parenting classes (which had little to no impact in changing these stuck cycles). Therapists implementing the Integrative Team Treatment model actively assist children in overcoming emotional and social skills deficits, increasing attachment security, and healing their trauma. Children with challenging behaviors and a history of attachment trauma and losses have been derailed from the typical developmental trajectory. The families are desperate, and they need a therapeutic approach that is effective and efficient. The Integrative Team Treatment model has had significant success in treating these hurt families.

We hope that therapists working with this population find one or more colleagues with whom they can collaborate to implement this protocol. Complex families require an enormous amount of thought and patience during the process of healing, and the family therapist and EMDR therapist collaboration is critical to success. Working with a fellow therapist allows for the brainstorming, support, and encouragement that bring energy and excitement to the work. The work accomplished in family sessions supports and expedites the work implemented in the EMDR sessions, bringing new hope and happiness to the family.

We hope that the practical suggestions and examples in this manual provide you with new inspiration. Our work is challenging—with natural setbacks and complications along the way. But with perseverance, determination, and teamwork, we can improve the lives of children and families.

Appendix A

HISTORY-TAKING CHECKLIST

Name _____

DOB _____ ID _____

Parents/Guardians _____

Current or Recent Behaviors
___Indiscriminate affection with strangers and others
___Clingy and attention-seeking with parent
___Arguing
___Defiance
___Destruction of property
___Quick to anger
___Meltdowns
___Aggression toward people or animals
___Acute jealousy toward siblings
___Stealing
___Lying
___Running away
___Whining
___Difficulty concentrating

___Hyperactivity

___Excessive masturbation

___Sexualized behaviors toward others

___Defiance/opposition

___Difficulty falling asleep

___Difficulty staying asleep

___Nightmares

___Enuresis

___Encopresis

___Other abnormal bathroom behaviors such as urinating in odd places or smearing feces

___Controlling/bossy toward others

___Does not go to parents for comfort

___Will not accept closeness or comfort

___Other _____

Current Triggers (situations that seem to lead to acting-out behaviors)

___Mom/dad/teacher saying no

___Mom/dad giving attention to a sibling

___Playing with siblings or peers

___Mom/dad/teacher giving a direction or redirection

___Mom/dad/teacher with an angry face

___Mom/dad sick, sad, preoccupied

___Receiving a consequence

___A family holiday or birthday

___A good grade

___A bad grade

___A criticism

___A compliment

___A transition from one activity to another

___Time to go to school

___Something exciting coming up

___Frustrating or confusing job or homework

___Bedtime

___Time to get up

___Other _____

Traumatic Past Events

___Loss of, and/or changes in, primary caregivers

___Temporary placement such as foster care or orphanage care

___Early experiences of abuse of any kind, neglect, or rejection by caregivers

___Early medical interventions

___Early experiences of pain that may have interfered with the child's ability to relax and bond, such as ear pain or colic

___Early separations from primary caregivers due to hospitalizations or any other reasons

___Frequent changes in day-care providers

___A frightening or chaotic environment, such as domestic violence, which may have interfered with the child's ability to relax and bond

___Parental addictions that may have removed the safe emotional presence of the parent

___Parental stressors such as illness in the family, death in the family, job loss, etc., that may have removed the safe emotional presence of the parent

___Parental emotional problems such as PTSD that may have removed the safe emotional presence of the parent

___The child's overhearing of information that interfered with feelings of safety and trust in parents

___Ridicule or rejection from classmates or teachers

___Other _____

Negative Cognitions (NCs)
(Think about the child's history and his/her current behaviors and hypothesize which upsetting thoughts and beliefs may be driving the child's actions.)

___"I'm not safe."

___"I cannot trust Mom/Dad."

___"I cannot trust or depend on anyone."

___"I have to get what I need/want for myself."

___"It's not safe to be close."

___"It's not safe to be vulnerable."

___"I'm powerless."

___"I'm bad/evil."

___"If I make a mistake, I *am* a mistake."

___"I need food/stuff to be OK."

___"She/he is out to hurt me."

___"She/he is against me."

___"Moms/dads are mean."

___"Moms/dads will leave."

___"She/he deserves to be punished."

___"I have to be in control."

___"I should have done something."

___"I'm not good enough."

___"I don't belong."

___"Something is wrong with me."

___"My feelings are bad/unsafe/scary."

___"It's not safe to share my feelings."

___"It's not safe to love or accept love."

___"I don't deserve love."

___"I don't deserve to be complimented."

___"A compliment is unsafe."

___"Bad things always happen."

___"Good things are not safe."

___"I'll disappear if you don't see me and hear me."

___"I don't deserve to be here."

___"Biological kids are more special than adopted kids."

___Other _____

Desired Positive Cognitions (PCs)
(Hypothesize the thoughts/beliefs the child may need to adopt or strengthen in order to feel and behave better.)

___"I'm safe."

___"I can trust my mom/dad."

___"I can relax and depend upon my mom/dad to give me what I need."

___"It's safe to be close."

___"It's OK to be vulnerable."

___"I have choices."

___"I have a good heart."

___"My mom/dad wants the best for me."

___"My mom/dad is on my side."

___"My mom/dad will always be here for me."

___"I'm loved."

___"I'm lovable."

___"I did the best I could."

___"I don't have to be perfect."

___"I belong."

___"I'm fine as I am."

___"My feelings are normal and OK."

___"It's safe to share my feelings."

___"It's safe to love and be loved."

___"I deserve love."

___"I deserve compliments."

___"Compliments are safe."

___"Mostly good things happen."

___"Good things are safe."

___"I'm here even when you don't see me or hear me."

___"I deserve to be here."

___Other _____

Future Templates (behaviors you would like the child to adopt)

___Cooperating while getting ready for bed

___Cooperating about getting ready in the morning

___Saying "OK" when Mom/Dad says "no" or makes a request

___Sharing, taking turns

___Finding something else to do when Mom/Dad pays attention to a sibling

___Coping with homework frustration

___Accepting a compliment

___Expressing hurt or angry feelings appropriately

___Coping when Mom/Dad is sick, sad, preoccupied, or angry

___Joining in the fun on a family holiday or birthday

___Handling criticism skillfully

___Handling a consequence

___Saying "I'm sorry" and correcting the situation

___Coping skillfully with a bad grade

___Coping skillfully with a good grade

___Asking for something appropriately

___Seeking help or comfort

___Other _____

List any strengths/positive behaviors:

Appendix B

USEFUL ASSESSMENTS

CHILD ASSESSMENTS

Adolescent Dissociative Experiences Scale (Armstrong, Putnam, Carlson, Libero, & Smith, 1997).

A 30-item self-report screening tool for children ages 11–18 that assesses a range of dissociative symptoms. Can be ordered through Sidran Institute, P. O. Box 435, Brooklandville, MD 21022-0436.

Attachment Disorder Assessment Scale—Revised (ADAS-R)

A 40-item questionnaire completed by parents that indicates severity of attachment disorder in children. It takes about 10 minutes to complete. Can be ordered through Acacia Publishing in Phoenix, Arizona by calling 866-265-4553 or online at www.acaciapublishing.com.

Child Behavior Checklist for Ages 6–18 (CBCL; Achenbach, 1991).

A 113-item assessment completed by parents to assess children's level of competency and overall emotional and behavioral symptoms. Can be ordered online from ASEBA at www.ASEBA.org.

Randolph Attachment Disorder Questionnaire (RADQ)

A 30-item assessment completed by parents to determine if there are behaviors that correlate with the diagnosis of attachment disorder. Can be purchased through the Institute of Attachment and Child Development, Littleton, Colorado, or online at www.info@instituteforattachment.org.

The Child Dissociative Checklist (Putnam & Peterson, 1994)

A 20-item screening tool for children ages 5–11 that is completed by the parent. One online source: http://cw.routledge.com/textbooks/eresources/9780415889957/AppendixD.pdf

Trauma Symptom Checklist for Young Children (Briere, 1996)

An assessment of trauma symptoms for children ages 3–12, completed by the parents. Includes scales for sexualized behaviors and dissociation. Ordered through PAR, 16204 N. Florida Ave., Lutz, Florida 33549; phone 1-800-331-8378 or online at www.parinc.com.

USEFUL PARENT ASSESSMENTS

OQ45 (Lambert et al., 1996)

A 45-item self-report questionnaire that measures symptom distress and interpersonal and social functioning. Order online at www.OQMeasures.com.

Experiences in Close Relationships Scale (Brennan, Clark, & Shaver, 1998)

A 36-item self-report measure. See http://internal.psychology.illinois.edu/~rcfraley/measures/ecrritems.htm.

Appendix C

HANDOUTS FOR PARENTS

HANDOUT 1: HOW TO PREPARE FOR YOUR CHILD'S THERAPY

As your child begins therapy, it can be anxiety-producing for both you and your child. Parents are vital to the therapeutic process, and we want you to feel as comfortable as possible. The program we offer includes exercises for creating experiences of closeness, connection, and trust between you and your child. The following will prepare you for this very powerful attachment work. We ask that you review these items, jot down your thoughts as needed, and be prepared to share them with your child during the sessions. If you have any questions about this process, please ask.

1. Brainstorm positive memories you have about the first time you met your child. Think about the "story" of how he/she came to grow in your heart(s). If your son/daughter is biological, brainstorm positive memories about the pregnancy, birth, and early years.
2. Think of positive experiences you and your child have shared. Notice how those times made you feel, and recall the joy you and your child experienced. These can be small things like singing songs in the car on family vacations. Overall, brainstorm times you and your child have felt connected.

3. List the things you and your child have in common—for example, foods, songs, outings you both enjoy, etc.

4. List the things you most enjoy doing with your child. Consider how you feel when you are doing these things.

5. Brainstorm attributes you love most about your child. You could start your list with, "I love you because . . . "

6. Think about the hopes and dreams you have for your child's future.

7. List recent or past triumphs your child has achieved. Even small things are important. Example: "He put his clothes in the hamper without being asked."

8. One of the exercises involves creating a safe/calm place for your child's "baby self" within. Think about how you would decorate a safe place for your child as a baby. List things you would do for the baby in this safe place. Examples: playing peek-a-boo, counting toes, feeding, rocking, etc.

9. Complete the following: "I noticed you _____. When you did this, I felt _____. I feel that feeling in my _____, and it feels _____." For example: "When you brushed your teeth without being asked, I felt proud. I felt that pride in my heart and it feels warm.

10. Think of early positive stories/memories you have of your child. List as many as you can.

HANDOUT 2: HOW TO HELP YOUR CHILD STRENGTHEN HIS/HER ATTACHMENT WITH YOU

Find ways to connect throughout the day:

- Brush your child's hair; paint your daughter's nails.
- Brush your teeth together.
- Share a hobby or sport or a passion of yours with your child.
- Play a board game or card game.
- Rock, cuddle, hold.
- Tuck your child in bed.
- Help your child with chores for no reason.
- Occasionally, excuse your child from chores and do something fun.

- Leave your child sticky notes with positive affirmations or nurturing messages. (Example: *I had so much fun playing that game with you.*)
- Think of books you and your child read together and/or used to read. Pull those books out. Sometimes even "big" kids enjoy having a story read to them.
- Find a lotion (with a particular smell) that both you and your child enjoy.
- Make up a family handshake that is special to your family.

Attune to your child:

- "It's hard to be little."
- "I notice you look a little sad today. Do you want to talk?"
- "It looks like you are having a hard time."
- "Help me understand what you are feeling."
- "I am here for you when you want to talk."

"Notice" things your child does "right":

- "I notice you did a great job making your bed."
- "I noticed you used your polite words today."

Follow the 10–20–10 method (adapted from Forbes, 2009)

- 10 minutes in the morning—Go in and sit with your child in the morning before he/she gets up and rub his/her back, stroke his/her hair, and give him/her nurturing messages.
- 20 minutes after school—Sit and share a snack, have light, pleasant conversation, and DON'T ASK ABOUT SCHOOL OR HOMEWORK.
- 10 minutes at night—Tuck him/her in, sit and rub his/her back, stroke his/her hair, and give him/her nurturing messages.

Appendix D

INTEGRATIVE TEAM TREATMENT CONSULT MEETING PLANNING SHEET

Clinician_____Date_____

I. Safety issues (suicidal/self-harming behavior, aggressive behavior, imminent placement outside of home): Clients _____

   Notes _____

   _____

II. Case management issues (concerns regarding appropriateness of a placement, need for psychiatric referral, school issues): Clients ___

   Notes _____

   _____

III. Parent behaviors that interfere with progress (missed sessions, parent anger, inability to incorporate integrative parenting techniques): Clients _____

   Notes _____

   _____

IV. Stuck behavioral cycles in child or family as a whole: Clients _____

   _____

   Notes _____

   _____

V. Important updates: Clients _____

   Notes _____

   _____

VI. Countertransference concerns: Clients _____

    Notes _____

    _____

VII. New cases/new referrals: Clients _____

     Notes _____

     _____

Appendix E

THERAPEUTIC STORY OUTLINES

These story outlines are adapted from the work of Joan Lovett (1999).

FOR GIRLS

Once upon a time, there was a young girl who lived with . . .

Like all children, she had some wonderful things and some confusing things happen in her life.

A wonderful thing was that she was born . . .

A confusing thing was . . .

If this little girl could have put her feelings into thoughts with words, she might have said (NCs):

The truth is (or what we want her to know is) (PCs):

A wonderful thing that happened was . . .

Another confusing thing that happened was . . .

The little girl felt . . .

If the little girl could have put her feelings into thoughts with words, she might have said (NCs):

The truth is (PCs):

Then some other wonderful things happened . . .

Today, the young girl still struggles with believing . . .

But, she has a family who loves her and they continue to help her understand things.

The girl's mother says, ". . .

The girl's father says, ". . .

As the young girl grows, she is gradually learning . . .

FOR BOYS

Once upon a time, there was a young boy who lived with . . .

Like all children, he had some wonderful things and some confusing things happen in his life.

A wonderful thing was that he was born . . .

A confusing thing was . . .

The little boy felt . . .

If this baby boy could have put his feelings into thoughts with words, he might have said (NCs):

The truth is (or what we want him to know is) (PCs):

A wonderful thing that happened was . . .

Another confusing thing that happened was . . .

The little boy felt . . .

If the little boy could have put his feelings into thoughts with words, he might have said (NCs):

The truth is (PCs):

Then some other wonderful things happened . . .

Today, the young boy still struggles with believing . . .

But, he has a family who loves him and they continue to help him understand things.

The boy's mother says, ". . .

The boy's father says, ". . .

As the young boy grows, he is gradually learning . . .

Appendix F

DEANNA'S STORY

Once upon a time, there was a young girl named Deanna who lived with her forever mom. Deanna enjoyed playing with her friend Emily and Emily's young nephew Will. Like all children, Deanna experienced some wonderful things in her life and some things that were confusing and hard to understand.

One wonderful thing was that Baby Deanna was born lovable and beautiful to a birth mother who loved her. One confusing thing was that her birth mother was not able to take care of her because the birth mother's life was too difficult. However, the birth mother loved her baby and wanted her to get good care. So the birth mother took her baby to an orphanage, where good people would find a loving forever mom to care for her baby and give her a good home. Baby Deanna felt sad when she didn't see the birth mother anymore. She thought, "I can't trust moms to take care of me. I must not be good enough." However, the truth was that Deanna's birth mother had made a loving decision to help her find a mom who could give her everything she needed. The truth was that Deanna was lovable and deserving of love.

In the orphanage, there were too many babies and not enough caregivers. The little baby Deanna felt alone. If Baby Deanna could have put her feelings into words, she would have said, "I am not safe. These other crying babies are arguing with me. No one loves me. I must not be good enough." Big Deanna is learning that the caregivers were good people trying to care for her. They just had too many babies. The truth was that she was safe—the babies were crying because they felt all alone, too.

Then one wonderful day, a new mother came to bring Deanna home. She was in love with Baby Deanna. Deanna's new mother was very happy to hold her and be with her. She adopted Deanna officially and became her official forever mother. She would always take care of her and make sure Deanna was safe and healthy.

As Deanna gets older, her forever mom continues to love her and care for her each and every day. Sometimes Deanna still has difficulty believing that she can trust her mom to always care for her and keep her safe. However, her mom does take good care of her, and she keeps her safe forever and always. Deanna's mother says, "You can depend on me to keep you safe and give you what you need." Deanna is gradually learning that she can trust her mom to be in charge, and when she lets her mom be in charge, Deanna relaxes and feels better. Deanna still sometimes struggles with understanding that crying babies are not arguing with her. But as Deanna grows, she is gradually learning the truth—that the crying babies just want to be loved. Sometimes Deanna struggles with believing her teachers at school can keep her safe, but as Deanna grows, she is learning that she can relax and rely on her teachers and be more successful. Deanna's mom loves her so much, she will continue to help her feel loved, lovable, and safe. Deanna has a safe school and a loving family, and she will grow up and have a good and happy life.

JOSEPH THE GUINEA PIG

Once upon a time, there was a mommy guinea pig who didn't have enough food for her baby guinea pig, named Joseph. So she took Baby Joseph to a guinea pig orphanage where there were some wonderful guinea pigs who would care for him and find him a forever home.

There were lots of baby guinea pigs there at the orphanage, all crying out to be held and fed at the same time, and they were loud. Baby Joseph felt scared and so he didn't cry out, but instead, he looked around and found a funny looking coat covered with sharp pointy quills. A porcupine coat! This was just what he needed! He put it on, and suddenly he didn't feel so scared anymore. *This will stab and hurt anyone who comes near me*, he thought.

The porcupine coat helped him survive in the guinea pig orphanage with the crowd of little guinea pigs. Then one day a new guinea pig mommy came to the orphanage and fell in love with little Baby Joseph. She noticed he was wearing a very uncomfortable-looking coat covered with sharp quills, but she thought, *I love this baby guinea pig, even with his porcupine coat*!

The mommy guinea pig adored the little guinea pig wearing the porcupine coat. The mommy guinea pig knew just what she needed to do to take care of the little guinea pig. She knew she had to find a porcupine coat she could wear, so that she could love and hug and care for the little guinea pig Joseph without getting pricked. She went into the forest and gathered porcupine quills from the ground. Next, she went home and found an old coat, and then she started sewing on one quill at a time until it was nicely covered.

The new mommy guinea pig loved her new child more than anything. At first, she had to wear her own porcupine coat every day. It made her tough as nails, and the little guinea pig's quills didn't bother her one bit. But some days, the little guinea pig's coat fell away, and the guinea pig's fur beneath the prickly coat was smooth and soft. On THOSE days, the mommy guinea pig smiled, threw off her own porcupine coat, and cuddled with her new child. They both enjoyed the closeness and the love they shared on those special days.

One day the mommy guinea pig felt sad for the little guinea pig. She noticed that the other guinea pigs avoided the little guinea pig when he was wearing the porcupine coat, because they didn't want to get poked. She looked in the little guinea pig's eyes and said, "Honey, why don't you take your coat off to play? Then the other guinea pigs will stick around because they won't be afraid of getting poked. And you will have a lot more fun."

There are two endings to this story. You get to pick.

Ending #1. They continued the rest of their days together, mommy guinea pig and little guinea pig. The little guinea pig continued to take his porcupine coat off on some days, and those were the days they both enjoyed the best. They laughed together, played games, and had a great time. On the other days, the little guinea pig woke up wearing his porcupine coat, and on those days, he sometimes wore the prickly coat all day long. Sometimes, he wore his coat for several days in a row. Those were not the most enjoyable days for either of them, but the mommy guinea pig loved her child no matter what, and all she had to do was wear her own porcupine coat. It made her as tough as nails so she could handle her prickly little guinea pig child just fine, caring for him, teaching him, and helping him grow. But she still felt sad for him, because on the days he wore his prickly coat, the other little guinea pigs stayed away, and he was lonely. He didn't have as much fun as he could have had.

Ending #2. They continued the rest of their days together, and soon, the little guinea pig's porcupine coat was left in the bottom of the closet and forgotten. The mommy threw her porcupine coat in the bottom of the closet, too, and before long, birds were flying off with the discarded quills to use in their nests. The mommy guinea pig and her child had lots of good times together. Once in a while the little guinea pig got grumpy, but never so grumpy that the porcupine coats came out of the closet. The mommy and child liked to cuddle, play, and talk. And the little guinea pig had lots and lots of friends, too, and they all enjoyed playing together each day, without having any old spiky prickles getting in the way.

Appendix H

THE TALE OF THE HAMSTER AND THE PORCUPINE COAT*

Once upon a time, there were a great many hamsters who lived in the forest near the Inky Black Lagoon. All the hamsters had been told from as early as they could remember, never EVER drink from the Black Lagoon. Any hamsters who drank from the Inky Black Lagoon could NEVER stop, because it tasted SO great. But the great-tasting black water from the Inky Black Lagoon caused hamsters to get mixed-up thoughts and do strange things, so it was very dangerous.

Once upon a time there was a mommy hamster and a daddy hamster who drank from the Inky Black Lagoon. It was a very sad thing, because they had a baby hamster who needed them and depended upon them. But when the mommy and daddy hamster drank the great-tasting black water, they became mixed-up and confused. They soon stopped taking care of their baby hamster, and sometimes they left him [her] all alone.

The baby hamster became hungry, and he [she] was afraid of all the other animals who lived around the Inky Black Lagoon because he had no one to keep him safe. He had to do something to protect himself. One day, he was rooting around in the yard looking for something to eat, when he found a funny-looking coat covered with sharp pointy quills. A porcupine coat! This was just what he needed! He put it on, and suddenly he didn't feel so scared anymore. *This will stab and hurt anyone who comes near me*, he thought.

*Originally presented at the 2006 annual meeting of the EMDR International Association, Philadelphia, PA.

One day, a group of very nice hamster supervisors came to the yard where the baby hamster was looking for something to eat. They were shocked that no one was taking care of the baby hamster! They said, "You come with us, little one! We will find you a forever mom and dad to take care of you."

The supervisor hamsters searched for a new hamster family for the little hamster. The little hamster was moved to one family and then another, but they had not yet found just the right family. The supervisors noticed that the little hamster was wearing a very uncomfortable-looking coat covered with sharp quills, and they knew they needed to find just the right mommy and daddy hamster who knew how to take care of a baby hamster wearing such a coat. One day a mommy and daddy hamster saw the little hamster playing outside, and they fell in love with the baby hamster. They said, "We want to raise this baby hamster as our own, forever!" The supervisors looked at each other, and then they looked at the mommy and daddy and they said, "You are the ones we have been looking for!"

The mommy and daddy hamster noticed that the little hamster was wearing a porcupine coat. The mommy hamster knew just what she needed to do to take care of the little hamster. She knew she had to find a porcupine coat that she could wear, so that she could love and hug and care for the little hamster without getting pricked. She went into the forest and gathered porcupine quills from the ground, and then she went home and found an old coat, and then she started sewing on one quill at a time until it was nicely covered.

The new mommy hamster loved her new child more than anything. At first, she had to wear her own porcupine coat every day. It made her tough as nails, and the little hamster's quills didn't bother her one bit. But some days, the little hamster's coat fell away, and the hamster fur beneath the prickly coat was smooth and soft. On *those* days, the mommy hamster smiled and threw off her own porcupine coat, and she cuddled with her new child. They both enjoyed the closeness and the love they shared on those special days.

One day the mommy hamster felt sad for the little hamster. She noticed that the other hamsters playing outside avoided her little hamster when he was wearing the porcupine coat, because they didn't want to get poked. She looked in her little hamster's eyes and said, "Honey, why don't you take your coat off to play? Then the other hamsters will stick around because they won't be afraid of getting poked! And you will have a lot more fun."

There are two endings to this story. You get to pick.

Ending #1. They continued the rest of their days together, mommy hamster and little hamster. The little hamster continued to take his porcupine coat off on some days, and those were the days they both enjoyed the best. They laughed together, played games, and had a great time. On some days, the little hamster wore the prickly coat all day long. Sometimes he wore the coat for several days in a row. Those were not the most enjoyable days for either of them, but the mommy hamster loved her child no matter what, and all she had to do was wear her own porcupine coat. It made her as tough as nails so she could handle her prickly little hamster child just fine, caring for him, teaching him, and helping him grow. But she still felt sad for him, because on the days he wore his prickly coat, the other little hamsters stayed away and he was lonely. He didn't have as much fun as he could have had.

Ending #2. They continued the rest of their days together, and soon, the little hamster's porcupine coat was left in the bottom of the closet and forgotten. The mommy threw her porcupine coat in the bottom of the closet, too, and before long, birds were flying off with the discarded quills to use in their nests. The mommy hamster and her child had lots of good times together. Once in a while the little hamster got grumpy, but never so grumpy that the porcupine coats came out of the closet. The mommy and child liked to cuddle, play, and talk. And the little hamster had lots and lots of friends, too, and they all enjoyed playing together each day.

REFERENCES

Achenbach, T. M. (1991). *Manual for the Child Behavior Checklist/4–18 and 1991 Profile*. Burlington, VT: University of Vermont Department of Psychiatry.

Adler-Tapia, R., & Settle, C. (2008). *EMDR and the art of psychotherapy with children*. New York, NY: Springer.

Ahmad, A., Larsson, B., & Sundelin-Wahlsten, V. (2007). EMDR treatment for children with PTSD: Results of a randomized controlled trial. *Nordic Journal of Psychiatry, 61*, 349–354.

Ainsworth, M. D. S. (1967). *Infancy in Uganda: Infant care and the growth of love*. Baltimore, MD: Johns Hopkins Press.

Ainsworth, M. D. S. (1982). Attachment: Retrospect and prospect. In C. M. Parkes & J. Stevenson-Hinde (Eds.), *The place of attachment in human behavior* (pp. 3–29). New York, NY: Tavistock.

American Psychiatric Association. (2013). *Diagnostic and statistical manual of mental disorders* (DSM-5). Washington, DC: Author.

Armstrong, J., Putnam, F. W., Carlson, E., Libero, D., & Smith, S. (1997). The adolescent dissociative experiences scale. *Journal of Nervous and Mental Disorders, 185*(8), 491–497.

Armstrong, S. (2011). *EMDR resource development activities*. Unpublished paper.

Attachment and Trauma Center of Nebraska. (2011). *EMDR and family therapy integrative model for the treatment of attachment trauma in children: Treatment manual*. Omaha, NE: Author.

Block, R. W., & Krebs, N. F. (2005). Failure to thrive as a manifestation of child neglect. *Pediatrics, 116*, 1234–1237.

Bossini, L., Fagiolini, A., & Castrogiovanni, P. (2007). Neuroanatomical changes after EMDR in posttraumatic stress disorder. *Journal of Neuropsychiatry and Clinical Neuroscience, 19,* 457–458.

Bowlby, J. (1973). *Attachment and loss: Vol. 2. Separation: Anxiety and anger.* New York, NY: Basic Books.

Bowlby, J. (1989). The role of attachment in personality development and psychopathology. In S. I. Greenspan & G. H. Pollack (Eds.), *The course of life: Vol. 1. Infancy* (pp. 119–136). Madison, CT: International Universities Press.

Brennan, K. A., Clark, C. L., & Shaver, P. R. (1998). Self-report measurement: An integrative overview. In J. A. Simpson & W. S. Rholes (Eds.), *Attachment theory and close relationships* (pp. 46–76). New York, NY: Guilford Press.

Briere, J. (1996). *Trauma Symptom Checklist for Children (TSCC) professional manual.* Odessa, FL: Psychological Assessment Resources.

Briere, J., Kaltman, S., & Green, B. L. (2008). Accumulated childhood trauma and symptom complexity. *Journal of Traumatic Stress, 21*(2), 223–226.

Cassidy, J. (1988). Child–mother attachment and the self in six year-olds. *Child Development, 59,* 121–135.

Chemtob, C. M., Nakashima, J., & Carlson, J. G. (2002). Brief-treatment for elementary school children with disaster-related PTSD: A field study. *Journal of Clinical Psychology, 58,* 99–112.

De Roos, C., Greenwald, R., den Hollander-Gijsm, M., Noorthoorn, E., van Buuren, S., & de Jongh, A. (2011). A randomized comparison of cognitive behavioural therapy. *European Journal of Psychotraumatology, 2,* 5694–5704.

Dodge, K. A., Bates, J. E., & Pettit, G. S. (1990). Mechanisms in the cycle of violence. *Science, 250,* 1678–1683.

Dozier, M., Albus, K. E., Stovall, K. C., & Bates, B. (2001). Attachment for infants in foster care: The role of caregiver state of mind. *Child Development, 72,* 1467–1477.

Egeland, B., & Sroufe, A. (1981). Developmental sequelae of maltreatment in infancy. *New Directions for Child Development, 11,* 72–92.

Elmud, A., Linblad, F., Vinnerljung, B., & Hjern, A. (2007). Intercountry adoptees in out-of-home care: A national cohort study. *Acta Paediatrica, 96*(3), 437–442.

Felitti, V. J., Anda, R. F., Nordenberg, D., Williamson, D. F., Spitz, A. M., Edwards, V., et al. (1998). Relationship of childhood abuse and household dysfunction to many of the leading causes of death in adults: The Adverse Childhood Experiences (ACE) study. *American Journal of Preventive Medicine, 14*(4), 749–379.

Field, T., & Fogel, A. (1982). *Emotion and early interaction*. Hillsdale, NJ: Erlbaum.

Fonagy, P., Target, M., Steele, M., Steele, H., Leigh, T., Levinson, A., et al. (1997). Morality, disruptive behavior, borderline personality disorder, crime, and their relationships to security of attachment. In L. Atkinson & K. Zucker (Eds.), *Attachment and psychopathology* (pp. 223–274). New York, NY: Guilford Press.

Forbes, H. T. (2009). *Beyond consequences, logic, and control: A love based approach to helping children with severe behaviors*. Boulder, CO: Beyond Consequences Institute.

Gomez, A. M. (2010, September/October). *Treating children with pervasive emotion dysregulation: EMDR and adjunctive approaches*. Paper presented at the annual meeting of EMDR International Association, Minneapolis, MN.

Gomez, A. M. (2013). *EMDR therapy and adjunct approaches with children: Complex trauma, attachment, and dissociation*. New York, NY: Springer.

Greenwald, R. (2009). *Treating problem behaviors: A trauma-informed approach*. New York, NY: Routledge.

Gunnar, M. R., & Barr, R. G. (1998). Stress, early brain development, and behavior. *Infants and Young Children, 11*(1), 1–14.

Hesse, E. (1999). The Adult Attachment Interview: Historical and current perspectives. In J. Cassidy & P. R. Shaver (Eds.), *Handbook of attachment: Theory, research and clinical applications* (pp. 395–433). New York, NY: Guilford Press.

Hofmann, A. (2009). The inverted EMDR standard protocol for unstable complex post-traumatic stress disorder. In M. Luber (Ed.), *Eye movement desensitization (EMDR) scripted protocols: Special populations* (pp. 313–328). New York, NY: Springer.

International Society for the Study of Dissociation. (ISSTD). Task Force on Child and Adolescents (2003). *Guidelines for the evaluation and treatment of dissociative symptoms in children and adolescents*. Retrieved from http://www.isst-d.org/education/treatmentguidelines-index.htm

Jaberghaderi, N., Greenwald, R., Rubin, A., Dolatabadim, S., & Zand, S. O. (2004). A comparison of CBT and EMDR for sexually abused Iranian girls. *Clinical Psychology and Psychotherapy, 11*, 358–368.

Kemp, M., Drummond, P., & McDermott, B. (2010). A wait-list controlled pilot study of eye movement desensitization and reprocessing (EMDR) for children with post-traumatic stress disorder (PTSD) symptoms from motor vehicle accidents. *Clinical Child Psychology and Psychiatry, 15*, 5025.

Korn, D. L., & Leeds, A. M. (2002). Preliminary evidence of efficacy for

EMDR resource development and installation in the stabilization phase of treatment of complex post-traumatic stress disorder. *Journal of Clinical Psychology, 58,* 1465–1487.

Kübler-Ross, E., & Kessler, D. (2005). *On grief and grieving: Finding the meaning of grief through the five stages of loss.* New York, NY: Simon & Schuster.

Lambert, M. J., Burlingame, G. M., Umphress, V., Hansen, N. B., Vermeersch, D. A., Clouse, G. C., & Yanchar, S. C. (1996). The reliability and validity of the outcome questionnaire. *Clinical Psychology and Psychotherapy (3)*4, 249–256.

LeDoux, J. (1996). *The emotional brain: The mysterious underpinnings of emotional life.* New York, NY: Touchstone.

Linehan, M. M. (1993). *Skills training manual for treating borderline personality disorder.* New York, NY: Guilford Press.

Liotti, G. (1999). Disorganization of attachment as a model for understanding dissociative psychopathology. In J. Solomon & C. George (Eds.), *Attachment disorganization* (pp. 291–317). New York, NY: Guilford Press.

Lovett, J. (1999). *Small wonders: Healing childhood trauma with EMDR.* New York, NY: Free Press.

Lovett, J. (2009, October). *Using EMDR to treat trauma and attachment in children and adults.* Paper presented at the Attachment and Trauma Center of Nebraska, EMDR Specialty Workshop, Omaha, NE.

Lyons-Ruth, K., Alpern, L., & Repacholi, L. (1993). Disorganized infant attachment classification and maternal psychosocial problems as predictors of hostile-aggressive behavior in the preschool classroom. *Child Development, 64,* 572–585.

Lyons-Ruth, K., & Jacobvitz, D. (1999). Attachment disorganization: Unresolved loss, relational violence, and lapses in behavioral and attentional strategies. In J. Cassidy & P. R. Shaver (Eds.), *Handbook of attachment: Theory, research and clinical applications* (pp. 520–554). New York, NY: Guilford Press.

Madrid, A., Skolek, S., & Shapiro, F. (2006). Repairing failures in bonding through EMDR. *Clinical Case Studies, 5*(4), 271–286.

Magid, K. (1988). *High risk: Children without a conscience.* New York, NY: Bantam Books.

Main, M., & Hesse, E. (1990). Parents' unresolved traumatic experiences are related to infant disorganized attachment status: Is frightened and/or frightening parental behavior the linking mechanism? In M. Greenberg, D. Cicchetti, & E. M. Cummings (Eds.), *Attachment in the pre-school years: Theory, research, and intervention* (pp. 161–182). Chicago, IL: University of Chicago Press.

Main, M., & Solomon, J. (1990). Procedures for identifying infants as disorganized/disoriented during the Ainsworth Strange Situation. In

M. Greenberg, D. Cichetti, & M. Cummings (Eds.), *Attachment in the preschool years: Theory, research, and intervention* (pp. 121–149). Chicago, IL: University of Chicago Press.

Paulsen, S. L. (2010, June). *The embodied self: Somatic methods for EMDR practitioners.* Workshop presented in Omaha, NE.

Paulsen, S. L. (2012, April). *When there are no words: EMDR for early trauma and neglect.* Workshop presented in Omaha, NE.

Perry, B. D. (1996). *Maltreated children: Experience, brain development, and the next generation.* New York, NY: Norton.

Perry, B. D. (1997). Incubated in terror: Neurodevelopmental factors in the "cycle of violence." In J. Osofsky (Ed.), *Children, youth and violence: The search for solutions* (pp. 124–148). New York, NY: Guilford Press.

Polansky, N. A., Gaudin, J. M., & Kilpatrick, A. C. (1992). Family radicals. *Children and Youth Services Review, 14*, 19–26.

Popky, A. J. (2009). The desensitization of triggers and urge reprocessing (DeTUR) protocol. In M. Luber (Ed.), *Eye movement desensitization (EMDR) scripted protocols: Special populations* (pp. 489–511). New York, NY: Springer.

Porges, S. W. (1995). Orienting in a defensive world: Mammalian modifications of our evolutionary heritage: A polyvagal theory. *Psychophysiology, 32*, 301–318.

Potter, A. (2011a). *The anatomy of a meltdown.* Unpublished paper.

Potter, A. (2011b). *The domino effect.* Unpublished paper.

Potter, A., Davidson, M., & Wesselmann, D. (2013) Utilizing dialectical behavior therapy and eye movement desensitization and reprocessing as phase-based trauma treatment: A case study series. In L. C. Stewart (Ed.), *Eye movement: Developmental perspectives, dysfunctions, and disorders in humans* (pp. 49–72). New York, NY: Nova Publishers.

Putnam, F., & Peterson, G. (1994). Further validation of the Child Dissociative Checklist. *Dissociation, 7*(4), 204–211.

Robredo, J. (2011, June). *EMDR and gender violence: Brief and intensive treatment for children exposed to gender violence.* Paper presented at the annual meeting of the EMDR Europe Association, Vienna, Austria.

Schore, A. N. (1994). *Affect regulation and the origin of the self: The neurobiology of emotional development.* Mahwah, NJ: Erlbaum.

Schore, A. N. (1996). The experience-dependent maturation of a regulatory system in the orbital prefrontal cortex and the origin of developmental psychopathology. *Development and Psychopathology, 8*, 59–87.

Schore, A. N. (1997). Early organization of the nonlinear right brain and development of a predisposition to psychiatric disorder. *Development and Psychopathology, 9*, 595–631.

Schore, A. N. (2001). The effects of early relational trauma on right brain development, affect regulation, and infant mental health. *Infant Mental Health Journal, 22*, 201–269.

Schweitzer, C. (2012). *Self-regulation skills teaching.* Unpublished paper.

Shapiro, F. (2001). *Eye movement desensitization and reprocessing: Basic principles protocols, and procedures.* New York, NY: Guilford Press.

Shapiro, F. (2007). EMDR and case conceptualization from an adaptive information processing perspective. In F. Shapiro, F. W. Kaslow, & L. Maxfield (Eds.), *Handbook of EMDR and family therapy processes* (pp. 3–34). Hoboken, NJ: Wiley.

Siegel, D. J. (1999). *The developing mind: Toward a neurobiology of interpersonal experience.* New York, NY: Guilford Press.

Siegel, D. J. (2001). Toward an interpersonal neurobiology of the developing mind: Attachment relationships, mindsight, and neural integration. *Infant Mental Health Journal, 22*(1–2), 67–94.

Siegel, D. J. (2007). *The mindful brain: Reflection and attunement in the cultivation of well-being.* New York, NY: Norton.

Siegel, D. J. (2010). *Mindsight: The new science of personal transformation.* New York, NY: Bantam Books.

Siegel, D. J., & Bryson, T. P. (2011). *The whole-brain child: 12 revolutionary strategies to nurture your child's developing mind.* New York, NY: Bantam Books.

Smith, S. L. (2010, October). *Keeping the promise: The critical need for post-adoption services to enable children and families to succeed.* New York, NY: Evan B. Donaldson Adoption Institute.

Taylor, R. J. (2002). Family unification with reactive attachment disorder: A brief treatment. *Contemporary Family Therapy: An International Journal, 24*, 475–481.

Teicher, M. H. (2002). Scars that won't heal: The neurobiology of child abuse. *Scientific American*, March, 68–75.

Tinker, R. H., & Wilson, S. A. (1999). *Through the eyes of a child: EMDR with children.* New York, NY: Norton.

Tronick, E. Z., Als, H., Adamson, L., Wise, S., & Brazelton, T. B. (1978). The infant's response to entrapment between contradictory messages in face-to-face interaction. *Journal of American Academy of Child Psychiatry, 17*, 1–13.

U.S. Department of Health and Human Services, Administration for Children and Families, Administration on Children, Youth and Families, Children's Bureau. (2012). *Child Maltreatment 2011.* Retrieved from http://www.acf.hhs.gov/programs/cb/research-data-technology/statistics-research/child-maltreatment.

van der Kolk, B. A. (1989). The compulsion to repeat the trauma: Reenactment, revictimization, and masochism. *Psychiatric Clinics of North America, 12*(2), 389–411.

van der Kolk, B. A. (2002). Beyond the talking cure: Somatic experience and subcortical imprints in the treatment of trauma. In F. Shapiro (Ed.), *EMDR as an integrative treatment approach: Experts of diverse orientations explore the paradigm prism* (pp. 57–84). Washington, DC: American Psychological Association.

van der Kolk, B. A. (2005). Developmental trauma disorder: Toward a rational diagnosis for children with complex trauma histories. *Psychiatric Annals, 35*(5), 401–408.

van der Kolk, B. A., & Fisler, R. (1992). Dissociation and the fragmentary nature of traumatic memories: Overview and exploratory study. *Journal of Traumatic Stress, 8*(4), 505–525.

van IJzendoorn, M. H. (1992). Intergenerational transmission of parenting: A review of studies in nonclinical populations. *Developmental Review, 12*, 76–99.

Weinberg, K., & Tronick, E. Z. (1998). The impact of maternal psychiatric illness on infant development. *Journal of Clinical Psychiatry, 59*, 53–61.

Wesselmann, D. (1998). *The whole parent: How to become a terrific parent even if you didn't have one.* Cambridge, MA: Da Capo Press.

Wesselmann, D. (2006, September). *Strengthening parent–child attachments with EMDR.* Paper presented at the annual meeting of the EMDR International Association, Philadelphia, PA.

Wesselmann, D. (2007). Treating attachment issues through EMDR and a family systems approach. In F. Shapiro, F. W. Kaslow, & L. Maxfield (Eds.), *Handbook of EMDR and family therapy processes* (pp. 113–130). Hoboken, NJ: Wiley.

Wesselmann, D. (2013). Healing trauma and creating secure attachment through EMDR. In M. Solomon & D. S. Siegel (Eds.), *Healing moments in psychotherapy: Mindful awareness, neural integration, and therapeutic presence* (pp. 115–128). New York, NY: Norton.

Wesselmann, D., Davidson, M., Armstrong, S., Schweitzer, C., Bruckner, D., & Potter, A. (2012). EMDR as a treatment for improving attachment status in adults and children. *European Review of Applied Psychology, 62*,(4), 223–230.

Wesselmann, D., & Potter, A. E. (2009). Change in adult attachment status following treatment with EMDR: Three case studies. *Journal of EMDR Practice and Research, 3*, 178–191.

Wesselmann, D., Schweitzer, C., & Armstrong, S. (2014). *Integrative parenting: Strategies for raising children affected by attachment trauma.* New York, NY: Norton.

Wesselmann, D., & Shapiro, F. (2013). EMDR and the treatment of complex trauma in children and adolescents. In J. Ford & C. Courtois (Eds.), *Treating complex traumatic stress disorders in children and adolescents* (pp. 203–224). New York, NY: Guilford Press.

Winnicott, D. W. (1965). *Maturational processes and the facilitating environment.* Madison, CT: International Universities Press.

Zarghi, A., Zali, A., & Tehranidost, M. (2013). Methodological aspects of cognitive rehabilitation with eye movement desensitization and reprocessing (EMDR). *Basic and Clincal Neuroscience, 4*(1), 97–103.

Zeanah, C. H., & Boris, N. W. (2000). Disturbances and disorders of attachment in early childhood. In C. H. Zeanah (Ed.), *Handbook of infant mental health* (2nd ed., pp. 353–368). New York, NY: Guilford Press.

INDEX